Also available at all good book stores

9781785316470

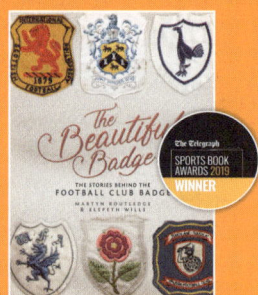
9781785313929

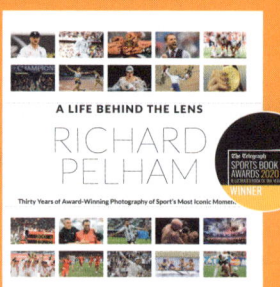
9781785315466

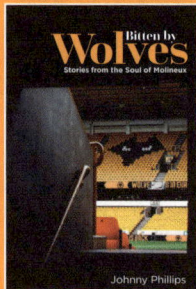
9781785316142

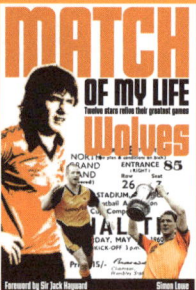
9781908051752

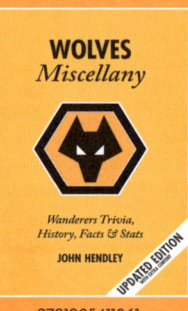
9781905411061

9781905411122

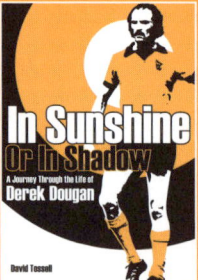
9781785314056

9781785315312

9781785314902

GREATEST GAMES
WOLVES
JOHN HENDLEY

First published by Pitch Publishing, 2012
Reprinted 2020

Pitch Publishing
A2 Yeoman Gate
Yeoman Way
Worthing
Sussex
BN13 3QZ
www.pitchpublishing.co.uk
info@pitchpublishing.co.uk

© John Hendley, 2012

Every effort has been made to trace the copyright. Any oversight will be rectified in future editions at the earliest opportunity by the publisher.

All rights reserved. No part of this book may be reproduced, sold or utilised in any form or transmitted in any form or by any means, electronic or mechanical, including photocopying, recording or by any information storage and retrieval system, without prior permission in writing from the Publisher.

A CIP catalogue record is available for this book from the British Library.

ISBN 978-1-90805-189-9

Typesetting and origination by Pitch Publishing

Printed and bound in India by Replika Press Pvt. Ltd.

CONTENTS

Foreword	4
Introduction	5
Acknowledgements	6
The Matches:	
Wolves 1 Aston Villa 1	7
Wolves 1 Everton 0	9
Newcastle United 1 Wolves 3	11
Wolves 7 Bradford City 2	15
Wolves 2 Arsenal 0	17
Wolves 7 Everton 0	19
Wolves 5 Grimsby Town 0	21
Wolves 6 Arsenal 1	23
Liverpool 1 Wolves 5	25
Bolton Wanderers 0 Wolves 5	27
Wolves 1 Manchester United 1	29
Leicester City 1 Wolves 3	31
Wolves 6 Birmingham City 1	35
South Western Districts 0 Wolves 11	37
Wolves 5 Chelsea 3	39
Huddersfield Town 1 Wolves 7	41
Wolves 6 Manchester United 2	43
Wolves 8 Chelsea 1	45
Wolves 3 South Africa 1	47
West Bromwich Albion 0 Wolves 1	49
Wolves 4 West Bromwich Albion 4	51
Wolves 4 Moscow Spartak 0	53
Wolves 3 Honved 2	55
Wolves 6 Huddersfield Town 4	59
Cardiff City 1 Wolves 9	61
Wolves 2 Moscow Dynamo 1	63
Wolves 5 Luton Town 4	65
Chelsea 3 Wolves 3	67
Wolves 4 Preston North End 3	69
Wolves 3 Real Madrid 2	71
Wolves 6 Chelsea 1	73
Wolves 7 Portsmouth 0	75
Wolves 6 Arsenal 1	77
Wolves 5 Luton Town 0	79
Wolves 3 Nottingham Forest 1	81
Manchester City 4 Wolves 6	83
Wolves 9 Fulham 0	85
Chelsea 1 Wolves 5	87
Blackburn Rovers 0 Wolves 3	89
Wolves 4 Everton 1	93
Wolves 3 Tottenham Hotspur 1	95
Wolves 8 Manchester City 1	97
Wolves 7 West Bromwich Albion 0	99
Wolves 4 West Ham 3	101
Wolves 8 Portsmouth 2	103
Wolves 1 Everton 1	105
Portsmouth 2 Wolves 3	107
Wolves 4 Hull City 0	109
Wolves 4 Bury 1	111
Aberdeen 5 Wolves 6	113
Wolves 3 West Bromwich Albion 3	115
Wolves 5 Newcastle United 0	117
Wolves 3 Nottingham Forest 3	119
Wolves 3 Chelsea 0	121
Wolves 3 Manchester United 2	123
West Bromwich Albion 2 Wolves 4	125
Heart of Midlothian 1 Wolves 3	127
Wolves 0 Heart of Midlothian 1	127
Wolves 5 Arsenal 1	129
Manchester United 1 Wolves 3	131
Wolves 2 Leeds United 1	133
Wolves 1 Tottenham Hotspur 2	135
Tottenham Hotspur 1 Wolves 1	135
Wolves 5 Stoke City 3	139
Wolves 2 Coventry City 0	141
Arsenal 1 Wolves 3	143
Manchester City 1 Wolves 2	145
Wolves 4 Newcastle United 2	149
Wolves 7 Chelsea 1	151
Burnley 1 Wolves 5	153
Wolves 3 Charlton Athletic 0	155
Hereford United 1 Wolves 6	157
Bolton Wanderers 0 Wolves 1	159
Everton 2 Wolves 3	161
Norwich City 0 Wolves 4	163
Nottingham Forest 0 Wolves 1	165
West Bromwich Albion 1 Wolves 3	169
Liverpool 0 Wolves 1	171
Wolves 3 Stockport County 1	173
Burnley 0 Wolves 2	175
Wolves 6 Mansfield Town 2	179
West Bromwich Albion 1 Wolves 2	181
Newcastle United 1 Wolves 4	183
Derby County 1 Wolves 2	185
Wolves 6 Newcastle United 2	187
Wolves 3 Millwall 1	189
Wolves 1 Sheffield Wednesday 1	191
Port Vale 2 Wolves 4	193
Wolves 3 Birmingham City 2	195
West Bromwich Albion 2 Wolves 4	197
Norwich City 0 Wolves 2	199
Leeds United 0 Wolves 1	201
Bristol City 1 Wolves 6	203
Wolves 3 Newcastle United 2	205
Sheffield United 0 Wolves 3	207
Wolves 4 Leicester City 3	211
Wolves 1 Manchester United 0	213
Charlton Athletic 2 Wolves 3	215
Derby County 2 Wolves 3	217
West Ham 1 Wolves 3	219
Wolves 2 Manchester United 1	221
Wolves 3 Tottenham Hotspur 3	223

FOREWORD

LOOKING BACK, when I joined Wolves from Huddersfield Town as a 20-year-old in 1968, never in my wildest dreams did I imagine that I would have such a long and enjoyable stay with the club or that I would become the man who has played more times in gold and black than any other. It is an honour I cherish.

In total I played 609 times for the club and they were very special days. Yes, there were disappointments along the way but I was proud to be in a team that, in the early seventies, were one of the best in the country. Losing out in the FA Cup and League Cup semi-finals was a bitter blow in 1973, but from the depths of despair we fought back to get to Wembley the next year.

It had always been my dream to play there and to do so against a highly-rated Manchester City side, and to beat them in a game regarded by many as one of the best at the stadium in years, was something that I recall with great pride. We did it again six years later when we were again the underdogs, this time against Brian Clough's Nottingham Forest, and once again we came out on top.

It wasn't just those high profile matches that gave me so much pleasure. Many of the 609 I played, whether it be a league or a cup game, helped me to put together a career that most people would have given their eye teeth for. I wound up my playing days with a short spell at Stoke and I have to say when it was all over, there was a big void in my life.

It wasn't just playing in the games that I missed. The everyday banter that is part of a footballer's life in training and in the dressing room is something that I still yearn for to this day. My job was fun – you had to work hard to stay fit, but it was fun and I loved it.

When Foz, sorry it doesn't sound right when I say John, told me he was writing a book about 100 Wolves games, many of which I played in, I made him promise me a copy.

By way of return he asked me to write this foreword and it's something that I'm only too happy to do. Foz is as passionate about Wolves as I was, and indeed still am. Over my years with them, like myself, a lot of the players were at Molineux for a long time. Men like John Richards, Kenny Hibbitt, John McAlle, Waggy and dear old Frank Munro are examples.

There were many more and we weren't just work colleagues, we were all friends which is one of the reasons that we did so well. We were all in it together and we fought as a team. I still live in the area and still enjoy the lads' company every now and then.

It's always good to talk about Wolves games gone by and now, thanks to this book, I'm looking forward to reading about some of them too.

Derek Parkin – Wolverhampton Wanderers 1968-1982

INTRODUCTION

ONE OF the things that I love about football is the memories that it evokes – especially the good time memories. I suppose it falls under the heading of nostalgia to recall victories against all the odds, footballers idolised from the stands and, yes, the terraces. For all the comforts of modern stadia, how I miss the atmosphere provided by standing supporters in the old North and South Banks at Molineux.

I thoroughly enjoy reading old match reports or watching DVDs of games gone by and it was while viewing a replay of Derek Dougan's home debut against Hull City, shown on *Match of the Day* that evening, that I thought "why not write about some of these games?"

You will notice from the cover of this book, that the title doesn't include the word "the" before 100 greatest games. I haven't seen every game that Wolves have played and, even if I had done, then it would only be my opinion as to which are the greatest and I don't believe that is my right. Every Wolves fan will have their own thoughts on the best games they have seen. There would always be questions asked about omissions which is why I left the title open.

So, how have I selected 100 games? Obviously I went for the cup successes and I have made a point of including details of the all rounds leading up to the respective finals.

There is just one defeat featured in the 100 games, the Uefa Cup reversal against Spurs. Such were the performances of Wolves both on the road to, and in the final, I felt it needed to be included. I selected a handful of pre-war matches and a plethora from the glory days of the 1950s.

While I don't wish to be any older than I already am, I would have loved to have seen Wolves' teams playing in the 15 years that followed the war. While my supporting days didn't begin until 1965, I have watched some great players wearing gold and black and although I have had my share of bitter disappointments, many times have I enjoyed the feeling that a good performance or result can bring.

I hope this book brings back memories of games that you have seen, or will give you an insight into those that you missed.

John Hendley

ACKNOWLEDGEMENTS

ONCE MORE I offer my truly grateful thanks to my good friend Steve Gordos. He witnessed the floodlit friendlies and glory games of the 1950s watching some of football's greats as they plied their trade wearing the gold and black of Wolverhampton Wanderers. His advice while I have written this book has been invaluable as has his proof-reading skills.

Thanks also to father and son photographers Dave and Sam Bagnall who have supplied any pictures I requested from them without fuss and in the blink of an eye. Also many thanks to AMA Sports Photo Agency for the use of some of their excellent work, and to Wolverhampton Wanderers for allowing me to dip into their vast archive.

Then there are the players that I've pestered in compiling this book. Derek Parkin, who has been kind enough to write the foreword, John Richards, John McAlle, Phil Parkes and Dave Wagstaffe have all received telephone calls and been asked about incidents from games that they played in. Considering that they played over 2,300 times for Wolves between them, it was amazing how easily they recalled things. So to Squeak, JR, Scouse, Lofty and Waggy, many thanks lads.

Last but not least thanks to Paul Camillin of Pitch Publishing for his patience and for letting me write this book. It has been a labour of love.

Wolves 1 (Cox OG)
Aston Villa 1 (Green)
Football League
Saturday 8th September 1888

IT WAS a little over 12 years since the club began under the guise of St Luke's FC that Wolves were invited to be one of the 12 clubs who founded the Football League. In 1879, St Luke's amalgamated with the nearby Wanderers Cricket Club which was situated adjacent to the Fighting Cocks pub on Goldthorn Hill. Two years later the team moved to a new ground on Dudley Road across the road from the pub having outgrown the two fields they used in Lower Villiers Street.

The ground ran alongside Dudley Road from the corner of Goldthorn Hill to a point between Wanderers Avenue and Hawthorne Road. Facilities for spectators were sparse with just a lean-to shed for cover and a boarded area of terrace that cost extra for fans who wanted to keep their feet dry and boots clean! The players used the Ring O'Bells public house for their dressing rooms.

In the winter of 1888, William McGregor, a member of the Aston Villa committee and the Birmingham FA, canvassed clubs in the Midlands and the north west with a view to starting a league involving teams playing each other on a home and away basis.

And so the Football League was born with Wolves being joined by neighbours Aston Villa and West Bromwich Albion along with fellow Midlanders Derby County, Notts County and Stoke City. Making up the inaugural 12 were six clubs from Lancashire; Accrington, Everton, Burnley, Blackburn Rovers, Bolton Wanderers and Preston North End.

Wolves' first fixture saw a home meeting with Villa and, despite the bumpy pitch, the game was played at a brisk pace throughout and was evenly contested with, at the conclusion, a draw deemed the correct result.

There was a slope on the pitch which Wolves played down in the opening half with the wind against them. The home side enjoyed much of the early play and Villa keeper Jimmy Warner had to punch the ball out to quell the danger of a sustained attack in the opening minutes.

Villa remained on the defensive until they broke free and Tommy Green had a shot at goal that lacked the power to threaten home keeper Jack Baynton. Then, after a run through the heart of the defence, Nicholas Anderson slipped a short pass to Alf Cannon who looked on to open the scoring until Villa full-back Gershom Cox ran across to get in a fine tackle.

Another Anderson run was followed by a cross that again required the clenched fist of Warner to clear. But Anderson did beat the keeper moments later only for his low shot to come back off the foot of a post. As the game progressed, Villa began

Wolves' Greatest Games

to make inroads on the home defence and Wally Garvey dribbled his way through before forcing a fine save from Baynton with a powerfully struck drive.

Villa threatened through Alf Brown, who shot over the bar before Frankie Dawson twice tried his luck with his first effort flying narrowly wide while the second was way off target. Baynton had to clear a low cross from Denny Hodgetts before Wolves hit back with a shot from Jeremiah Cooper. Then Cox's attempt at clearing a shot from Wally White led to the opening goal.

The ball went as far as Cooper on the right wing and when he returned it to the goalmouth White headed the ball down. In the scramble that followed the ball struck the body of Cox and bounced into the net to give Wolves their first league goal and the advantage after 30 minutes' play.

The goal seemed to inspire Wanderers to achieve greater things and Cox made amends for his faux pas as he and Frank Coulton worked doggedly at preventing further goals. Shortly before the break, Villa drew level. Garvey worked a shooting position for himself and when Green got in the way of his team-mate's shot, the ball rebounded to Brown. He crossed hard and low for Green to side-foot the ball past Baynton off the inside of the post.

After the interval it was Villa who posed much of the attacking threat although when they got within shooting distance of the goal the visiting forwards lacked the killer touch. For Wolves, Cooper twice tested Warner with long-range efforts. Despite their best efforts, neither set of forwards could find a winning goal.

For a drawn league game each team has always secured a point although it wasn't until ten weeks into that first season that a points system of two for a win, one for a draw and nothing for a defeat was devised. Wolves won eight and drew two of their 11 home fixtures with the only defeat coming against eventual champions Preston North End. On their travels there were victories at Burnley, Everton, Stoke and West Bromwich as the team finished in a creditable third place 12 points behind unbeaten Preston at the top and a point behind second-placed Aston Villa.

In the FA Cup, Wanderers made it through to the final where they were unable to stop Preston achieving the double as they went down 3-0 at Kennington Oval. Two Wolves players, Harry Allen and Dickie Baugh, took part in all 22 league games and they also were ever presents in the six-game cup run and a total of 19 players were used in the 28 league and cup games played.

Wolves: Baynton, Baugh, Mason, Fletcher, Allen, Lowder, Hunter, Cooper, Anderson, White, Cannon.
Villa: Warner, Cox, Coulton, Yates, Devey, Dawson, Brown, Green, Allen, Garvey, Hodgetts.
Attendance: 2,500.

Wolves 1 (Allen)
Everton 0
FA Cup Final
Fallowfield, Manchester
Saturday 25th March 1893

IN 1893, for the first and only time in its history, the FA Cup Final was played at Fallowfield, Manchester. It was that year that Wolves brought the trophy back to Molineux for the first time although the game was almost demoted in status to that of a friendly because of crowd problems at the Lancashire venue.

The cup run that season had begun at Bolton where extra time couldn't separate the sides in a game that finished with Jack Johnson getting the visitors' goal in a 1-1 scoreline. The replay, in front of an 18,000 crowd at Molineux, took place a week later and the home support went home happy after seeing their team winning by 2-1 – Harry Wood and David Wykes the scorers.

A second-round home tie with Middlesbrough was the reward for the replay victory and, in a tight match, Wanderers overcame the north-eastern opposition to progress through to the quarter-final stage of the competition. Wykes was on the mark once more along with Joe Butcher in another 2-1 win.

The quarter-final draw gave Wolves a home tie this time against another northern team – one long since a Football League memory – Darwen. They were ruthlessly swept aside by Wanderers who scored five without replay – Wykes, Butcher, Alf Griffin and Dick Topham with a brace the goalscorers. For the semi-final Wolves were paired with Blackburn Rovers in a game played at Nottingham Forest's Town Ground.

The Wolves side was comprised entirely of Englishmen with seven of the players born within six miles of Molineux while Rovers, who were out-and-out favourites to reach the final, included eight Scots, a Welshman and just two Englishmen. Wolves edged a tight contest 2-1, with Topham and Butcher on the mark. It wasn't all good for the 18-year-old Butcher, however, as he finished the game with a broken nose and some loose teeth!

On the day of the final, it soon became apparent that the Fallowfield authorities were going to struggle to cope with an attendance far higher than they had anticipated. By noon the ground was packed and wooden barriers gave way under the pressure resulting in spectators encroaching on the pitch. It was at this point, with the police struggling to keep control, that the question was asked as to whether or not a game of such importance should be allowed to take place in such chaotic surroundings – or should it just be played as a friendly?

When officials asked the referee, Mr CJ Hughes, what the status of the game was to be, he replied sharply that it was his business. Such was the chaos that three Wolverhampton councillors scaled a tree to get a vantage point while press reports of the game contained little detail as reporters' view from the pavilion that housed them was almost entirely blocked by the throng.

Wolves' Greatest Games

However, the game got under way and the Merseysiders, with their neat, close passing, began to make inroads on the Wanderers rearguard. Both defences played well and when chances were created, the two keepers dealt with anything that came their way. Everton did have a goal ruled out but the interval arrived all square although the Liverpudlian team shaded it in terms of possession and attacking play.

Despite the close proximity of the crowd to the pitch, the spectators behaved impeccably and none trespassed on to the playing area so the referee confirmed during the break that the game was being played as the final and not a friendly. After the restart it was Wolves who began to get the upper hand with Wykes heavily involved in most of the forward moves.

The only goal came on the hour mark from the Wolves captain, Harry Allen. Everton keeper Richard Williams appeared to lose sight of the central defender's speculative long-range shot in the bright sunlight and he stood motionless as the ball went past him.

A goal down, and with the Wolves defence coping with the few threats that came their way, with 15 minutes remaining Everton lodged a protest about the conditions that the game was being played in. Wolves held on and at the final whistle there was more confusion as to whether the cup was to be presented or not.

No-one appeared to know whether Everton's appeal had been upheld or not and FA officials said that the trophy couldn't be handed over without the permission of Lord Kinnaird, the FA president. Thereby lay a problem as he had left the ground and gone home. But Wolves president Sir Alfred Hickman made his feelings known in no uncertain circumstances and the coveted trophy was finally handed over to Allen.

The team travelled back by rail that evening with the Great Western Railway marking their achievement by placing fog detonators on the line. The triumphant party made the short journey from the town's Low Level station where they were greeted by Swan Bank Band playing the music of Handel while the Victoria Hotel's facade was festooned with decorative Chinese lanterns. After acknowledging the cheering crowd that had lined the streets from the station, the players and officials went inside to enjoy a banquet and celebrate the club's first major honour.

The gate receipts were £2,559 but in those days the takings weren't shared between the respective clubs, instead kept by the FA. Just £10 was all that went into the Molineux coffers from that afternoon, but it mattered not. Wolves had won the FA Cup!

Wolves: Rose, Baugh, Swift, Malpass, Allen, Kinsey, Topham, Wykes, Butcher, Wood, Griffin.
Everton: Williams, Kelso, Howarth, Boyle, Holt, Stewart, Latta, Gordon, Maxwell, Chadwick, Milward.
Attendance: 45,067.
Referee: CJ Hughes.

Newcastle United 1 (Howie)
Wolves 3 (Hunt, Hedley, Harrison)
FA Cup Final
The Crystal Palace
Saturday 25th April 1908

IT DIDN'T need a football genius to predict the likely outcome of the 1908 FA Cup Final. In opposition were the previous season's league champions, Newcastle United, who had followed that up with a fourth-placed finish in the top flight, and a Wolves side who were situated in mid-table of the Second Division at the end of the campaign. Twenty-four places separated the teams as they headed to The Crystal Palace to compete for the trophy.

Newcastle's side was laced with English and Scottish internationals with six of the team coming from north of the border. The Wanderers' 11 were all of English descent, two of them Wolverhampton-born and a further four hailed from the local vicinity.

Seven of the Geordie team, goalkeeper Jimmy Lawrence, Alec Gardner, Colin Veitch, Peter McWilliam, Jock Rutherford, Jimmy Howie and Bill Appleyard, had played in the 1905 Cup Final defeat against Aston Villa, and a year later all but Appleyard tasted defeat again, this time at the hands of Everton, again at The Crystal Palace. So, for the six it was a case of hoping for third time lucky in the space of four years.

All four of United's games leading to the semi-final were played at St James' Park. They beat Nottingham Forest and West Ham, both 2-0, in the first and second rounds respectively before seeing off the threat of Liverpool, 3-1, and Grimsby Town 5-1 in the next two stages. The semi-final was played at Anfield where Fulham were demolished 6-0.

Wolves met fellow Second Division side Bradford City in the opening round and George Handley's goal at Valley Parade turned out to be the only one conceded by Wanderers on the way to the final. Jack Shelton was on target for the visitors and, in the replay, a George Hedley goal put Wolves through to a home meeting with top flight Bury who succumbed to a brace from Walter Radford.

Next up at Molineux were Southern League club Swindon Town and another 2-0 win saw Wolves through to the quarter-final with Hedley and Billy Harrison the scorers. A Staffordshire derby at Stoke was the reward. The Potters, like Wanderers, were stationed in mid-table in the Second Division and a goal from Radford was all that separated the teams after a closely competed game between evenly matched sides.

Now, all that stood between Wolves and a fourth FA Cup Final was another Southern League side, Southampton. The Southern League was a strong one at the time and it boasted the likes of Tottenham Hotspur, who won the competition in 1901, while the Saints were losing finalists in 1900 and 1902. The semi-final was played at Stamford Bridge and Hedley and Radford scored, without reply, to book a return trip to London four weeks later.

Wolves used just 12 men in the entire cup saga. Percy Corbett played at inside-left in the two games against Bradford before Radford took over the role. The other ten positions remained the same throughout.

Considering that it was late April, the weather was awful with snow falling on the morning of the game and then giving way to rain. It was cold and bleak. The Newcastle team stayed in the capital overnight while Wolves made the trip to Euston on the day of the game heading straight to The Crystal Palace on arrival. Billy Wooldridge led his men out to a rousing reception and they were followed by United skipper Gardner and his team.

From the kick-off Newcastle went forward and Ted Collins had to stop Howie in his tracks. Collins fed Wooldridge who was fouled but the free kick was easily cleared. Then Kenneth Hunt sparked an attacking move when he passed to Hedley whose cross, intended for Radford, was headed away by a defender. It took the combined efforts of Dick Pudan and Peter McWilliam to stop Harrison's charge down the left flank as Wolves enjoyed the best of the opening exchanges with Wooldridge keeping a tight check on the dangerous Appleyard.

Pudan and his fellow full-back McCracken were kept at full stretch as Harrison and Jack Pedley delivered a series of low crosses intended for Hedley. When Newcastle did threaten, Wooldridge headed clear from Appleyard who had run past Collins. The north-eastern team suddenly sprang to life and they should have opened the scoring through Rutherford but he fired wastefully over the bar from just six yards out.

Following a Rutherford corner, Collins cleared the ball upfield to Hedley who played Harrison through. Hampered by Pudan, the winger fired wide. Appleyard led Newcastle's next attack and although he had Wooldridge and Bishop either side of him, the striker still hit a shot that had Tommy Lunn on his knees as he saved. The keeper had to receive treatment for a facial injury shortly afterwards but he was soon able to resume.

Harrison was fouled by Gardner outside the area and from Hunt's free kick, Radford headed wide. In the 42nd minute, Harrison crossed to Radford who drove a shot goalwards with Lawrence parrying his effort. The loose ball ran to the unmarked Hunt and his shot was so powerful that although Lawrence caught the ball, he couldn't hold it and it went through his arms and over his head into the net.

The goal clearly rattled the United players and with the cheers of the Wolves supporters still ringing in their ears they suffered another crushing blow as the game was about to enter injury time. Hedley picked the ball up and, from an acute angle, he struck a magnificent shot that beat Lawrence all ends up to give Wanderers a 2-0 interval lead. It has always been said that to concede just before the break is the worst possible time to do so. The Geordies had twice been breached and a major shock suddenly seemed a distinct possibility.

v Newcastle United, 1908

Credit to Newcastle, however, who started the new half in a determined fashion and there was a terrific scramble in Lunn's goalmouth that went on for several seconds before the keeper finally emerged with the ball safely in his arms before he launched it upfield. However, Wolves were giving as good as they got and after Radford had fired fractionally wide, Harrison, with a burst of speed, beat McWilliam before he found his progress barred by Pudan.

The Molineux defenders were playing with extreme confidence but they were finally beaten in the 65th minute when Howie scored with a low shot that Lunn got a hand to, but was unable to divert wide of the post. Even after that setback, Wooldridge and his men refused to be shaken, throwing themselves into tackles and cutting off the source of attacks before there were any real opportunities although Appleyard looked odds on to equalise before he shot wide from just eight yards out.

A number of Newcastle corners were cleared and then, just four minutes from the end, Harrison eased any nerves in the Midlands section of the crowd as he scored Wanderers' third goal. With United pushing up looking for a leveller, Harrison slipped past Pudan and homed in on the unprotected Geordie goal before stroking the ball past the advancing Lawrence. Wooldridge almost got in on the act himself in the final minute, but he was denied by the keeper. However, it mattered not for the FA Cup was returning to Wolverhampton along with the delighted 3-1 victors.

The Lord Mayor of London, Sir Henry Bell, presented the trophy to Wooldridge in the main stand. The Wolves captain gave a brief speech saying: "Ladies and gentlemen. I have great pleasure in accepting the English Cup. I hope it won't be the last time I shall have the honour of doing it."

Speaking to the press later, Wooldridge added: "The best team won. We seemed to be trained better than they were. We lasted better. George Hedley was the man. He did good work by swinging the ball about. Harrison played well."

Newcastle skipper Gardner responded: "I have very little to say. The better team won, simply because they took advantage of their opportunities. I can't say too much in favour of them. They really played a good game."

Back in Wolverhampton, news of the game had been relayed back to the offices of the *Express and Star* and through an open window, staff relayed the score to the thousands of supporters that had packed Queen Street for news of the game. On hearing of Harrison's late strike that settled matters, the crowd broke into a rousing chorus of "for he's a jolly good fellow".

The ringing of a hand bell signalled the end of the game from the office window and as homing pigeons were released to convey the news throughout the local area, two huge gold and black flags were unfurled and carried triumphantly along Queen Street.

Kenneth Hunt returned to Wolverhampton that evening and, on the following Monday morning, he looked back at the cup glory from his St Mark's Vicarage home. When asked how he felt he admitted: "Oh, all right; only a bit stiff. I think it was one of the best games we have played in the cup ties. Certainly it was much better than against Southampton. We seemed to settle down very much quicker than usual.

Wolves' Greatest Games

"We realised that our only chance was to bustle them. We never intended to do anything but bustle. I spoke to three people afterwards who kept statistics of the fouls. One gentleman said there were five against the Wanderers and three against Newcastle, and the other two both gave three against the Wanderers and three against Newcastle. That shows it was not a foul game."

On Monday afternoon a film of the final was shown at the Empire Palace to a full house who, it was reported, cheered each goal and the final whistle as if the proceedings were live. Further showings were planned for that evening with the screening doubtless coming after the team returned to High Level station in preparation for a horse-drawn coach trip through the streets of the town. The Reverend Hunt met his team-mates at the station so, as he put it, "to be in the swim".

Praise for Wolves' victory was national and summed up by the editor of the *Athletic News* who wrote: "The Wolverhampton Wanderers never give themselves airs. They never anticipate triumphs. They merely do their duty and win. For instance, they passed last week at their own quarters [stayed at home], they journeyed up to London on Saturday morning, and they had not even ordered a repast for the evening or a bed for the night. They will return to their town today as conquerors in the great match of the English season as the guardians of the guerdon coveted by all clubs."

One quirk of the final was that the four men playing whose surnames began with the letter H scored the four goals.

Newcastle: Lawrence, McCracken, Pudan, Gardner, Veitch, McWilliam, Rutherford, Howie, Appleyard, Speedie, Wilson.
Wolves: Lunn, Jones, Collins, Hunt, Wooldridge, Bishop, Harrison, Shelton, Hedley, Radford, Pedley.
Attendance: 74,967.
Referee: TP Campbell.

Wolves 7 (Phillipson 5, Bowen, Weaver)
Bradford City 2 (Moore 2)
Football League Second Division
Saturday 25th December 1926

TOM PHILLIPSON and his Wolves team-mates made sure it was a very unhappy Yuletide for Bradford City when the sides met on Christmas Day in 1926. A below average crowd turned up for the match with many doubtless consigned to the home for family duties. But those that didn't make the game with The Bantams not only missed Wolves' best win of the season, but also the chance of seeing only the second man in the club's colours to hit five goals in a game.

Phillipson had joined Wolves from Swindon Town in December 1923, for a £1,000 fee. That was a lot of money in those 1920s days yet Phillipson's signing could still be easily considered as a snip. By the time he left for Sheffield United in 1928, he had amassed 111 goals from just 159 appearances and, in the process, had made himself the club's all-time leading scorer.

His 12 goals in what remained of the 1923/24 season following his move from the Wiltshire club helped Wanderers secure the Third Division North title. He followed that up with a further 16 as Wolves finished fourth on their return to the Second Division. But it was in 1924/25 that he really opened the eyes of the football world scoring 37 goals in league and cup.

All but four of the goals came in an incredible 25-game run in which he failed to hit the target in just five. It began on Christmas Day at Oldham where he scored both in a 2-1 win at Boundary Park. There was a spell of ten consecutive games that he scored in and his profitable spell included hat-tricks against Middlesbrough and Stockport County, as well as a four-timer against Barnsley.

After a slow start in 1926, with just two goals against his name from eight outings, a hat-trick in the 9-1 demolition of Barnsley at Molineux sparked another run of scoring in consecutive league games – a run that was to give him an English league record that stands to this day. And poor Bradford found themselves right in the middle of it. And yet Wolves' form had been anything but consistent and the four games leading up to the Bradford visit had yielded just a single point for the Molineux men despite Phillipson's heroics.

The visitors made some early threats with Peter Bennie prompting his forwards while Fred Moore gave home keeper Jack Hampton a few anxious moments. But, from the quarter-hour mark, when Phillipson fired Wolves into the lead, there was only going to be one winner although there was to be a scare along the way. Walter Weaver crossed for Tommy Bowen to tee the ball up for Phillipson who beat City keeper Len Boot with a low shot.

Fifteen minutes later it was 2-0 with Phillipson again the scorer. Albert Kay picked out Harry Lees and his accurate through ball left Phillipson with just Boot to

15

Wolves' Greatest Games

beat which he did with consummate ease. But ten minutes before the break Bradford pulled a goal back. Ted Richardson crossed and Bennie held the ball up nicely for Moore who ran in and beat Hampton from eight yards.

Another two minutes passed by and Hampton was again picking the ball out of the net after fragility in the home defence allowed Moore to pick his spot for his second of the morning. But, just before the break, Wolves regained the advantage as Phillipson completed his hat-trick by shooting home from 25 yards after a corner had been half-cleared to him.

In the second half, Bowen and then Weaver added further goals to put Wanderers 5-2 ahead before Phillipson got another two to complete his personal nap hand. He was only denied a sixth goal by the offside flag after he had forced the ball past the unfortunate Boot. The players were then afforded the luxury of having Boxing Day off before the return fixture at Valley Parade.

Whereas the Molineux gate was one of the lowest of the campaign, up in Yorkshire the near-28,000 that turned up was Bradford's highest gate. And they witnessed Phillipson carrying on with his remarkable run as he scored for the ninth consecutive game. Lees had given Wolves the lead with a simple tap-in after Boot had dropped Albert Legge's centre after 30 minutes' play.

Phillipson made it 2-0 four minutes after the break after he had taken a pass from Weaver and found the back of the net with a low, 15-yard drive. City pulled one back when a shot from Bert Smith struck the crossbar and then Hampton before bouncing into the net and although the Molineux keeper was busier than his counterpart for the remainder of the game, Wolves held on for the win.

The leading scorer carried his excellent form into the New Year netting two in a 5-2 home win over Hull City, the consolation in a 4-1 reversal at Swansea, a hat-trick in a 5-0 trouncing of Clapton Orient and a strike in a two-all draw at Notts County to complete the record of scoring in 13 consecutive league games. He finished the season with a total of 33 goals from just 35 appearances in league and cup.

Tom Phillipson joined Bilston and then Walsall after his Sheffield United stint, but returned to Wolverhampton where, for many years, he ran a tobacconist shop in the town centre. He also entered local politics and was made Mayor of Wolverhampton in 1944.

Wolves: Hampton, Watson, Shaw, McDougall, Mitten, Kaye, Legge, Bowen, Phillipson, Lee, Weaver.
Bradford City: Boot, Russell, Cheetham, Burkinshaw, Gilhooley, Lloyd, Bennie, Moore, Ormston, Batten, Richardson.
Attendance: 10,421.
Referee: HE Hull.

Wolves 2 (Jones, Brown)
Arsenal 0
Football League Second Division
Saturday 19th September 1936

ARSENAL WERE the team that everyone wanted to beat in the thirties. After winning their first championship in 1931, the Gunners were then runners-up before reeling off three consecutive top spots. Wolves on the other hand, had only rejoined the top flight in 1932 after a 26-year absence and in the eight meetings between the clubs leading in to the 1936/37 campaign, had managed just one win and two draws against them.

That solitary victory was by 2-1 at Highbury in Wolves' first season back in the First Division. It was part of a decent run-in by Major Frank Buckley's team with five wins from the last eight games, starting with the one at Arsenal, preventing a quick return to the Second Division. Just two points separated Wanderers and the relegated pair of Bolton and Blackpool.

In the three years since that close call, there had been a steady improvement in Buckley's team and, for the visit of Arsenal, hopes were boosted when Bryn Jones passed a fitness test on the morning of the game. He returned to the side in place of Bob Iverson as the only change to the 11 who had won 3-1 at Preston seven days earlier. At kick-off time there were still hundreds of supporters queuing to get into the ground.

Arsenal won the toss and, on a near perfect afternoon, they elected to attack the South Bank end but after three minutes Wolves threatened. George Ashall fired over a cross that was just too high for Tom Waring and Gordon Clayton. In the next attack, Clayton was about to get a shot away when Eddie Hapgood stuck out a foot to block. Norman Sidey had obviously been ordered to man mark Waring as he shadowed the centre-forward constantly.

Cecil Shaw had to clear from Jack Crayston but little was seen of the Arsenal attack in the opening stages of a game that was being played at a terrific pace. The Gunners did go close when George Laking's headed clearance fell to Alex James who cleared the bar by inches after hitting a shot from 25 yards. For Wolves, Tom Galley was just as close with a first-time drive that was no more than a foot wide.

Jones put Wolves ahead in the 12th minute after a build-up involving Ashall, Waring and Smalley. When the ball was played through to Jones he squeezed it between visiting keeper George Swindin and the near post. Arsenal's response was through Cliff Bastin who lifted a shot over the bar and then forced a fine save from Alex Scott who turned aside a rising drive.

In the 19th minute, Jackie Brown got a second for Wolves after exchanging passes with Clayton before driving home a low shot that was well out of the reach of Swindin. The goal seemed to shake the visitors' attack into life and Ray

Wolves' Greatest Games

Bowden should have pulled one back but he shot wide when unmarked in front of goal.

Scott had little trouble in fielding a 30-yard effort from Crayston before the Arsenal goal escaped when, following a corner from Brown, Hapgood had to clear Waring's flick off the line. Play continued to swing from end to end and just before the half-time break, Scott made a spectacular save, turning James's goalbound shot around the post.

Shortly after the resumption, Scott was called into action again saving this time from Ted Drake who had forged a path through the heart of the Wanderers defence.

Waring fired six inches wide of the post after some good work by Jones set up the chance. Jones then damaged an ankle and was forced out onto the wing with Ashall moving inside as cover.

Despite his handicap, Jones still managed to put over a fine cross that Waring allowed to run through to Clayton whose powerful shot forced Swindin into a first-rate save. Moments later the keeper showed that he was fallible as he dropped another Jones centre and only just managed to drop on the ball in time as Waring ran in.

Apart from when the goals were scored, the biggest cheer of the afternoon was reserved for Scott as he made a fantastic double save. The first came when Bastin crossed to Drake who was inside the six-yard box and unmarked. He hit the ball with fearsome power but Scott leapt to push it away. But it only went as far as the head of Pat Beasley who tried to nod back into the net only for the keeper to save once more.

Jones appeared to have shaken off his injury and he returned to his normal inside-right position to look a threat once again against the side destined to sign him two years later. Arsenal's main threat, in the time that remained, came from Beasley and Bastin on the wings. But the home defence held on as Wolves enjoyed their first home win over Arsenal in 31 years.

The attendance of 53,097 was a ground record beating the previous best against Aston Villa on Boxing Day 1932 by almost 1,000. Arsenal got their revenge in the return fixture winning 3-0 but they failed to add the Football League title to their honours list as they finished in third place behind winners Manchester City and runners-up Charlton Athletic. Wolves finished in a creditable fifth position as their reputation continued to grow on the way to becoming one of England's finest.

Wolves: Scott, Laking, Shaw, Smalley, Morris, Galley, Ashall, Jones, Waring, Clayton, Brown.
Arsenal: Swindin, Male, Hapgood, Crayston, Sidey, Copping, Beasley, Bowden, Drake, James, Bastin.
Attendance: 53,097.
Referee: J Wiltshire.

Wolves 7 (Westcott 2, Dorsett 4, McIntosh)
Everton 0
Football League First Division
Wednesday 22nd February 1939

WOLVES HAD finished runners-up the previous season to the mighty Arsenal but should have won the title, going down 1–0 at Sunderland in their final match, enabling the Gunners to be champions by a point. Many experts thought Major Buckley's side would make amends the following season but it was a team without a manager who set the early pace. It was not until the end of the 1938/39 season that Theo Kelly was named Everton manager, having previously been secretary at Goodison Park.

The team selection was in the hands of senior trainers and boardroom executives and they clearly got it right as Everton began the campaign with six successive wins. Their exciting young centre-forward Tommy Lawton was on target in all six, collecting eight goals. It was form that soon earned him his first England cap.

In contrast Wolves had a disappointing start. They drew their first four games before winning at Brentford only to then lose the next two. So they were six points behind Everton at that stage and, with only two points for a win, it was quite a gap. And it quickly became eight points when the clubs met on Merseyside and Lawton scored the only goal of the game. By the time of the return at Molineux, Wolves had steadily made inroads into Everton's total and, with 28 matches gone, were then four points adrift. It was vital for the home side to get a win and though many thought they would do so few could have predicted the ensuing goal avalanche.

The match was played on a Wednesday afternoon as both clubs had been in action in the fifth round of the FA Cup the previous Saturday when they were scheduled to have met in the league. Everton drew 2-2 at Birmingham while Wolves beat Liverpool 4-1.

Everton came into the league match with five successive wins behind them. Lawton was played at inside-forward for the first time that season. It was because of an injury to Stan Bentham who missed his only game of that season. It was a landmark for Lawton – his 100th league game and he was still only 19. The game was watched by several club managers, it being a weekday afternoon, and also present was Football League secretary Fred Howarth. They had hardly sat down when Wolves took the lead.

Tom Galley brought Jimmy Mullen into the action and when the right-half came into possession for the second time he drew left-half Jock Thomson and gave Mullen the ball once more. The winger hit it first time with his left foot and dropped the ball straight on to Dennis Westcott's head and he nodded past Harry Morton. Dicky Dorsett then had a shot deflected by Welsh international centre-half Tommy Jones

Wolves' Greatest Games

to Teddy Maguire who should have scored but shot wide. When Stan Cullis headed away a centre from Wally Boyes the Wolves skipper was temporarily stunned.

Former Villa goalkeeper Morton, deputising for England international Ted Sagar, had to punch the ball off Dorsett's head from another fine Mullen centre, and Wolves were kept waiting until the 26th minute for their second goal. Galley found Westcott and the centre-forward bided his time before making an accurate pass which slipped Dorsett through and he made no mistake.

Dorsett was denied by Morton shortly afterwards but his second goal duly arrived on 33 minutes. Westcott again slipped the ball through to him and again there was no stopping the shot that followed. It was nearly four just before the break when a Galley clearance found Westcott who drew Morton before putting the ball into the net only to be ruled offside. A minute into the second half there came some light relief. Full-back Bill Morris, who had won his first England cap earlier in the season, robbed Bunny Bell and put the ball well upfield where Norman Greenhalgh took it on his head and then started laughing – the ball had burst.

The half was only three minutes old when Dorsett completed a genuine hat-trick. Westcott again put him through after the inside-left had run into a perfect position as Everton appealed in vain for offside. Another five minutes and Wolves struck again. Mullen beat Greenhalgh and raced on before delivering the perfect pass to the feet of Alex McIntosh. He trapped the ball with his left foot and then steered it just inside a post with his right.

There was always a threat of more goals, Westcott getting clean through only to miss his kick while Mullen cut in and fired a shot just wide. With 13 minutes to go Dorsett collected his fourth and Westcott nipped in for his second seven minutes from time. Twelve days later the teams met again and Wolves triumphed 2–0 at Molineux thanks to two Westcott goals to earn a place in the FA Cup semi-final. Yet Everton would have the last laugh as they won the league by four points.

After the game manager Major Frank Buckley modestly said of his team: "They played well don't you think?" When Everton half-back Joe Mercer was asked what had happened to his team he responded: "What happened? You can't play against a team like this."

John Macadam of the *Daily Express* wrote: "Let it be said at once, on this form Wolves are the greatest thing that ever struck the football game. They didn't simply beat Everton, they demolished them."

Wolves: Scott, Morris, Taylor, Galley, Cullis, Gardiner, Mullen, McIntosh, Westcott, Dorsett, Maguire.
Everton: Morton, Cook, Greenhalgh, Mercer, Jones, Thompson, Gillick, Lawton, Bell, Stevenson, Boyes.
Attendance: 39,734.
Referee: AW Barton.

Wolves 5 (Westcott 4, Galley pen)
Grimsby Town 0

FA Cup semi-final
Old Trafford
Saturday 25th March 1939

MANCHESTER WAS victim to light rain and sleet on the morning of the FA Cup last four meeting of Wolves and Grimsby Town. But the bad weather, albeit temporarily, relented as a record crowd of 76,962 packed into Old Trafford.

All four of Wolves' cup ties that year had taken place at Molineux with a total of 187,910 supporters watching the games against Bradford City (3-1), Leicester City (5-1), Liverpool (4-1) and Everton (2-0). The fifth-round match against Liverpool attracted a ground record of 61,315. The Mariners' road to Manchester saw then beating Tranmere Rovers, Millwall, Sheffield United and Chelsea.

Town were without regular keeper George Tweedy who was out injured. He was replaced by George Moulson who was destined for an unhappy afternoon. Grimsby were the first to show with right wing raids by Jimmy Boyd that resulted in obstruction decisions going against Joe Gardiner and Frank Taylor. Boyd took the free kicks himself, the first being headed clear by Stan Cullis and the other by Taylor.

Tom Galley's attempt to get his forwards moving petered out and there was a chance for Grimsby when Bill Morris's clearance rebounded off Fred Crack who controlled the ball and crossed for Tommy Jones to get in a header that was taken by Wolves keeper Alex Scott. Then Fred Howe fired wide with a low drive as the East Coast club continued to have the best of the game's early moments.

A cross from Teddy Maguire forced Harry Betmead into a rushed clearance as Alex McIntosh threatened and Dickie Dorsett ran in to shoot powerfully over the bar. Town hit back when Boyd beat Taylor and raced off towards goal but the full-back recovered and got back to divert the ball out for a corner. Scott missed his punch from Boyd's flag-kick and Howe got in a header that Morris managed to boot clear even though he was facing his own goal.

Dennis Westcott was inches away from giving his side the lead with a terrific drive after he had been put through by McIntosh. The Wolves players had settled into the game now and were starting to threaten while the defence was coping confidently with any threats. But, after 15 minutes, the game took an unexpected and ugly turn.

McIntosh slipped a pass to Dorsett who, as he shot, collided with Moulson. The ball bounced up for McIntosh whose header went over the vacant net. Both trainers raced on to the field to tend to their stricken men. Dorsett was carried to the touchline and he was immediately followed by Moulson who was taken to the dressing room. Town full-back Jack Hodgson went in goal with Buck dropping back into defence as cover while Wolves played with four forwards. Howe then missed the

Wolves' Greatest Games

best chance of the game when he beat Cullis and had time to pick his spot only to shoot wide.

Dorsett was then carried from the touchline to the dressing room on the shoulders of the trainers as the sleet that had been falling again gave way to snow. Wolves began to do the majority of the pressing while the Grimsby defence were doing all they could to protect their stand-in keeper. Hodgson received a hearty cheer with his first real action as he ran out to catch a Maguire centre.

But he was helpless as Wolves moved into a 32nd-minute lead. McIntosh beat Jones and Betmead before slipping the ball to Westcott who drew Hodgson from his line before finding the net. Dorsett had returned to the field with his left leg heavily bandaged just prior to the goal and he was limping heavily. There was, however, to be no return for Moulson that afternoon.

Despite the disadvantage, Town were still a threat and Scott had to run from his goal to block as Crack went through in a move that saw Maguire taking a knock that needed attention. Just as Maguire rejoined the fray, Westcott made it two in the 40th minute. Again McIntosh supplied the telling pass sending the centre-forward clear of the defence before he beat the advancing Hodgson. Just on the break Betmead headed a Jimmy Mullen shot off the line.

Almost straight from the restart, Morris had to clear a shot from Crack for a corner. But in the 48th minute, a Galley penalty gave Wanderers a clear sight of the twin towers of Wembley. Westcott was about to profit on a poor header from Buck when he was fouled by Betmead and Galley expertly despatched the spot-kick.

Credit to Grimsby who didn't throw in the towel with Scott having to save a header from Crack who then had a well struck drive blocked by the legs of Cullis. Scott was also called upon to save at the feet of Boyd but there was to be no consolation for the ten men. Instead they were punished further with four minutes remaining when Westcott took a pass from Maguire and calmly sidestepped Ned Vincent before netting.

A minute later Westcott got his fourth goal of the afternoon after Gardiner's long ball put him in the clear. He was obviously in no mood for mistakes as he once more drew the hapless Hodgson before finding the net. The massive crowd had witnessed a drama-packed game that yielded gate receipts of £8,193. There was to be no happy ending to the cup trail for Wolves, however, as they went down by 4-1 to underdogs Portsmouth in the final the following month.

Grimsby: Moulson, Vincent, Hodgson, Hall, Betmead, Buck, Boyd, Beattie, Howe, Jones, Crack.
Wolves: Scott, Morris, Taylor, Galley, Cullis, Gardiner, Maguire, McIntosh, Westcott, Dorsett, Mullen.
Attendance: 76,962.
Referee: FW Wort.

Wolves 6 (Pye 3, Westcott 2, Mullen)
Arsenal 1 (Lewis)
Football League First Division
Saturday 31st August 1946

THE RAIN that fell on Molineux as the kick-off to the new season approached in 1946 didn't deter the fans as a crowd of 50,000 packed the ground for the game with Arsenal. And no-one could blame the throng for wanting to see their team in first class action again because, after all, they had been waiting for 2,444 days.

That was the amount of time lost between the 2-2 draw with Arsenal in August 1939, and the return of the Gunners. The fixtures for the 1946/47 campaign mirrored those of the 1939/40 campaign when only three games were completed with the outbreak of the Second World War bringing the game, as people knew it, to a halt. All results from that truncated season were to be expunged from the records.

Five of the side that played in the eve of war contest between Wolves and Arsenal, Bill Morris, Stan Cullis, Tom Galley, Dennis Westcott and Jimmy Mullen, were in the team for the restaging while another four, Bert Williams, Billy Wright, Fred Ramscar and Angus McLean, had all played wartime football for the club.

Making their full debuts were Rotherham-born Jesse Pye, and Johnny Hancocks who was more of a local man as he hailed from Oakengates. The duo had been signed from Notts County and Walsall respectively and both had played in the five-game pre-season tour to Sweden that the club had embarked upon.

Welsh international Bryn Jones, who had moved from Molineux to Highbury for a record transfer fee in 1938, watched the game from the stands while another member of the Arsenal team, Ian McPherson, was a fighter pilot ace who had earned two DFCs during the hostilities.

With less than a minute gone, new boys Pye and Hancocks combined with the latter delivering a centre that George Swindin had to turn behind for a corner. The keeper then had to deal with a ball from the left which had been fired over by Mullen. Arsenal's first threat came when McPherson beat McLean on the right wing but his pass found Reg Lewis in an offside position.

Williams had to race from his goal to save bravely at the feet of Cliff Bastin and Swindin was in action too as he turned a powerful effort from Galley around the post. The keeper then had to be at his best to keep out a fierce drive from Pye.

As Wolves upped their game, Swindin was by far busier than Williams who watched from the South Bank end as his counterpart saved from Ramscar and Galley and, just before the break, from Pye whose shot was turned against the bar. When the ball dropped down into the goalmouth, it was smothered by the keeper.

The only real surprise was that the opening 45 minutes had passed by without a goal. But the lead that had eluded Wanderers finally arrived two minutes after the resumption. Hancocks switched the ball inside to Wright and he in turn laid it into the path of Pye who took aim from 25 yards before hitting a shot that hit the diving Swindin before continuing over the line.

Hancocks was quickly establishing himself as a crowd favourite and he supplied an inch-perfect cross for Pye to head home the second, from an acute angle, on 54 minutes. It was very much one-way traffic now and Swindin made an excellent save to deny Pye his hat-trick. But then a centre from Hancocks completely deceived the keeper who was relieved to see the ball bouncing off the bar and going behind.

With 65 minutes gone Westcott made it three after he took a pass from Mullen and swivelled before powerfully striking the ball past the helpless Swindin. And it was Mullen who supplied the cross for Pye to complete his dream debut with a hat-trick goal just three minutes later.

The four-goal burst in a 21-minute spell had the Arsenal defence reeling but Wolves were in no mood to show mercy and with a quarter of an hour left on the Molineux Street Stand clock, Westcott met a perfect cross from Mullen to head Wanderers into a five-goal advantage.

Little was seen of the Arsenal attack and three dangerous raids from the home forwards led to three corners in as many minutes that were only cleared with an air of desperation and difficulty. In a rare move into the Wolves half of the field, there was a chance for Lewis but he squandered it by firing wide from 15 yards out.

Mullen, who had supplied the centres for three of the five goals, got on the scoresheet himself with just four minutes remaining. Wright found Ramscar on the left wing and he in turn fed Mullen who showed no signs of fatigue given his contribution to the game as he powered the ball past Swindin.

Two minutes from the end, in a breakaway move, the Gunners grabbed a consolation goal as Lewis ran clear and drew Williams from his goal and dummied the keeper before turning the ball into the empty net.

Unfortunately, Wolves didn't carry any momentum into the five games that followed in the next 16 days with just one point and two goals gleaned from them before the team rediscovered the form that had destroyed Arsenal on that opening day.

Wolves: Williams, Morris, McLean, Galley, Cullis, Wright, Hancocks, Pye, Westcott, Ramscar, Mullen.
Arsenal: Swindin, Scott, Male, Nelson, Joy, Curtis, McPherson, Sloan, Lewis, Logie, Bastin.
Attendance: 50,845.
Referee: G Tedds.

Liverpool 1 (Balmer pen)
Wolves 5 (Westcott 4, Mullen)
Football League First Division
Saturday 7th December 1946

CHRISTMAS CAME two weeks early for Wolves and in particular Dennis Westcott when the team travelled up to Merseyside to take on league leaders Liverpool at their Anfield fortress. The Reds had a game in hand to Wanderers with both sides locked on 24 points at the top and separated only by goal average.

The chase for league honours was hotly contested and going into that afternoon's programme of games, just six points divided the top six. Wolves were in superb form, losing just once and drawing once in a 12-match run leading up to the visit to Anfield.

The previous weekend they had enjoyed a 3-2 Molineux victory over high-flying Manchester United with Westcott hitting his 13th and 14th goals of the season.

Unsurprisingly, Ted Vizard named an unchanged team – in fact, it was the fourth successive game that he had done so. Early morning rain had given way to bright sunshine as a cavalcade of coaches ferried Wolves supporters to the ground while the railway also did a roaring trade in return tickets from Wolverhampton High Level to Liverpool Lime Street.

Liverpool had lost just one home game up to that point coincidently against the only team to beat Wolves in their profitable 12-game run – Middlesbrough. And the home side got off on the front foot with inside-left Cyril Done failing to get his head to an early free kick into Bert Williams's area.

Wolves responded with a thrust down the left flank by Jimmy Mullen who lifted a cross over for Jesse Pye to head inches over the bar. In the next attack by the visitors, Westcott was fouled right on the edge of the Liverpool area. Johnny Hancocks, rather than trying a shot, instead tried a short cross that was cleared by Ray Lambert.

Despite the heavy pitch, the game was being contested at a fair pace with play swinging from end to end. Angus McLean was penalised for handling as he challenged Billy Liddell and when Bernard Ramsden took the resultant free kick, he saw the ball deflected away off team-mate Jack Balmer. Williams had to rush from his line to save at the feet of Done and when the keeper cleared the ball upfield he found Hancocks whose angled drive was just off target.

In the 14th minute Westcott opened the scoring following a foul on Tom Galley. Hancocks took the free kick and although the ball was returned to him from a defender's half-clearance in the congested area, the winger sent it back into the middle and Westcott leapt to send a powerful header past Cyril Sidlow, the one-time Wolves keeper.

Sidlow had to be at his best shortly after the goal as he dived full length to save a low shot from Hancocks and, when Liverpool went in search of an equaliser, Liddell

Wolves' Greatest Games

fired over the bar. A great run by Mullen, in which he beat three defenders, ended when a fourth Liverpool man took the ball off his foot as he was lining up a shot.

Williams held on to a header from Done and Billy Wright went forward to shoot over as the entertainment continued. Such was the strength of the attacking play from both sides another goal had to come and when it did it was in Wolves' favour and again it was Westcott that did the damage. Thirty-three minutes had gone when Mullen and then Hancocks had shots charged down but it was a case of third time lucky when the ball rebounded to Westcott who calmly picked his spot before beating Sidlow. And five minutes later, the big striker completed his hat-trick. Mullen ended a typical solo run with a precision pass to Westcott whose power and pace took him past Laurie Hughes and Sidlow before stroking the ball into the net.

Westcott was obviously not in the mood to ease up against the tormented Liverpool defence and he added his fourth just two minutes later when, with a burst of speed on the muddy surface, he snapped up Wright's pass and sidestepped Sidlow before shooting into the empty goal. It was his fourth strike in just 28 minutes and it looked as if he had got a fifth when he netted again just before the break. But this time the linesman's flag for offside quelled the cheers of the travelling supporters.

Liverpool, despite facing a hopeless task, made a bright start to the second half but Stan Cullis and his defence thwarted any hopes that the home forwards had of creating a foundation to build on. In fact, when the next goal did arrive it was a fifth for Wolves on 56 minutes and it deservedly went to the hard-working Mullen. He ran onto a slide rule pass from Willie Forbes and beat Sidlow with a left-foot drive.

Legendary Anfield striker Albert Stubbins had the chance of pulling one back for his side but he dallied allowing McLean to nip in and rob him of the ball. Williams made a tremendous save from a Balmer piledriver and then the keeper turned a header from the same player against the crossbar before the ball was cleared.

Liverpool finally did get a goal after Balmer was fouled by Cullis in the box. Balmer picked himself up and beat Williams from the spot for a consolation goal. But the afternoon belonged to Wolves and, in particular, to the striking talents of one Dennis Westcott.

Liverpool: Sidlow, Lambert, Ramsden, Taylor, Hughes, Paisley, Eastham, Balmer, Stubbins, Done, Liddell.
Wolves: Williams, McLean, Crook, Galley, Cullis, Wright, Hancocks, Pye, Westcott, Forbes, Mullen.
Attendance: 52,512.
Referee: J Briggs.

Bolton Wanderers 0
Wolves 5 (Hancocks 2, Pye, Mullen 2)
Football League First Division
Saturday 28th August 1948

AT THE end of the 1947/48 season, Ted Vizard ended his four-year spell as manager of Wolves, leaving his assistant Stan Cullis, who was still only 31 years of age, to take up the reins. But the man who had excelled as a player and captain at Molineux, and was to excel as a manager too, didn't have the happiest of introductions to life in the hot seat as, from his opening two games, both at home, Wolves took just a single point.

After an opening day draw with neighbours Birmingham City in front of a 54,000-plus crowd, a midweek single goal defeat by Sunderland invited heavy criticism from sections of the crowd and questions were already being asked as to whether the appointment had been made on sentiment rather than on Cullis's skill as a manager. Over the years those critics would be forced to eat their words on more than one occasion.

The third game of the campaign was against Bolton at Burnden Park. The Trotters had won one and drawn the other of their first fixtures but they were dealt a blow shortly before the kick-off when skipper Don Howe failed a fitness test and was replaced by John Aspinall. Cullis made just one change to his starting line-up with Bill Crook coming in for Jimmy Dunn. The new manager did, however, shuffle his pack moving Willie Forbes from right-half to inside-left and Sammy Smyth from inside-left to inside-right.

In an uneventful opening few minutes, the first threat came from Wolves when Smyth and Crook set up the chance for Johnny Hancocks to deliver a dangerous cross but the move came to a halt when the referee spotted a push by Jesse Pye in the Bolton box. Another Hancocks cross was headed away by Ralph Banks straight to the feet of Smyth who immediately fired at goal but straight into the arms of Bolton keeper Stan Hanson.

Nat Lofthouse was well wide with a hurried shot as Bolton went on the attack but the home team were soon forced back with Hancocks again crossing for Smyth to shoot too close to Hanson once more. There was a chance for Pye who ran onto Smyth's through ball and shot as he was tackled with his effort just going wide of the angle.

Then came a sustained spell of Bolton pressure during which Vince Dillon headed wide, Jack Bradley fired over the bar and Bert Williams was forced to scramble along his line to save a drive from Tom Woodward after the keeper's punch from a corner had landed in the Bolton winger's path. When Wolves went back on the front foot, Forbes wasted a good chance by snatching at the ball after he had taken a pass from Pye.

Wolves' Greatest Games

Wolves had played by far the better football and they moved into the lead with 37 minutes gone. Billy Wright found Pye and he quickly slipped the ball to Hancocks who cut inside and hit a shot that flew past the static Hanson. The keeper did, however, make a smart save to prevent Jimmy Mullen from netting a second goal shortly before the interval.

Seconds after the resumption, Smyth drove inches wide of the post before, in the next attack, he cleverly back-heeled the ball to Hancocks whose centre was caught by Hanson. Bolton then temporarily lost the services of Dillon who was hurt in a collision with Hancocks. But despite being a man down they should have been level when Woodward found himself with only Williams to beat but he screwed his shot wide.

Dillon returned on the hour mark, after a ten-minute absence, just before Wolves moved into a two-goal lead. Smyth sent Hancocks away down the right flank and, after running to the line, he hit a low cross that hit the inside of the far post and bounced up into the net. The ball was over the line before Smyth arrived to apply the finishing touch.

It was one-way traffic now and Hanson had to punch away a long-range effort from Angus McLean from under the bar before using his fists again to clear a Hancocks centre from a crowded area. But he was beaten once more in the 67th minute by a peach of a goal. Mullen and Pye ran from inside their own half to the edge of the Bolton box, exchanging passes along the way, before Pye blasted the ball home.

The savage assault on Hanson's goal continued and the home defence gave way again with 80 minutes gone with Pye crossing to Mullen who ran in and clinically despatched the ball past the keeper. Four minutes later it was Mullen again who lifted the ball over the advancing Hanson's head to complete the rout.

Mullen did almost complete his hat-trick two minutes later, but he tapped the ball just the wrong side of the post with Hanson stranded. But the winger must have been well satisfied with not only his performance and a brace of goals, but the showing of the team after such an unhappy opening week.

And the day before the Bolton game, he received a benefit cheque of £750 from Wolves chairman James Baker having completed ten years' service at Molineux. It must have been a sweet trip back to Wolverhampton for the Geordie.

Bolton: Hanson, Roberts, R Banks, Aspinall, Gillies, Murphy, Woodward, Dillon, Lofthouse, Bradley, Moir.

Wolves: Williams, McLean, Springthorpe, W Crook, Shorthouse, Wright, Hancocks, Smyth, Pye, Forbes, Mullen.
Attendance: 33,856.
Referee: HI Wright.

Wolves 1 (Smyth)
Manchester United 1 (Mitten)
After extra time
FA Cup semi-final, Hillsborough
Saturday 26 March 1949

AFTER A ten-year gap, six of which had been lost through the Second World War, Wolves got through to the last four of the FA Cup. But whereas the 1939 drubbing of Grimsby Town was made easier after the Mariners had lost their keeper through injury, this time it was Wolves who struggled in those pre-substitute days as they had one man reduced to a virtual passenger in the early stages, and another after the interval.

With 11 fit men Wanderers were in for a testing time for the game at Hillsborough because their semi-final opponents were Manchester United – the holders of the Cup. Johnny Hancocks returned after a three-game injury absence, and Jesse Pye passed a fitness test by the club doctor on the day, after he had been a bedridden midweek flu victim.

Just six minutes had gone when disaster struck for the first time in the game for the men in old gold. Charlie Mitten sent over a cross from the left and Jimmy Delaney and Roy Pritchard collided as they went for the ball. Delaney was unharmed but the Wolves left-back had to leave the field after receiving treatment. Mitten lifted a centre on to the roof of Bert Williams' net and Bill Shorthouse had to intervene when Delaney took advantage of Billy Wright's miskick as the ten men reorganised.

United keeper Jack Crompton caught a Hancocks cross underneath the bar before Pritchard limped back onto the pitch to take up a position on the left wing. Jimmy Dunn dropped back to left-half and Billy Wright to Pritchard's left-back slot. Amazingly, given the problems they had suffered, it was Wolves that broke the deadlock after just 12 minutes. Jimmy Mullen found Hancocks and he slipped the ball through in front of Pye and United defender Allenby Chilton.

The centre-half won the chase but his attempt to find his keeper was under-hit and Pye was on the ball like a flash, beating John Aston before finding Sammy Smyth on the edge of the box. He calmly trapped the ball before beating Crompton with a low shot.

United were soon threatening an equaliser and when Bert Williams couldn't hang onto a stinging effort from Mitten, Bill Crook ran over to clear the loose ball.

Crompton saved at Mullen's feet after a neat flick from Pye sent him through, and then Wright cut the ball out when Delaney looked to be in with a chance. But United had been threatening and they drew level after 23 minutes. A deep cross from the right landed at Mitten's feet and he had the time to control before lobbing the ball over Williams.

Crompton made a spectacular save as he tipped a Mullen drive over the bar, and then Stan Pearson screwed the ball wide as he failed with an attempted half-volley.

Wolves' Greatest Games

Despite having Pritchard struggling to make any contribution such was the severity of his injury, Wolves were giving as good as they got with Mullen's crosses a real cause for concern for the opposition defence. And Hancocks too was in a determined mood and after he had slipped by Aston his low centre was cleared by Johnny Carey who got to the ball a fraction before Pye could.

At the other end, Wright cleared as Delaney threatened before a move involving Smyth and Mullen came to an end when the crippled Pritchard was unable to take advantage of Smyth's pass out wide. The interval arrived with Wanderers fully deserving to be on level terms despite their disadvantage.

Shortly after the resumption, there was a terrific scramble in the Wolves goalmouth after a run by Mitten. With the ball flying about it took a double fisted punch from Williams to clear the danger. Then, after Dunn had conceded a free kick which was taken by Mitten, the ball was half-cleared back to the winger. This time he crossed for Jack Rowley who headed wide from a good position.

Crompton turned a Pye header over the bar and, from Hancocks' corner, the keeper just beat the incoming Mullen and Smyth to the ball. But then Wolves were hit with another major setback. The half was at its midway stage when Lol Kelly went down near the halfway line. He was surrounded by players from both sides and, after his leg was put into splints, he was carried off on a stretcher.

More reorganisation followed with Pritchard returning to his original position and Wright moving over to right-back – his third position of the game. Shortly afterwards, the skipper's mistimed pass fell to Delaney but to the relief of the Molineux supporters in the crowd, he wasted the chance by shooting wide. After ten minutes off the field, Kelly hobbled back on but he was in obvious discomfort as he took up a right-wing position, struggling to put his right foot to the ground.

Extra time arrived and the main chances, perhaps unsurprisingly, fell to United. Rowley found the net but was ruled offside as he ran through, and Williams, twice in quick succession, saved from Bill McGlen's dipping shot and then Delaney's well struck drive.

But Wolves held on, despite only having nine fit men at the end of the game, to earn a replay at Goodison Park when they moved through to the final at Wembley courtesy of a Smyth goal just four minutes from the end in front of a 72,000 crowd.

Wolves: Williams, Kelly, Pritchard, Crook, Shorthouse, Wright, Hancocks, Smyth, Pye, Dunn, Mullen.
United: Crompton, Carey, Aston, Cockburn, Chilton, McGlen, Delaney, Anderson, Rowley, Pearson, Mitten.
Attendance: 62,250.
Referee: JH Parker.

Leicester City 1 (Griffiths)
Wolves 3 (Pye 2, Smyth)
FA Cup Final
Wembley
Saturday 30th April 1949

IT MADE a change for Wolves to go into an FA Cup Final as odds-on favourites. Generally speaking, through the course of the club's history, it has been the other way around. Wanderers were heading for a top six finish in the First Division but their opponents at Wembley, Leicester City, were in danger of relegation from the Second Division and lay three off the bottom on the day of the final.

Stan Cullis, in his first season in charge at Molineux, became the youngest ever manager to take a side to a Wembley Cup Final at the age of 32. And whereas he missed out on the major domestic honours of the game as a player either side of the Second World War, Cullis was finally able to taste success.

There was a comfortable dawn to the final when the third-round draw paired Wolves with Chesterfield of the Second Division. Over 46,000 packed into Molineux for a one-sided game that saw Wolves cruising to a 6-0 victory. It took Wanderers just 13 minutes to open their account as Johnny Hancocks dribbled past three men as he cut in from the wing before beating Ray Middleton with a low shot.

Four minutes later the home side doubled their score with Jesse Pye running onto Billy Wright's forward pass and drawing Middleton from his line before slotting the ball home. Such was the dominance enjoyed by Cullis's men, the only real surprise was that it took until six minutes before the break before the third goal arrived. The scorer was Jimmy Mullen who ran in from the left and unleashed a shot that went in off the underside of the bar.

Pye notched the fourth four minutes after the interval and again it was Wright who provided the telling pass. The skipper found Pye with his back to goal but the centre-forward quickly turned and rifled the ball past Middleton. It was left to Sammy Smyth to complete the rout with goals in the 73rd and 75th minutes. Mullen retrieved the ball after his shot had hit the post and he crossed for Smyth to sidestep his marker before scoring with a cross-shot. Smyth then headed the sixth from a Hancocks cross.

A trip to Bramall Lane for a fourth round tie with Sheffield United was the reward for Wolves and in front of another huge crowd the visitors were relieved to go into the half-time break level pegging. The Blades had dominated the opening 45 minutes and Bert Williams had to be at his best as the home forwards pounded his goal although he was relieved to see a George Jones header come back off the crossbar.

There was a dramatic change to the scenario in the 49th minute when Hancocks latched on to a long through ball and fired low into the net past home keeper John Smith. Once again the woodwork came to the visitors' rescue with Jimmy Hagan

Wolves' Greatest Games

hitting the foot of the post. Spurred by the stroke of luck, Wolves went two up in the 62nd minute when Jimmy Dunn smashed the ball home after Smith, under pressure from Smyth, had failed to clear properly. Hancocks wrapped things up in the 75th minute when he scored from a tight angle after a low cross from Mullen.

It was back to Molineux for the fifth round and the visit of Liverpool. The Reds were very much second best in the opening half which was in its final minute when Wolves moved into a deserved lead. Centres rained into the Liverpool box and, try as they might, the Merseysiders just couldn't clear their lines and they were punished when Dunn's waist-high shot flashed past former Molineux keeper Cyril Sidlow.

Liverpool fought back after the interval and they drew level in the 62nd minute when Cyril Done took the ball round Williams before turning it into the net. It took just ten minutes for Wolves to regain the lead. Hancocks beat Ray Lambert and crossed for Mullen to send in a header that Sidlow looked to have caught. But the ball bounced out of his arms and Smyth was there to slam it home. In the 79th minute Mullen settled the tie when he didn't spurn the opportunity created by Dunn's run and pass.

Cup fever hit South Staffordshire in a big way when Wolves were drawn at home to Second Division side West Bromwich in the quarter-final. The game was played at a terrific pace and the first half was a pretty even contest. However, after the break Wolves began to impose their authority on the proceedings and the only goal of the game arrived in the 59th minute with Mullen racing past Jim Pemberton's challenge before beating keeper Jim Sanders.

Details of the dramatic semi-final against Manchester United have been covered in the previous chapter of this book. The crowds from the two games, at Hillsborough and Goodison Park, boosted the aggregate attendance from the six games leading up to the final to an amazing 341,580.

Leicester's path to Wembley was an adventurous one. It took three bites of the cherry before the Foxes got past First Division side Birmingham City. Two 1-1 draws, at Filbert Street and St Andrew's, came before Leicester finally prevailed 2-1 back at St Andrew's. Another top flight team, Preston North End, went down 2-0 at Filbert Street before an incredible fifth round tie with Luton Town.

It finished 5-5 at Kenilworth Road and the respective defences were exposed again in the replay with City coming out on top by 5-3. Brentford failed to make the most of home advantage in the quarter-final with Leicester winning 2-0 before the East Midlands club pulled off a major shock by beating league champions-elect Portsmouth by 3-1 at Highbury to reach Wembley.

On the big day the teams were introduced to the Dukes of Gloucester and Edinburgh before Pye kicked off for Wanderers, attacking the tunnel end after Norman Plummer had won the toss for City. Jack Lee broke up Wolves' first attack as he cut out Smyth's attempted pass to Mullen and Bill Shorthouse stopped Leicester's first probe when he intercepted a long through ball.

The opening minutes were littered with misplaced passes and the first time that Williams handled the ball was when he fielded a deep pass into the box from Lee.

v Leicester City, 1949

When Mal Griffiths threatened, Terry Springthorpe was there to clear the danger. Neat work between Wright and Dunn opened up an opportunity for Mullen who cut inside before hitting a shot that was no more than a yard wide.

The Foxes began to settle into the game and Griffiths brushed off the challenge of Springthorpe before shooting over the bar and, as the rapid pace of the early exchanges showed little sign of abating, City keeper Gordon Bradley cleared as Pye burst through the middle onto Dunn's through pass. Williams, with customary bravery, saved at the feet of Charlie Adam who then collided with the keeper.

Pye and Dunn both had shots blocked before Wolves moved ahead in the 12th minute with a goal of the highest quality. Hancocks sprinted past Alex Scott on the right before delivering a cross that was met by Pye who bulleted an unstoppable header past Bradley.

A foul by Wright on Walter Harrison led to a Ted Jelly free kick that Williams had to punch away with Shorthouse completing the clearance. It then took a fine save from Bradley to prevent a second Wolves goal, the keeper pushing out a Mullen drive with no gold shirted players on hand to snap up the loose ball. Then Dunn fired narrowly wide after Pye's hassling caused Jelly to miskick, and when a Wright flick gave Pye a chance he fired over the bar.

Leicester's best opening up to that stage came when Ken Chisholm found John King in the Wanderers box but the left-half's firm shot struck Shorthouse and bounced away. Wolves were enjoying much of the attacking play without having too many goal attempts although Bradley did well to keep out a drive from Hancocks.

The City defence had a reprieve when Jelly's attempted clearance from Pye fell to Mullen. He quickly set up Dunn whose low shot went across the face of goal and wide of the far post. However, three minutes before the break, Pye got a second goal. City failed to clear Hancocks' corner and after a brief scramble the ball was half cleared to Wright. His shot went to Pye who, with his back to goal, turned and beat Bradley from close range.

After the break, City made a strong start to the new half and they pulled a goal back after three minutes' play. Griffiths began the move with a terrific run from deep inside his own half. He slipped a pass to Chisholm whose shot was pushed aside by Williams. Griffiths had continued his run through and he raced onto the loose ball to force it home with Roy Pritchard's attempted clearance off the line hitting the post and going in.

Hancocks shot wide and Mullen was dispossessed by Plummer as he was about to shoot after latching on to Pye's nod on. Then Bradley threw himself at Smyth's feet to prevent the Ulsterman from getting in a shot, and Mullen fired just over the bar as Wolves sought a third goal. However, there were a few hearts in mouths in the Wolves section of the crowd when Chisholm slotted an angled shot past Williams only to have his effort disallowed for offside.

In the 66th minute Smyth eased the tension with a brilliant solo effort. Running from halfway, he beat challenge after challenge before calmly slotting the ball past Bradley. Shortly afterwards Pye should have made it four but he skied the ball over the bar with the goal at his mercy. Not that Leicester had given up with Williams having to save from Adam and Griffiths as the brave City team looked to get back into the game.

However, there was to be no comeback as Wolves held on to their advantage and Wright led his men up the Wembley steps to receive the trophy from Princess Elizabeth. For City, at least they were to have the consolation of clinging on to their place in the Second Division albeit by just a single point.

Wanderers returned to Low Level station the following day and an open topped coach took them through the crowded town centre to North Street and the town hall. From the balcony, Stan Cullis said: "On behalf of the boys and myself, I thank you for the wonderful reception you have given us today. You have all done a lot by your support to contribute to our success. My part has been a small one. It is the players that deserve the credit, and I express my gratitude to them for the way they have played this season."

City: Bradley, Jelly, Scott, W Harrison, Plummer, King, Griffiths, Lee, J Harrison, Chisholm, Adam.
Wolves: Williams, Pritchard, Springthorpe, Crook, Shorthouse, Wright, Hancocks, Smyth, Pye, Dunn, Mullen.
Attendance: 98,920.
Referee: RH Mortimer.

Wolves 6 (Pye 2, Mullen 2, Walker, Swinbourne)
Birmingham City 1 (Trigg)

Football League First Division
Saturday 6th May 1950

AFTER FINISHING as runners-up in the First Division in the two seasons leading up to the outbreak of the Second World War, and then missing out on title honours in the campaign after hostilities had ended when victory in their final game would have sealed the championship, Molineux supporters must have despaired of ever seeing their team sit proudly at the top of English football.

So how the home faithful must have felt to see their team miss out again for the fourth time in six seasons is hard to imagine. And this time it was just goal average, the deciding factor in the days before goal difference, that denied Wolves the prize that they coveted.

Going into the final game and on the same points total as Portsmouth, Wolves entertained a Birmingham City side that lay at the bottom of the First Division table and, before a ball was kicked that afternoon, were already condemned to the drop. By coincidence, Pompey were at home against City's near neighbours and bitter rivals, Aston Villa.

Assuming that Wolves could despatch the Blues, the question home supporters were asking was could mid-table Villa upset the form book on the south coast? Bettering their rivals' goal average was out of the question as Wanderers would need to score more than 20 goals to overturn the superior average held by Portsmouth. Torrential rain in the hours leading up to the game left pools in the goalmouths and centre circle and, as the teams ran onto the field, the ground staff were still hard at work in trying to disperse the water.

Fred Harris, a Birmingham player for 17 years, had announced his retirement and this was to be his last game. He was named as honorary skipper for the day and he received a huge ovation from both sets of supporters. He won the toss and set his side to attack the South Bank end. But, just 90 seconds after the start, Harris was watching his keeper Gil Merrick picking the ball out of the net after Jesse Pye had given Wolves the lead. Jimmy Mullen's corner was only partially cleared to Billy Wright who returned the ball to the winger. He beat Len Boyd and found Pye who sidestepped his marker before scoring via the underside of the bar.

Wolves kept up the pressure but there was a threat from City as Bob Brennan's drive had Bert Williams at full stretch to turn the ball behind. But the home side soon picked up the pace again and after he had skipped past Dennis Jennings, Johnny Hancocks fired into the side netting. The winger's next involvement saw him setting up the second goal on ten minutes when Pye let his cross run through to Mullen who made no mistake.

Wolves' Greatest Games

There was a shock for the home fans five minutes later when Wolves were awarded a penalty from which the usually reliable Hancocks struck the base of the post with the ball bouncing clear. When Blues went on the attack, Cyril Trigg had a few home hearts in mouths as he shot into the side netting after cutting in from the left. Trigg then headed over following a cross from Jackie Stewart shortly before Mullen put Wolves three goals to the good. Roy Swinbourne fed the winger who rounded Ken Green before hitting a cross-shot that went in at the far post.

Wolves were well on top and a fourth goal wasn't long in coming as Walker sprinted clear and drew Merrick from his line before confidently beating the Blues keeper with 31 minutes gone. Moments later Merrick had to be at his best to save from Pye after Mullen had thrilled the crowd with some intricate wing play before setting up the chance.

Harris then wasted the opportunity of marking his finale with a goal when he shot wide of an open net after his initial shot had rebounded back to him off Williams. Instead of celebrating a goal, Harris was in position to restart the game just seconds later after Swinbourne had headed number five following a cross from Mullen. Within a minute Mullen almost grabbed his second of the game after running onto a through pass from Pye but Ted Duckhouse got his foot to the winger's shot to divert the ball away from goal.

The team ran in at the break to a tremendous ovation although the mood of the crowd was somewhat deflated by the news that Portsmouth were two up on Villa. But that didn't stop Wolves starting the new half where they had left off – on the attack with Swinbourne firing wide after John Walker's shot had been blocked.

With Merrick out of position, Ray Ferris had to clear from under the bar after Walker had nodded Mullen's centre into the goalmouth and then Mullen took a through pass from Bill Crook and hit a fierce shot inches wide. Blues had made the occasional threat on the break and they finally pulled a goal back when Trigg took advantage of Chatham's brief hesitation as he ran onto Stuart's through pass before his low shot flew past the diving Williams.

Five minutes from time Pye wrapped up the proceedings with a fine individual effort. He took the ball from just inside the Birmingham half to the edge of the box and despite the close attention of both Duckhouse and Green, he beat Merrick for Wolves' sixth. But an almost identical score from Fratton Park, where Pompey had thrashed Villa 5-1, meant that it had all been in vain with the only consolation being that of second place.

Wolves: Williams, McLean, Shorthouse, Crook, Chatham, Wright, Hancocks, Walker, Swinbourne, Pye, Mullen.
Blues: Merrick, Green, Jennings, Boyd, Duckhouse, Ferris, Stewart, Brennan, Trigg, Harris, Berry.
Attendance: 42,935.
Referee: A Bond.

South Western Districts 0
Wolves 11 (Walker 3, Broadbent 3, Mullen, Dunn 2, Smyth, Cullis)

Tour friendly, Mossel Bay, South Africa
Wednesday 6th June 1951

WOLVES' TOUR to South Africa in 1951 was historic in more ways than one. It was the first time an English club had been invited for an extended visit there and also brought a landmark goal for one of the greatest names in football. In a distinguished playing career with Wolves, Stanley Cullis had never managed to score a goal in 171 league and cup appearances (apart from an own goal against Leicester in the record 10-1 win in 1938). Nor did he find the net in his 12 full internationals and 20 wartime games for England.

Yet in the harbour town of Mossel Bay one of the greatest names in Wolverhampton Wanderers' history at last managed to hit a goal for the club he would serve for 30 years. Cullis had hung up his boots in dramatic style at the end of the 1946/47 season. Before the final game he announced he was retiring. He hoped to go out on a high note as just a draw against Liverpool at Molineux would have made Wolves champions of England for the first time in their history.

However, Liverpool won 2-1 and eventually took the title. Cullis then became Wolves' assistant manager and in 1948 was named boss when Ted Vizard and the club parted company. Cullis then set about the task of bringing to Molineux the honours that had eluded him as a player, having twice seen his side pipped for the title before the war and also lose to Portsmouth in the 1939 FA Cup Final.

Cullis's first season in charge saw the FA Cup return to Wolverhampton for the first time in 41 years and it was the nucleus of the side who triumphed over Leicester at Wembley who formed the tour party. The new boss was always ready for a challenge and welcomed the invitation from the South African Football Association believing it would help build team spirit as well as spreading the soccer gospel.

Whether Cullis had planned in advance to play again after a four-year gap, no-one knows but for the sixth match of the tour he decided to don his boots once more – against South Western Districts. He explained later that he felt some of the players needed a rest and some of the team had suffered minor knocks. Wolves had made a wonderful start to the tour, winning their first five games, scoring 22 goals and conceding only two.

Johnny Walker, who had been a key figure in the side's progress to the FA Cup semi-final in the season just ended, started the Mossel Bay goal avalanche after only five minutes when he fired home from point-blank range. Peter Broadbent, who three weeks earlier had celebrated his 18th birthday, soon doubled the lead and the home defence had little answer to the combination play of Walker, Sammy Smyth and Jimmy Mullen. Scottish inside-left Walker and left-winger Mullen soon got their names on the scoresheet.

Wolves' Greatest Games

Jimmy Dunn, playing on the right wing, then connected with a Mullen cross to make it 5–0. Wolves' regular in the number seven shirt Johnny Hancocks had a phobia about flying so did not go on the tour. Mullen turned provider once more when he centred for Smyth to make it six just before half-time. Irishman Smyth was playing at centre-forward for the second game running so that Roy Swinbourne could be given a break. Swinbourne had scored nine goals in the opening four games.

In the second half Wolves continued to entertain a crowd of only 1,500 packed into the small ground. With the politically incorrect laws of those days, the black fans were crammed into their own enclosure and they did not give any support to the home side – they cheered Wanderers throughout. Wolves' ball control and swift passing won much admiration from all the home fans, however, and it was no surprise when Dunn made the total seven. Then came Cullis's magic moment.

The manager fired home a cracker to make it 8-0. Mullen, who was allowed to fly home a few days later as his wife Joan was expecting their second child, confirmed it was no ordinary goal.

"He beat the goalkeeper with a scorching 25-yard shot and the crowd went frantic," Mullen reported. The winger added that Cullis showed he was still a master half-back with all the old touches.

After the Cullis moment, which saw him receive numerous pats on the back from his team, Walker completed his hat-trick and Broadbent did likewise with two more goals. Maybe Cullis benefited from playing in the new lightweight boots the team wore because of the hard pitches in South Africa. Mullen reckoned the boots would be a must back in England with the heavier boots relegated to use only on muddy pitches.

Cullis had played right-half in this match and decided to do so again two games later. However, the opposition, Border, were a much stronger outfit. Wolves won the game in East London 2-0 but this time Cullis found the going much tougher and was clearly wilting midway through the second half.

Sensibly, the manager, though still only 34, decided there would be no more comebacks and he would concentrate on becoming the most successful manager in Wolverhampton Wanderers history. Amazingly, the win at Mossel Bay was not the biggest on a tour which saw Wolves win all 12 games. In Benoni they hammered Eastern Transvaal 13-0 with Swinbourne grabbing six goals.

Wolves: Parsons, Short, Pritchard, Cullis, Shorthouse, Deeley, Dunn, Broadbent, Smyth, Walker, Mullen.
Attendance: 1,500.

Wolves 5 (Dunn, Wilshaw, Pye 2, Hancocks)
Chelsea 3 (Bentley, Campbell, J Smith)
Football League First Division
Saturday 22nd September 1951

AFTER THE disappointing end to the 1950/51 campaign in which they had finished 14th, Wolves made a fair start to the new season by winning four and drawing one of the opening seven games. A home triumph over Liverpool and a 3-2 victory over Portsmouth at Fratton Park preceded the visit to Molineux of a Chelsea team stationed four places off the bottom of the table.

Roy Swinbourne, feeling that he was out of form, had asked to play in the reserves, and otherwise Stan Cullis was able to send out his strongest side while Chelsea boss Billy Birrell fielded the 11 that had beaten Huddersfield at Stamford Bridge seven days earlier. Just one goal was scored in the opening half and there was no indication of the scoring glut after the interval that included one of the fastest bursts of goals from any team at Molineux.

The first threat of the game came from Chelsea's Bill Dickson whose shot was deflected behind for a corner. Jim Smith took the flag kick and Roy Bentley rose to send in a powerful header that bounced down off the bar before being cleared by a defender. Wolves replied with two shots in quick succession from Johnny Hancocks with the ball rebounding off a defender on each occasion.

Bert Williams was called into action as he saved a shot from Bentley after a long throw from Dickson, and then Bill Crook just managed to take the ball off Jim Smith's foot as he was about to try a shot on the run. Bentley almost prospered after Bill Shorthouse and Roy Pritchard had collided, but Pritchard recovered in time to boot the ball out for a throw-in before the centre-forward could get in an effort on goal.

Jack Short ran down the wing and crossed to Jesse Pye who was well off target with his normally trusty head, and when Billy Wright's pass was nodded down by Dennis Wilshaw to Jimmy Dunn, the move was ended by Derek Saunders who had read the situation and had nipped between the pair to clear the danger.

But he could do nothing to prevent Wolves taking a 21st-minute lead. Pye harried Sid Bathgate into conceding a corner that was taken from the left by Jimmy Mullen and converted by Dunn who beat Chelsea keeper Bill Robertson with a perfectly flighted header.

A breakaway by Chelsea almost led to a quick riposte but Williams got down well to save a flick from Bob Smith. Pritchard then ran from inside his own area to the edge of Chelsea's before laying off a pass to Wilshaw who set up Hancocks for a centre that had Robertson moving smartly from his line to collect before Pye could get to the ball.

Despite holding a goal advantage, the home attack had looked none too convincing but they suddenly clicked into gear and began to give the Chelsea rearguard a hard time. Hancocks scraped the top of the bar with a powerful drive and Wright saw his shot deflected behind for a corner. Wilshaw's return pass to Pye was too strong, allowing Robertson to claim, then the keeper had to save a first time effort from Mullen.

Chelsea were dangerous on the break and Short had to hook the ball behind as Jim Smith was preparing to shoot. The unfortunate Bathgate took a full blooded shot from Mullen in the midriff and clearly winded, he had to receive attention before he could continue. Just before the interval Robertson made a fantastic save after Hancocks had steamed in and lashed the ball towards goal.

Wilshaw had a goal disallowed two minutes after the restart for a push on Saunders, but when the striker found the net again four minutes later, this time it counted as he beat Robertson with a right-foot shot after taking a pass from Crook. And the crowd were still acclaiming the goal when, within two minutes, Pye took a pass from Hancocks and sidestepped his marker before sending an angled drive into the net.

Hancocks was giving Syd Tickridge a torrid time on the right wing and one through ball from the little man released Pye who was crowded out before he could get a shot away. Another Hancocks centre picked out fellow winger Mullen whose volley was headed away by Phil McKnight. On 77 minutes, a Hancocks' throw to Dunn was followed by a cross that was headed home by Pye.

Then Wolves were awarded an 83rd-minute penalty which was the start of four goals in a five-minute spell. After he had been fouled by Dickson, Hancocks blasted the spot kick past Robertson for Wolves' fifth. Then the home defence must have taken their foot off the gas as Chelsea bagged three consolation goals.

Bentley got the first as he headed Bill Gray's centre beyond the reach of Williams, then the keeper saved well from a Bentley shot but couldn't hold on to the ball and Bob Campbell ran in to seize on the opportunity to tap home from close range. Jim Smith quickly added a third with a cross-shot.

Given the way that they had been overpowered, especially after the break, no-one could have expected such a quickfire response from Chelsea. It was Wilshaw that wound up proceedings in front of the breathless crowd by running virtually the length of the field before putting the ball a yard wide of Robertson's goal.

Wolves: Williams, Short, Pritchard, Crook, Shorthouse, Wright, Hancocks, Dunn, Wilshaw, Pye, Mullen.
Chelsea: Robertson, Bathgate, Tickridge, McKnight, Saunders, Dickson, Gray, Campbell, R Smith, Bentley, J Smith.
Attendance: 35,184.
Referee: BAE Buckle.

Huddersfield Town 1 (Metcalfe)
Wolves 7 (Mullen 2, Dunn 3, Pye, Hancocks)

Football League First Division
Saturday 29th September 1951

JUST A week after the eight-goal entertainment against Chelsea at Molineux, Wolves were involved in another spectacular game, this time at Huddersfield Town's Leeds Road home, when once again the ball hit the back of the net eight times. Wolves beat the London side 5-3 but the game against the Terriers was to be a lot more one-sided.

Twenty-four hours before the fixture, Wanderers had bid a fond farewell to Cup Final star Sammy Smyth. The Northern Irish striker ended his four-year stay with the club when he joined bottom-of-the-table Stoke City for a £20,000 fee. He had played 116 league and cup games for Wolves and scored 43 goals which included that memorable solo effort at Wembley. While his former team-mates were taking on Huddersfield, he inspired the Potters to a 2-1 victory over Burnley, their first league success of the season.

Sent to face a slight breeze by former Wolves full-back Lol Kelly, the visitors went straight onto the attack and Kelly was penalised in the first minute for deliberately handling a Johnny Hancocks cross. Billy Wright ended a threatening build-up between Harold Hassall and Vic Metcalfe, and then, in Town's next attack, Hassall let fly with a long-range shot that was just too high.

Wolves moved into a fifth-minute lead after a move that began with Roy Swinbourne. He found Jimmy Dunn who in turn passed to Wright. The skipper wasted no time in slipping the ball to Jimmy Mullen who ran past the challenge of Don Howe and rammed a cross-shot past Town keeper Jack Wheeler.

Metcalfe was in line for a quickfire equaliser when he turned the ball past Bert Williams after meeting John McKenna's cross, but Bill Shorthouse had spotted the danger and positioned himself on the line to clear. In the 14th minute Dunn put Wanderers two in front. Wright won the ball from John Battye and gave possession to Hancocks who slid a pass into the path of Dunn and the inside-forward got his shot in to score just as he was tackled.

Shorthouse successfully dispossessed Metcalfe who had run into the Wolves area and Williams caught a lofted free kick from Bill McGarry as Huddersfield tried desperately to get the goal that would keep them in touch. Then Williams pushed out a Metcalfe free kick and when the ball ran to McKenna, the keeper saved the resulting follow-up shot. A fierce Metcalfe drive was uncomfortably close to the post and then Hassall, who had been struggling to shake off the effects of a knock, smashed a 20-yard free kick against the bar. But the Town players' efforts were in vain as Wolves went three up when Kelly missed a long through pass and Jesse Pye outpaced Don McEvoy before burying a shot beyond the range of Wheeler.

Wolves' Greatest Games

Pye, his appetite whetted, tested Wheeler with a half-volley, and at the other end Williams was relieved to see a Metcalfe shot flash across the face of his goal and wide of the far post. But the keeper was beaten in the 35th minute with the persistent Metcalfe pulling one back for Town. Hassall passed into the area and although Metcalfe's first effort was kicked off the line by Roy Pritchard, the winger regained possession and made sure with his second attempt.

McGarry hit the bar with a long-range shot and a Hancocks free kick bounced clear off the wall after Pye had been fouled as the action continued unabated. And just before the break Dunn restored Wolves' three-goal cushion when, from 30 yards, he hit a shot so powerful that although Wheeler got both hands to it, he couldn't prevent the ball from dropping behind him and going over the line.

After such an eventful opening half, the second period started relatively slowly with the only real goalmouth action coming when Shorthouse had to clear a free kick from McKenna. But when things began to warm up once more, Pye wasn't far off with a hooked shot that went over Wheeler but wide of the post. Shortly afterwards, the keeper needed two attempts to cling on to a low shot from the Wolves centre-forward.

Pritchard blocked a shot from Hassall before the industrious Swinbourne began a move that involved Hancocks and Pye and finished with a drive from Mullen that flew narrowly wide. Then there was a half chance for Town's Ron Burke but he blasted the ball high over the bar. In their next attack, Wolves scored a fifth goal through Hancocks. The game was 65 minutes old when the winger collected a Mullen cross and rounded Kelly before sending an angled shot past Wheeler.

Four minutes later Dunn completed his hat-trick after he had been put clean through by Hancocks but still the agony for Huddersfield continued as Mullen made it seven with nine minutes remaining. He stayed onside as he waited for Pye's pass before sprinting clear of the chasing defenders and lifting the ball over the head of Wheeler as he advanced from his line.

In the dying seconds Pye and Mullen combined to set up Swinbourne who was denied the goal he deserved by a fantastic Wheeler save. The win meant that Wanderers had won by 7-1 in an away game in three different divisions. They beat Ashington in January 1924, and Port Vale in December 1931 in doing so.

Town: Wheeler, Howe, Kelly, McGarry, McEvoy, Battye, McKenna, Taylor, Burke, Hassall, Metcalfe.
Wolves: Williams, Short, Pritchard, Wright, Shorthouse, Crook, Hancocks, Dunn, Swinbourne, Pye, Mullen.
Attendance: 32,496.
Referee: A Tootill.

Wolves 6 (Wilshaw 2, Swinbourne 3, Mullen)
Manchester United 2 (Rowley 2)
Football League First Division
Saturday 4th October 1952

WITH BILLY WRIGHT on England duty, Stan Cullis gave a debut to amateur Bill Slater for the visit of reigning league champions Manchester United. Slater had signed from Brentford at the start of the 1952/53 season. And with Bill Crook out injured, the Wolves boss brought Ron Flowers back into the team for only his second outing. Flowers had made a scoring debut in the 5-2 home defeat against Blackpool a fortnight earlier – Wolves' only loss in a six-game run leading up to the visit of United.

Another to make his debut in the game was United's 18-year-old winger John Scott. Leading the Reds' attack was Wolverhampton-born Jack Rowley who still holds the ground scoring record at Molineux. He guested for Wolves occasionally during the Second World War and, in November 1942, he hit all eight goals in a Football League North game against Derby County. And he was to give a reminder of his predatory skills on that autumn afternoon ten years on.

Visiting keeper Reg Allen had to be at his best to prevent Dennis Wilshaw from giving Wolves an early advantage. Roy Pritchard started the move with a fine pass to Jimmy Mullen who played a quick one-two with Les Smith before crossing to Wilshaw who hit a shot on the turn that Allen somehow got down to and saved one-handed.

Roy Swinbourne couldn't have been closer as he headed anther Mullen centre against the post, before Bert Williams was called into action, firstly cutting out a dangerous cross from John Berry before saving at the feet of Rowley with Bill Shorthouse, captain for the day in Wright's absence, completing the clearance. Williams then had to save a hard shot from Rowley after Berry had beaten three men on a run before crossing to the centre-forward.

Williams stuck out a foot to divert away an effort from Berry before Rowley opened the scoring in the 19th minute after Williams had been penalised for handling outside the box as he tried to prevent a corner. Scott's free kick ran through to Rowley to the right of the goal and he fired home through a sea of legs in the goalmouth. And the Scott/Rowley combination worked again less than a minute later with, from virtually the same position, Rowley meeting the winger's cross with a first time left-foot drive.

It took the home side just five more minutes to halve the deficit. Smith delivered a cross from the right that Allen could only punch into the air and, as the ball dropped, Wilshaw was waiting to nod it over the line. Shots from Mullen and Slater were both deflected behind for corners and from a Wilshaw cross, Peter Broadbent hooked the ball wide as Wanderers began to assume total command.

Wolves' Greatest Games

More excellent wing play from Smith ended with Allen cutting out his centre as Swinbourne and Mullen ran in before persistence was finally rewarded five minutes before the break. Wilshaw, out on the left wing, took the ball to the line before crossing for Swinbourne to smash an unstoppable shot past Allen.

In a rare United attack, a fine tackle by Shorthouse denied Rowley the chance of a clear run at goal and a possible hat-trick. Then, right on half-time, Slater dispossessed Tom McNulty and forced a save from Allen. The loose ball ran to Mullen who wasted no time in returning it into the middle where Swinbourne fired inches wide. It took Wolves just 30 seconds of the second half to move ahead for the first time.

Smith won possession in a coming-together with Aston and he started a quickfire passing move up the field involving Swinbourne, Wilshaw and Broadbent who laid a perfect ball for Mullen who ran in to lash an angled drive into the far corner of the net. The United defence was struggling to cope with the constant pounding and it caved in again in the 53rd minute after Broadbent beat John Aston before crossing for Wilshaw to direct a downward header past Allen.

Two minutes later came a fifth with a terrific strike from Swinbourne. Fully 35 yards out, he seemed to be looking at passing options when he suddenly let fly with a shot that entered the goal just below the bar as Allen waved his arms in a futile attempt to save. It was a brilliant strike and it fully deserved the prolonged bout of applause it drew.

John Downie had an excellent chance of pulling a goal back when he found himself just six yards out with only Williams to beat but he succeeded only in shooting straight at the keeper. Then the crowd were 'treated' to the unusual sight of the trainer running on to attend to the referee who was suffering from a nosebleed!

With six minutes remaining Wolves had two men down and in trouble from the same attack. Smith left the bamboozled Aston sat on the floor after tricking his way past him before passing to Broadbent whose shot struck Swinbourne full in the face. He dropped to the floor like a stone and, as the ball fell, Wilshaw ran in to head home before he collided with the post.

He too went down but his pain was not worthy of the effort as he had been flagged offside. Thankfully, both men were able to resume after treatment and Swinbourne completed his hat-trick two minutes from time as he headed in Mullen's centre. The win took Wolves to level top of the division with Liverpool whose goal average was slightly superior.

Wolves: Williams, Short, Pritchard, Flowers, Shorthouse, Slater, Smith, Broadbent, Swinbourne, Wilshaw, Mullen.
United: Allen, McNulty, Aston, Carey, Chilton, Gibson, Berry, Downie, Rowley, Pearson, Scott.
Attendance: 39,667.
Referee: BJ Flanaghan.

Wolves 8 (Hancocks 3, Wilshaw, Swinbourne 2, Broadbent, Mullen)
Chelsea 1 (Bentley)
Football League First Division
Saturday 26th September 1953

THE OPENING three games of the 1953/54 campaign for Wolves were all played away from Molineux and at first there was little to suggest that this was to be the season that they would at last, after so many near misses, capture the Football League championship. Defeats at Burnley and Sunderland came either side of a 4-0 win at Manchester City before the team really clicked into gear.

Five wins on the spin, four of them at home and the other coming against Arsenal at Highbury, hoisted Wolves up the First Division table and leading into the home clash with Chelsea there were away draws at Liverpool and then Blackpool. John Short and Dennis Wilsaw returned to the side to face Chelsea after recovering from their respective injuries and also back was Bill Slater who, while his team-mates were in action at Bloomfield Road, was skippering the England Amateur XI against South Africa.

It took just three minutes for Wolves to move ahead after Stan Willemse handled a Jimmy Mullen cross when he had all the time in the world to clear. Johnny Hancocks made no mistake from the spot. The winger figured heavily in the opening exchanges and he almost found the net again when he connected with a Mullen cross – his shot carrying so much power that it knocked Chelsea keeper Bill Robertson backwards as he turned the ball behind for a corner.

Robertson was soon in action again, saving Peter Broadbent's header on the line with one hand after a Hancocks lob into the area. Chelsea responded with a run from Frank Blunstone that was halted by a clinical tackle from Billy Wright. On ten minutes Roy Pritchard came to the rescue when he cleared from John McNichol after Bert Williams had failed to hold on to a cross in a congested goalmouth.

The England keeper athletically got down to smother a Jim Lewis drive while Robertson saved three times in succession from the irrepressible Hancocks. Then the keeper cut out a Wilshaw pass that was heading to Roy Swinbourne. Wolves moved into a two-goal lead in the 31st minute and it didn't come as any surprise that it was Hancocks who was on the mark again.

It came about after a mistake by Robertson, whose poor clearance went straight to the winger who was fully 35 yards out from goal. Without hesitating he took aim and hit a shot that was nestling in the back of the net before the keeper could get back in position. Shortly before the interval, Hancocks hit a free kick that flew inches over the upright.

Just three minutes after the game restarted, the winger played a part in Wolves' third goal. Broadbent played a short pass to Hancocks whose centre was headed out by Ron Greenwood but only as far as Mullen. He sent over a lobbed cross that

Wolves' Greatest Games

Wilshaw headed home just inside the far post. And, in the 54th minute, the inevitable happened as Hancocks completed his hat-trick. Mullen sent a deep cross into the area and, in the melee that ensued, Hancocks slammed the ball home from eight yards out.

Bobby Smith had to leave the field for treatment to a facial injury and, in his absence with the game just past the hour mark, Swinbourne made it five as he volleyed home after a run and squared pass from Slater. In a rare Chelsea attack, Roy Bentley set up a chance for Derek Saunders but the left-half's first-time shot flew inches wide.

Smith returned after a five-minute absence and he watched as Mullen's low cross went straight through the goalmouth with no-one able to get a touch. Then it was the turn of Greenwood to go off for attention to a facial injury and, while he was off, Peter Sillett cleared off the line from Swinbourne after a centre from Hancocks.

With 71 minutes gone Mullen created the sixth with a low cross that saw Broadbent getting to the ball just before Robertson. The inside-forward flicked the ball past the keeper and it rolled inside the post as Robertson made desperate but futile attempts to reach it. Five minutes later, Chelsea finally got off the mark. Short fouled Blunstone in the box and from Bentley's spot kick, Williams made a brilliant save. However, the ball ran back to the Chelsea striker who put away the rebound.

The goal simply stirred Wanderers into more attacking play and in the 79th minute Swinbourne headed in Mullen's cross to restore the six-goal advantage. With four minutes to go, when Mullen headed in a Broadbent centre, he became the last of the home forward line to get on the scoresheet. In the dying seconds Hancocks twice was close to his fourth goal but, on each occasion, a defender got in the way of his shots to block.

Going into the game Wolves were lying third in the table and the two points took them up another place nearer top spot which was occupied by West Bromwich Albion who were two points better off. The win was the eighth in what turned out to be an 18-game unbeaten run when just five points out of a possible 36 were dropped by Stan Cullis's men. When Burnley ended the run and completed the double over Wolves two weeks before Christmas, it also brought a halt to 15 consecutive home victories.

Wolves: Williams, Short, Pritchard, Slater, Shorthouse, Wright, Hancocks, Broadbent, Wilshaw, Swinbourne, Mullen.
Chelsea: Robertson, Sillett, Willemse, Armstrong, Greenwood, Saunders, Bentley, Smith, Lewis, McNichol, Blunstone.
Attendance: 36,134.
Referee: JH Clough.

Wolves 3 (Mullen, Broadbent, Hancocks)
South Africa 1 (Gibson)
Floodlit friendly
Wednesday 30th September 1953

IN THE winter of 1953, over a period of just 56 days, Wolves were invited to provide the opposition to mark the opening of floodlight systems at four different venues while construction of pylons at Molineux were still at the planning stages. But, although they weren't the first to use artificial light, when they did open it was to help propel the club into world status.

In January 1953, after the scheduled game was postponed through fog, the lights at Bristol City's Ashton Gate lit up a bright performance from Wanderers who won 4-1 with Ron Stockin, with a hat-trick, and Les Smith finding the net. Then, in March, Hull celebrated their new lights at Boothferry Park with Roy Pritchard netting in the visitors' surprise 3-1 defeat.

Just eight days later came the short trip to Bilston Town's Queen Street where a young Molineux team eased to a 4-2 triumph over their non-league neighbours. Eddie Stuart, Johnny Hancocks, Colin Booth and an own goal made up the visitors' tally before at Hednesford's Cross Keys home Wolves met West Bromwich Albion to mark Town's newly installed system. Wolves, through Stockin with a brace, Jimmy Mullen and a Jimmy Sanders own goal, came out on top by 4-2.

Players and public alike in Wolverhampton had their appetites whetted by the novelty of watching under floodlights along with the notion that they would be able to watch midweek football all the season through although it was to be 1956 before floodlit league matches were permitted. So it was with great anticipation that over the summer months of 1953, pylons began to grow in each corner of Molineux.

The last day of September was selected for the inaugural game and the chosen opposition were the South African national side. Wolves had won many friends when they toured the country in 1951 and the friendly was part of an eight-week South African tour. There were no professionals in the travelling party who included in their ranks diamond cutters, soldiers, students and policemen.

Before the game, which had a 7.45pm start, it was announced that Stuart, the South African defender signed by Wolves after he was discovered on the 1951 tour, was made captain for the night after Bill Shorthouse stood down. And it soon became apparent that although Wolves were quicker off the mark both in thought and in action, their amateur opposition included some very talented individuals.

The previous Saturday, Chelsea had limped away from Molineux on the back of an 8-1 mauling with Hancocks in peak form as he notched a hat-trick. The winger sparkled once again under the new lights as did Mullen, his partner on the opposite flank. South African skipper Ross Dow admitted after the game that the long cross-

Wolves' Greatest Games

field passes and interplay between the Wolves wingers and wing halves had a devastating effect on his team.

Playing in a fluorescent gold and black strip that shone superbly under the lights, Wolves enjoyed the best of the opening half hour. Mullen opened the scoring on 32 minutes before, just two minutes later, Peter Broadbent lashed a terrific cross-shot past impressive keeper Ken Rudham. Just three minutes into the second half Brian Gibson headed past Bert Williams to earn generous applause from the crowd before Roy Swinbourne wound up the scoring when he turned in a Hancocks cross four minutes from time. As well as Rudham's athleticism, inside-forwards Gibson and Walter Warren showed some exceptional ball control in a side who were never outplayed.

Of course, the main topic after the final whistle was the floodlights and in the local press Phil Morgan reported that he had nothing but praise for the set-up. Billy Wright said they were the best lights that he had played under in England while manager Stan Cullis said he was greatly impressed and felt that it was worth the wait until the club could be sure of getting the best system.

Acting skipper Eddie Stuart said after the game: "It was a great honour to be captain of Wolves in their very first floodlit game. Some may say it was the obvious thing to do so with me being a South African and the game being against South Africa but the club didn't have to do it. It was a tremendous gesture and so good of Bill Shorthouse to agree to step down. It's something I'll never forget. It was a very colourful occasion, us in our fluorescent shirts, South Africa in their famous green shirts and the novelty of the floodlights."

While the Molineux board were quietly disappointed with an attendance of over 33,000, they will no doubt have been a little happier when a further 8,000 turned up just a fortnight later to watch Wolves beat Celtic by 2-0 thanks to two Dennis Wilshaw goals. In between the two games, Wolves were invited to yet another opening of lights ceremony, this time at Bury's Gigg Lane where they suffered a 3-1 defeat with Stockin getting the consolation goal.

It wasn't until April 1956 that Wolves finally played a First Division game under lights. And they marked the occasion by rattling five goals past Tottenham Hotspur who could only respond once. A year later a new and taller quartet of pylons were erected at the ground with the old set being sold to Blackpool and reassembled at Bloomfield Road.

Wolves: Williams, Short, Pritchard, Slater, Stuart, Wright, Hancocks, Broadbent, Swinbourne, Stockin, Mullen.
South Africa: Rudham, Machanik, Jacobson, Dow, Naish, Jacques, Claassens, Warren, Salton, Gibson, Le Roux.
Attendance: 33,681.
Referee: F Read.

West Bromwich Albion 0
Wolves 1 (Swinbourne)
Football League First Division
Saturday 3rd April 1954

FOR SUCH a crucial fixture, it's hard to imagine that West Bromwich and Wolves went into a game missing two players each because of international needs. But it proved to be the case as the First Division title race hotted up with both teams having just half a dozen games to play before the conclusion of the 1953/54 season.

Going into the showdown at The Hawthorns, Albion headed Wanderers by two points at the top having missed the chance of extending their lead after suffering a midweek defeat at Sunderland, this after they had booked a place at Wembley in the FA Cup Final after beating Port Vale at Villa Park on the previous Saturday. It was after an FA Cup tie against Birmingham at the turn of the year that Wolves hit an erratic spell of form.

The Second Division Blues pulled off a shock 2-1 win at Molineux and, in the ten league games that followed, five of them ended in defeat for Stan Cullis's side. While Albion were dealing with Port Vale, Wolves took on relegation-haunted Middlesbrough at Molineux and despite two strikes from Peter Broadbent, they never recovered from conceding two goals in the opening 12 minutes, eventually ending on the wrong side of a 4-2 scoreline.

So, with Albion's Johnny Nicholls and Ronnie Allen joining Billy Wright and Jimmy Mullen at Hampden Park for the home international with Scotland, the stage was set at a Hawthorns that was predictably bursting at the seams. To add to the Baggies' woes, they were without the injured quartet of Norman Heath, Stan Rickaby, Frank Griffin and George Lee. For Wolves, Roy Pritchard came in at right-back with Bill Shorthouse moving to Wright's centre-half position, and Les Smith covered for Mullen although he played on the right wing with Johnny Hancocks moving to the left.

Defending the Birmingham Road end, Albion had the first attempt at goal with Ray Barlow shooting high over the bar before Shorthouse headed clear a Fred Cox corner. After eight minutes Barlow was hurt after a tackle from Shorthouse and although he carried on after treatment, he was limping heavily.

Albion keeper Jim Sanders had to beat away a fierce effort from Broadbent and then he dealt with shots from Ron Flowers and Roy Swinbourne. Across at the Smethwick End, Bert Williams was alert enough to spot the danger as he saved at the feet of Reg Ryan after the inside-right had cut into the area. Sanders saved well after Broadbent had breezed past Len Millard, before Wolves, through Hancocks, found the back of the Albion net.

Any celebrations were quickly curtailed though for after Smith had tapped the free kick to Hancocks and he had thumped the ball home from just outside the area,

Wolves' Greatest Games

the referee ordered that it be retaken. This time Smith touched the ball to Swinbourne but Jimmy Dugdale got in the way to block. Williams caught a hooked shot from Wilf Carter and although Barlow was still struggling to shake off his injury, he still climbed high to send a header two feet wide after a Cox corner.

A Broadbent-inspired attack opened the second half but the Baggies defence stood firm and when the home team retaliated, the offside flag brought their move to an abrupt halt. Then Broadbent robbed Joe Kennedy and sent Smith away down the right. The winger cut inside and released a shot that beat Sanders and the outstretched foot of Swinbourne before flashing just wide of the far post.

A low shot from Reg Cutler was safely collected by Williams before Wolves moved into a 58th-minute lead following a Smith corner. The ball was headed on to Swinbourne who hooked a waist-high shot past Sanders and just inside the upright. Virtually from the restart, Dennis Wilshaw went on a run that took him into the Albion box and a second goal looked odds-on until Stuart Williams robbed the striker with a meticulous tackle.

The home goal was soon under threat again following a Swinbourne throw which found Broadbent. He crossed low to Hancocks and his powerful shot was punched by Sanders onto the head of his own player, Millard, who nodded clear. Millard, like the keeper, was positioned on the line. Swinbourne then got the better of Dugdale and was clean through but he shot against the body of Sanders. The ball bounced into the path of Hancocks but he drilled his shot wide from a tight angle.

Sanders, standing in for regular custodian Heath, enjoyed a terrific game. But he had no chance with Swinbourne's winner and, moments before the end, he denied Hancocks with a great save after the Wolves man had been put clean through by Wilshaw. The victory gave Wolves the double over Albion, the only team to achieve that in the season with the game at Molineux also finishing 1-0 thanks to a Mullen goal.

Albion still headed the table that night but only on goal average. They were to have the consolation of winning the Cup Final at Preston North End's expense while Wolves won the title for the first time, finishing four points ahead of the second-placed Baggies. And, in the international, Wright captained England to a 4-2 victory over the Scots with Nicholls, Allen and Mullen all finding the net to do Staffordshire proud.

Albion: Sanders, Williams, Millard, Dudley, Dugdale, Kennedy, Cox, Ryan, Barlow, Carter, Cutler.
Wolves: Williams, Pritchard, Stuart, Slater, Shorthouse, Flowers, Smith, Broadbent, Swinbourne, Wilshaw, Hancocks.
Attendance: 49,884.
Referee: F Cowan.

Wolves 4 (Swinbourne 2, Deeley, Hancocks)
West Bromwich Albion 4 (Allen 3, Ryan)
FA Charity Shield, Molineux
Wednesday 29th September 1954

FOR A clash between Wolves and Albion to produce eight goals is rare. A game at Molineux did so in 1893 but all eight goals went to the men from West Bromwich and remains the Wanderers' heaviest home defeat. Eight goals were scored in a Molineux derby clash 61 years later but this time they were shared equally in a pulsating clash with the FA Charity Shield the prize at stake.

The reason for their meeting under the Molineux lights was that Wolves had pipped Albion the previous season to become champions of England for the first time while the Baggies had made up for their disappointment by winning the FA Cup. Albion's Wembley triumph was a dramatic one as they came from 2-1 down to beat Preston 3-2 thanks to a late goal from right-winger Frank Griffin.

These were great days for Black Country football and a crowd of 45,000 were at Molineux to see who would come out on top. Both sides were below strength. Wolves were without the injured Eddie Stuart and Jimmy Mullen while Billy Wright had to miss out because he was due to captain England against Northern Ireland three days later. That match also ruled out Bill Slater who was a travelling reserve for the international.

Another on duty for England was Albion left-half Ray Barlow. England legend Bobby Moore would years later cite Barlow as the half-back he most admired yet the Irish game would prove to be his only international. Albion also had to make do without the injured Johnny Nicholls, whose strike partnership with Ronnie Allen had proved lethal during the previous season and had brought both of them England caps.

Wolves began the game at a furious pace but it soon settled down to a ding-dong battle with starkly contrasting styles. Wolves favoured the long pass and more direct moves while the Baggies preferred the short pass, often across field or backwards. Two who stood out in a heartwarming encounter were among the youngest – Ron Flowers and Norman Deeley. The latter was much in evidence in the early exchanges, combining well with Dennis Wilshaw, Mullen's deputy on the left wing.

On the Baggies side Allen sparkled, along with the ice-cool full-back Stan Rickaby, who had missed out on Wembley through injury. Yet Allen, despite hitting a hat-trick, did not have it all his own way against another Wolves youngster, 19-year-old Peter Russell, deputising for Wright at centre-half. It was Russell's debut and he came through it well, but his opposite number, the far-more-experienced Joe Kennedy, found Roy Swinbourne quite a handful.

It was Swinbourne who opened the scoring on 12 minutes. He nipped past Kennedy to fire the ball home and the only surprise was that more goals did not

Wolves' Greatest Games

follow before half-time. The lead was doubled with the second half not even a minute old and it was thanks to a move between the smallest men on the field. Johnny Hancocks took a free kick and Deeley was in the clear to head home.

That was a signal for Albion to step up their efforts and two goals in a minute saw them wipe out the deficit. Allen scored them both, the first after 55 minutes. Wolves roared back and Swinbourne took a perfect Deeley pass to beat Jim Sanders once more. Then Swinbourne turned goal maker and put Hancocks through for number four.

Still Albion would not lie down and with six minutes to go the enterprising Rickaby got through only to see his shot hit the bar. The ever-alert Allen was on the spot to put home the rebound and it ended all-square. Allen might even have had a fourth goal and there was some mystery why his shot from a free kick that beat Bert Williams was not deemed a goal. Referee Gibson explained afterwards that Jimmy Dudley had nudged the ball to Allen but the ball had not travelled its full circumference which it must do from a free kick.

However, the official had then awarded the kick to Wolves but that was a wrong interpretation of the law. If the ball does not travel its full circumference, the procedure is for the free kick to be retaken. To add to the confusion, the original free kick was not indirect so there was no need for Dudley to play the ball before Allen took a shot at goal. No-one had thought of penalty shoot-outs to settle the issue in those days so the teams held the trophy for six months each.

Floodlit games were still very much a novelty – Wolves had only had lights for a year – and there was another new phenomenon that night. For the first time at Molineux, substitutes were used. Ken Hodgkisson, later a Walsall stalwart in well over 300 games, came on for Albion left-winger George Lee while Jimmy Dugdale came on for Jimmy Dudley. Russell had made an outstanding first-team bow and was given his league debut in a 4-2 home win over Manchester United three days later.

On the same day Barlow helped England beat Northern Ireland 2-0 in Belfast. However, that proved his last game for his country. Injury ruled him out of the next international – against Wales – and Slater made his England debut. Slater kept his place for the game against world champions West Germany but he and Barlow were out of the reckoning when England faced Scotland at Wembley the following April. The selectors instead went for a promising youngster – Duncan Edwards.

Wolves: Williams, Guttridge, Shorthouse, Flowers, Russell, Clamp, Hancocks, Broadbent, Swinbourne, Deeley, Wilshaw.
Albion: Sanders, Rickaby, Millard, Dudley (Dugdale), Kennedy, Brookes, Griffin, Ryan, Allen, Carter, Lee (Hodgkisson).
Attendance: 45,035.
Referee: G Gibson.

Wolves 4 (Wilshaw, Hancocks 2, Swinbourne)
Moscow Spartak 0
Floodlit friendly
Tuesday 16th November 1954

MOSCOW SPARTAK were the seventh team to visit Molineux for a floodlit friendly and there was little doubt that they would be providing the biggest test so far for Billy Wright and his men. The Russian giants had taken on – and beaten – Arsenal 2-1 a week earlier to give an indication of just how good they were. Other scalps taken in 1954 by the red-shirted Muscovites included a 6-2 home victory over the Norwegian national team, and in Belgium, wins against two top sides – 7-0 over Anderlecht 5-2 over Liege.

Nineteen days before Spartak's arrival, Wolves had thrashed Maccabi Tel Aviv 10-0 in a friendly at Molineux but Spartak were an altogether different kettle of fish. The importance of the game, not just locally, but nationally, was evident with the BBC broadcasting the entire match on radio and the second half live on television.

Spartak's team was studded with international players and were renowned for their fitness. But the fitness level was to be severely tested by a Wolves side at their best on a murky Wolverhampton night that saw fog swirling under the glow of the floodlights. Peter Broadbent and Johnny Hancocks were to be shadowed throughout the game by Igor Netto and Yruy Sedov respectively. But, come the final whistle, the Russians were on the point of exhaustion such was the run-around they had been given by the Molineux duo.

On a heavy surface Wolves' tactics were by far the superior and they moved the ball about with much greater accuracy than their Russian counterparts. Spartak's best football came in the opening half and they almost took the lead in the early stages through Nikita Simonian who lobbed the ball over Bert Williams but was denied by Bill Shorthouse who cleared off the line.

Then it took a last ditch tackle from Billy Wright to prevent Boris Tatouchine from having a clear run at goal. At the other end of the field, Spartak keeper Michael Piraev twice saved Bill Slater headers while Les Smith drove narrowly wide of the post. Roy Swinbourne was causing all kinds of problems for the Russian defence who had little thought for finesse as they desperately cleared their lines.

Inside-right Alexei Paramonov missed a good opportunity when he shot over the bar from eight yards out, then Williams made a good save from Anatoly Ilyin to ensure that the score was all-square at half-time. It was after the resumption that Wolves began to take command and as the hour mark was reached they were looking the more likely to make the breakthrough and they almost did when Hancocks smacked a 20-yard drive against the crossbar.

And, in the 66th minute, the pressure finally told as Dennis Wilshaw forced the ball home after Piraev had punched out a Shorthouse free kick. Then came a moment of controversy. Substitutes were allowed but only for an injury and the Russian trainer called Ilyin to the touchline and gave him a message. Ilyin sprinted across the field and had a word with Paramonov who immediately developed a limp. By the time he had hobbled to the bench the Russian trainer had Anstoly Isayev ready for action.

His presence had little effect and Wolves almost scored again when Wilshaw dribbled the ball round the keeper only for Bachachkine to clear from in front of the line. Wolves continued to dominate but Spartak almost drew level in the 81st minute when Eddie Stuart cleared off the line from Ilyin who had run in on to Boris Tatouchine's low centre. But whether or not fatigue had set in, no-one was expecting the Spartak defence to crumble the way that it did in the final six minutes.

Hancocks made it 2-0 in the 84th minute when he ghosted past two defenders and drew Piraev from his line before rolling the ball into an empty net. Just a minute later Hancocks headed a deep clearance on to Swinbourne who found the back of the net from just outside the box. Hancocks thought he had got a fourth when he beat Piraev only to be flagged offside. But he did have the last laugh when, in the seconds that remained, he completed the scoring. Wilshaw's pass took a deflection off a defender on the way to Hancocks who shot home from eight yards out.

The Spartak manager, Mr Antipenok, didn't take the defeat well and at first he refused to speak to the press before, begrudgingly offering: "Wolves played well and fully deserved their win. Spartak were satisfactory in the first half, but played very, very badly in the second. You cannot stand still in this game." When congratulated on his team's sporting attitude, he replied: "It is not enough to be sporting. It is necessary to play football as well."

So Wolves became the first British club to have beaten Spartak and on the front page of the next morning's *Daily Mail*, under the headline "Wolves Kick Spark Out Of Spartak" it read: "The Wolves, England's League Champions, last night beat Spartak, the pride of Russia, by four goals to nil, and in 90 minutes restored in full our lost football prestige."

Comments were made about the Russian substitution and the fact that Wolves manager Stan Cullis refused to send on a replacement for Stuart even though he was clearly dazed following a collision.

Wolves: Williams, Stuart, Shorthouse, Slater, Wright, Flowers, Hancocks, Broadbent, Swinbourne, Wilshaw, Smith.
Spartak: Piraev, Ogonkov, Sedov, Parchine, Bachachkine, Netto, Tatouchine, Paramonov (Isayev), Simonian, Vorichilov, Iline.
Attendance: 55,184.
Referee: BM Griffiths.

Wolves 3 (Hancocks (pen), Swinbourne 2)
Honved 2 (Kocsis, Machos)

Floodlit friendly
Wednesday 13th December 1954

IN NOVEMBER 1953, as Wolves were heading towards their first league championship, Hungary arrived in England to play the home country in a friendly at Wembley. Whatever result the footballing public were expecting, it certainly wasn't the one that occurred on that misty afternoon in north London. The final score of England 3 Hungary 6 was one which sent shockwaves through English soccer, thrusting the game into a deep depression. Any hope of exacting revenge the following summer in a return fixture in Budapest was destroyed along with the team, as this time the Hungarians humiliated England 7-1. English soccer had never been at a lower ebb.

On the domestic front, with the championship won, Wolves continued to play top opposition in a series of floodlit friendlies that were to gain them world renown. The opening of the lights in September 1953 was commemorated by the visit of the South African national side who were beaten 3-1. Other opponents were Glasgow Celtic, Racing Club of Buenos Aires, First Vienna, Maccabi of Tel Aviv and Moscow Spartak. All were beaten with the exception of Vienna who held Wolves to a scoreless draw.

When it was announced that the next team to try to achieve a victory at Molineux were to be the crack Hungarian side Honved of Budapest, the interest not just in Wolverhampton, but throughout the country, was immense. This was the chance to exact a little revenge and put some pride back into English soccer. However, the measure of the task that faced Wolves was clear. They were to face a side who included six of the team that had given England a footballing lesson at Wembley a year previously, as well as a regular from the team who missed the international through injury.

It was also a chance for Billy Wright to settle a few scores. He had been the only Wolves player in the team at Wembley and as the captain of both national and club sides he once more faced his Hungarian counterpart, the great Ferenc Puskas. As the teams walked out into the chilly December air in front of a capacity 55,000 crowd, Wolves wore satin shirts which they believed stood out more under the floodlights. At the start of that season they had changed their colours from the traditional old gold to a brighter gold. Honved were kitted out in white with two red hoops on their shirts.

The first ten minutes of the game was something of a midfield stalemate as the teams jousted for possession in the thick mud that soon churned up, making the centre of the park resemble a ploughed field. The atmosphere inside the ground was tremendous but it was muted in the tenth minute when, from a Puskas free kick fortuitously awarded on the edge of the box after the ball had hit Ron Flowers' hand, Sandor Kocsis headed home.

Within a minute Roy Swinbourne had the chance to level things but Lajos Farago smothered the centre-forward's shot. It proved to be a costly miss, for Honved counter-attacked brilliantly. With the crowd still talking of the Swinbourne chance, Honved took the ball to the other end of the field with some great touch football and Ferenc Machos slipped the ball past Bert Williams. Two down and the game still in its infancy, the team, and for that matter the crowd, refused to yield, and Wolves began to peg Honved back into their own half, restricting them to the odd breakaway.

Twice, Les Smith, keeping out England international Jimmy Mullen on the left wing, had good chances to pull a goal back, and Johnny Hancocks, Dennis Wilshaw and Swinbourne all brought the best out of Farago who was putting on a world class display in the visitors' goal. The interval arrived and Wolves still hadn't breached the Hungarian defence.

During the break, manager Stan Cullis told his team: "You are too nervous. Get out there and play your normal game." His words seemed to have the desired effect for within four minutes Wolves had pulled a goal back. Hancocks ran through into the area only to be pushed by Ferencs Kovacs. The referee awarded a penalty, a decision that did not please the Honved players. After their protests fell on stoney ground, the diminutive Wolves number seven steadied himself and blasted the ball home from the spot.

The penalty was the signal for an all-out assault on the Honved goal. The home defence were playing superbly when called upon although, by now, the Hungarians were restricted to sporadic attacks although they were still extremely dangerous on the break. The youthful Flowers and Bill Slater gave great support to Wright while Eddie Stuart and Bill Shorthouse gave solid displays in the full-back berths in a Wolves team that was comprised of 10 Englishmen and one South African.

Peter Broadbent was finding more and more space in the centre of the park and Puskas kept having to fall back to rally his beleaguered troops. Such was the importance of the game, it was broadcast on radio and shown on live television. The radio commentators in their excitement, as Wolves got more and more on top, kept referring to Honved as Hungary.

The commentators went as mad as the crowd did when Swinbourne got a deserved equaliser 14 minutes from the end. Wolves had forced a succession of corners, all of which had come to nothing. It seemed the goal just wouldn't come. Then Wilshaw's centre found the head of Swinbourne and, to the deafening roar of the crowd, the ball hit the back of the net. A minute later, Smith beat two men out on the left and then sent a diagonal through ball for Swinbourne to run on to, the centre-forward firing home from just inside the area.

The last ten minutes must have seemed like an eternity for the Wolves team and the crowd. The Hungarians broke out of defence to try to get an equaliser though it was still Wolves that looked the more dangerous side. When Welsh referee Mervyn

v Honved, 1954

Griffiths blew for time, the cheers that rose from the crowd shook the famous old ground to the rafters.

Billy Wright was met by Laszlo Marosi, the Honved manager, as he left the field. He warmly shook the Wolves skipper's hand, conceding that the better team had won. A delighted Wright said later: "I was so proud of the team. They all played a wonderful game. They were all wonderful, in fact everything's wonderful." Stan Cullis turned to his captain and simply said: "Magnificent."

A measure of Wolves' superiority was shown in that they had 28 attempts at goal, 14 in each half compared with Honved's 11 of which only two came following the interval. Wanderers also led the corner count by ten to three. Wing-Commander Charles Reep, described as Wolves' back-room boffin, was credited for his homework on the Hungarian team. He spent two long sessions with Cullis's men giving a detailed analysis of Honved's players and their style of play in the days leading up to the game. The following morning, Wolves commanded the headlines of the national press – not only back page but the front too. "Wolves champions of the World now" said the *Daily Mail*, while the *News Chronicle* led with "That's great Wolves, another boost for England: Honved hammered".

The villain of the day tag belonged to BBC *Light Programme* radio announcer Adrian Waller who faded out the broadcast to present the Cyril Stapleton Show Band programme with a minute of the game remaining and Honved piling on the pressure in search of an equaliser. Kenneth Adam, head of the *Light Programme* and Waller's boss, was one of the infuriated listeners who immediately called the BBC only to find the lines jammed by people wishing to complain.

Adams jumped into a taxi from his flat and raced to the nearby Broadcasting House where he was met by a remorseful Waller who asked permission to break into the Show Band recorded performance to apologise. He said: "This is a really repentant Adrian Waller saying I do realise I made a mistake in fading out that great match which the Wolves won by three goals to two. I know a good many listeners have phoned up about this and I am sorry to have put them to the trouble. It is the kind of mistake we only make once, and needless to say I shall be very wary about doing it again."

The fact that Waller's 'faux pas' made headline news illustrated the importance of the game to football in England, and Wolves had not failed in their duty.

Honved returned to Molineux twice more in the years to come, both for friendly games, the first of which was in December, 1962. It was a poor game which contained little of the skills and thrills of the one that had taken place eight years earlier. Honved went in front with just five minutes of the match left through right winger Nagy. Two minutes later, Alan Hinton slammed the ball home to level the scores. There had been little else to cheer the crowd of 13,914.

The third visit was in 1993 to mark the completion of the rebuilt Molineux. Guest of honour was Ferenc Puskas who met up with his old adversary Billy Wright who, at the time, was a director at the club and also amongst the capacity crowd were the other ten members of the 1954 Wolves team.

Wolves' Greatest Games

Ironically, after the original game became a legendary event under the floodlights, the new lights were struck down with an attack of the gremlins and the kick-off had to be delayed for 15 minutes as the crowd sat in darkness before they were partially restored so play could take place. It wasn't until the interval that the fault was completely repaired and full power was regained. By that time Honved were a goal up through Istvan Pisont who controlled Istvan Vincze's through ball before beating Mike Stowell on the half-hour mark.

Visiting keeper Istvan Brockhauser saved from David Kelly with his legs before Andy Thompson tapped the ball home in the 60th minute after both Kelly and Cyrille Regis had seen efforts come back off the woodwork. There were no further goals although, before the end, Molineux was treated to its first ever Mexican wave. The game itself was much more of a friendly than in 1954, but the 28,000 supporters seemed to go home in a contented mood. Well, after all, the new surroundings were a million miles away from the ruins of the old and once proud Molineux.

Nobody who was at Molineux on that Monday evening in December 1954 will surely ever forget the dramatic game in which Wolves helped restore the pride in English football.

Wolves: Williams, Stuart, Shorthouse, Slater, Wright, Flowers, Hancocks, Broadbent, Swinbourne, Wilshaw, Smith.
Honved: Farago, Palicsko, Kovacs, Bozsik, Lorant, Banyai, Budai, Kocsis, Machos, Puskas, Czibor.
Attendance: 55,000.
Referee: BM Griffiths.

Wolves 6 (Hancocks 3, Wilshaw 2, Slater)
Huddersfield Town 4 (Glazzard 3, Frear)
Football League First Division
Saturday 12th February 1955

JOE BAILLIE played just one senior game for Wolves – but what a game it was. After eight years at Celtic in his native Scotland, he was signed by Stan Cullis in December 1954 and he made his solitary outing the following February when Huddersfield Town visited a snowbound Wolverhampton.

Seven days earlier, Wolves had been humbled 6-1 by Bolton at Burnden Park and yet Cullis resisted making wholesale changes to his team which, had Eddie Stuart been fit, would have been unchanged. But the South African was ruled out and in came Baillie while former Molineux full-back Lol Kelly was given the captaincy of Huddersfield against his former club.

Around an inch of snow covered the playing surface and the lines and penalty spots had to be cleared before they were re-marked in yellow to aid visibility for the match officials and spectators. Despite the chill, the sun was shining as Kelly won the toss and opted to defend the hotel end. Within two minutes, he was watching as Town keeper Jack Wheeler was retrieving the ball from the back of the net.

Ron Simpson cut in from the left and fired wide from the kick-off before Bill Shorthouse's long punt upfield set up Johnny Hancocks for the opening goal with the winger drilling a low shot past Wheeler from just inside the area. A second looked a certainty after ten minutes after Ron Stanisforth had miskicked. Les Smith ran in and squared a pass for Roy Swinbourne who turned it towards goal only for the ball to hit the back of Kelly's feet as he ran back to cover.

Hancocks was a foot off target after he had met Swinbourne's low cross and then Bryan Frear almost levelled matters with a shot on the turn that Bert Williams was relieved to see go wide before Baillie had to receive attention after he collided with Simpson as he cleared. Billy Wright cleared a fierce Albert Hobson shot from just in front of the goal-line as the sun disappeared and the snow began to blow across the pitch.

Wheeler dived full length to turn a Smith effort around the post and from a corner Baillie sent a lob inches over the bar with Wheeler struggling to make his ground. Huddersfield had two good opportunities to open their account but Frear was denied by Williams who dived to save at the inside-left's feet before Simpson put the ball over the bar from 12 yards out with just the keeper to beat.

Considering the conditions, there was plenty for the crowd to enjoy and after Wheeler had used both fists to clear a Dennis Wilshaw drive, Williams had to save from Frear right under the crossbar. Then Peter Broadbent delivered a cross that Swinbourne diverted towards goal only for Wheeler to save on the line. Just before the break, Town's Jim Watson headed inches over.

Wolves' Greatest Games

After a one-goal opening half, the spectators were to witness a scoring spree which began within a minute of the restart. Baillie's pass fell nicely for Wilshaw who rode a tackle before finding the back of the net. Shortly afterwards Broadbent beat the offside trap and drew Wheeler from his line but his shot was off target.

With 53 minutes gone, Town pulled a goal back. Hobson looked to have fouled Wright wide on the right but the referee waved play on and the winger crossed for Jim Glazzard to head past Williams. It took Wanderers just seven more minutes to restore their two-goal cushion. Wilshaw won possession on the edge of the Huddersfield box and after he had cleverly sidestepped a defender he pushed the ball past Wheeler.

The Town defence were now at full stretch and on 64 minutes Kelly fouled Smith, who was in full flight heading towards Wheeler's goal, deep inside the box. Hancocks blasted the ball past the keeper for his second and Wolves' fourth of the game. The entertainment, however, was far from over and, just five minutes later, the visitors scored once again with Frear sending a 20-yard shot into the net via the underside of the bar.

Virtually from the restart Williams had to dive full length to turn away a drive from Watson as Town began to assume command with, perhaps, some of the home team having thought that the game was won. Far from it. Glazzard reduced the deficit to just one, shooting as he fell in meeting a cross from Simpson.

But the tension eased somewhat in the 78th minute as Bill Slater went up for a Hancocks corner and headed beyond Wheeler. And two minutes later, Hancocks completed his hat-trick with something of a freak goal. He turned Kelly inside out before hitting a cross that hit the inside of the far post and rebounded into the net just inside the opposite upright. With the last kick of the game, Glazzard too completed his hat-trick as he turned home a cross from the right. The win saw Wanderers moving to the top of the table above Sunderland.

While he had made a successful debut, Baillie immediately lost his place to the fit-again Stuart the following week. The Scot was transferred to Bristol City in June 1956 and he later played for Leicester and Bradford Park Avenue. He tragically lost his life in a car crash in his native Glasgow in 1966 at the age of just 37.

Wolves: Williams, Baillie, Shorthouse, Slater, Wright, Flowers, Hancocks, Broadbent, Swinbourne, Wilshaw, Smith.
Town: Wheeler, Staniforth, Kelly, McGarry, Taylor, Quested, Hobson, Watson, Glazzard, Frear, Simpson.
Attendance: 30,666.
Referee: FH Gerrard.

Cardiff City 1 (Stockin)
Wolves 9 (Hancocks 3, Mullen, Swinbourne 3, Broadbent 2)

Football League First Division
Saturday 3rd September 1955

IT WOULD be hard to imagine anyone in football making a more prolific contribution to a game than that of Jimmy Mullen on a sun-baked afternoon at Cardiff's Ninian Park shortly after the birth of the 1955/56 season. Until that day the record winning margin for an away team in a top flight game was eight goals.

The first team to achieve the feat were West Bromwich Albion with, unfortunately, Wolves being on the receiving end of the 8-0 thrashing at Molineux in December 1893. Then, in December 1908, in another local derby, Sunderland stunned Newcastle by winning 9-1 at St James' Park. There was no indication that Wolves were going to equal that record when they met the Bluebirds despite running into form prior to the game.

After picking up just a point from their first two games of the campaign, Molineux games against Manchester City and Portsmouth saw consecutive wins with a total of ten goals scored. Cardiff had won their two home fixtures, against Sunderland and Bolton, but had returned pointless from trips to Arsenal and Aston Villa. In the City forward line was former Wolves inside-forward Ron Stockin, who scored seven goals in 21 appearances before switching to Cardiff for a £12,000 fee in the summer of 1954.

Stockin was joined in the attack by one-time Kidderminster striker Gerry Hitchens who was drafted in at the last minute after Welsh international centre-forward Trevor Ford had failed a morning fitness test. Neither had time to draw breath before they found themselves restarting the game after Johnny Hancocks had given Wolves the lead inside the first minute.

Bill Slater initiated the move, finding Mullen with a long pass and when the winger's shot came back off the bar, Hancocks was waiting to send the rebound past home keeper Ron Howells. Billy Wright, with typical efficiency, broke up a dangerous Cardiff attack, steering the ball back to Bert Williams. Then it was Hancocks' turn to hit the bar although this time a defender was on hand to clear. But, in the tenth minute, he added his own and his team's second goal when he took a pass from Mullen and hit a shot from 12 yards that was so powerful that it lodged in the netting.

Four minutes and three Wolves corners later it was 3-0. Peter Broadbent and Hancocks gave Mullen the opportunity to rifle a left-foot shot into the roof of the net past the shell-shocked Howells. City tried hard to hit back and if Harry Kirtley had been a little faster with his reactions he could well have reduced the deficit. But the visitors were well on top with Hancocks and Mullen on the wings in devastating form with the Cardiff defenders seemingly powerless to stop them.

Wolves' Greatest Games

Just 19 minutes had gone when Roy Swinbourne got a fourth goal. Mullen crossed from the left and when Colin Booth dummied his marker, the ball ran through to Swinbourne who volleyed past Howells. Almost immediately John McSeveney was close to giving the home supporters something to shout about when he took the ball round Eddie Stuart but then fired over the bar. Then Derrick Sullivan paid the price for heading out a ferocious effort from Hancocks, as he was almost knocked out in the process such was the power of the shot.

At the other end of the field, Williams was becoming something of a spectator and when the home defence managed to break up an attack it earned ironic cheers from the City fans. Howells had his hands stung in saving another drive from Hancocks but he couldn't stop the winger from completing his hat-trick ten minutes before the break. Again Mullen was involved, this time picking out Hancocks with a pinpoint centre that was converted with a rare header by the shortest man on the park. The interval arrived with Wolves virtually using Howells' goal for shooting practice such was their domination.

There was no respite for the home team after the break and Ron Stitfall injured himself in challenging Swinbourne who would otherwise have been clean through. The full-back was able to resume after treatment. On 56 minutes Swinbourne made it six following a Hancocks corner who had earned the flag-kick with a run from halfway before his cross was turned behind. He lifted the ball into the middle and when the ball went out to Mullen he tried a shot that struck Swinbourne, who skilfully back-heeled the ball into the net.

Williams did have to punch clear a cross as Hitchens threatened but, midway through the half, Broadbent got in on the act with an easy finish from Mullen's corner. In the 75th minute Broadbent struck again, sweeping the ball into the net after taking yet another pass from Mullen. Six minutes later Swinbourne became the second visiting player to complete his hat-trick when he deflected Mullen's cross-shot beyond the reach of Howells. It was the striker's ninth goal from just five games.

With seven minutes remaining Stockin fired past Williams to give Cardiff a consolation on what, for them, had been an afternoon of horror. On the other hand, for Mullen, to have scored one and played a part in the other eight goals, was a terrific feat as Wolves became the third team to win away by eight goals. Amazingly, for the return fixture on New Year's Eve, Cardiff won 2-0 at Molineux.

Cardiff: Howells, Sherwood, Stitfall, Harrington, Gale, Sullivan, Dixon, Kirtley, Hitchens, Stockin, McSeveney.
Wolves: Williams, Stuart, Shorthouse, Slater, Wright, Clamp, Hancocks, Broadbent, Swinbourne, Booth, Mullen.
Attendance: 40,060.
Referee: J Kelly.

Wolves 2 (Slater, Mullen)
Moscow Dynamo 1 (Ilyin)
Floodlit friendly
Wednesday 9th November 1955

ALMOST A year after Spartak had been demolished by 4-0, it was the turn of their Moscow rivals Dynamo to visit Molineux and try to get the result that would exact some revenge for Russian football on its travels to England. But they faced a difficult task as Wolves' home form had been excellent with the last defeat in front of their own fans coming on Christmas Day almost 11 months earlier when Everton were 3-1 victors. During the summer of 1955, Wolves had embarked on a tour of Russia to play Spartak and Dynamo in Moscow. Spartak were comfortable 3-0 winners but the game with Dynamo was a much closer affair with Wanderers losing by the odd goal in five, Dennis Wilshaw getting both of their goals to become the first Englishman to score in the Soviet Union.

On a cold November evening Dynamo arrived at Molineux with an eye on an Anglo-Russian double. As usual for the time, and nature of the opposition, the gates were closed as Wolves looked the more impressive side in the opening stages as they attacked the North Bank end. With top scorer Roy Swinbourne missing with the injury that was to cruelly bring about a premature end to his playing days, Wolves gave a debut to 19-year-old Jimmy Murray.

For the Dover-born centre-forward, who was doing his national service, it was the start of what was to be a highly successful career at Molineux. And he gave no indication of nerves in the face of such notable opposition that night. But for a team noted for their discipline, Dynamo's defence were looking very ragged as they tried to cope with the wing threat from Johnny Hancocks and Jimmy Mullen.

A goal had to come and it duly arrived in the 15th minute. The move began and was ended by Bill Slater. He spread a pass out to the right where Hancocks advanced before crossing into the Russian area where Konstantin Krizhevsky headed behind. Hancocks took the corner and when the ball fell to Dennis Wilshaw at the far post, he sliced his goal attempt. But the ball spun away into the path of Slater whose first attempt was blocked but he made no mistake with the second, beating the legendary Russian keeper Lev Yashin from just eight yards out.

Four minutes later Mullen would have had a second but for the brilliance of Yashin who somehow got to the winger's on-target volley. Slater nearly did it again after Peter Broadbent had picked him out but Yashin dived low to save. But, in the 49th minute, Mullen made it two when he controlled Eddie Clamp's long through ball and dummied Igor Rodionov before planting a right-foot drive past the advancing Yashin and into the corner of the net.

Vladimir Ilyin broke into the left channel of the Wolves box but Williams dived forwards to save an angled shot, then a Broadbent header from Hancocks' corner struck the bar before being cleared by a defender. Yashin made another fine save to keep out Wilshaw's header before the Russians began to force the issue with some spirited attacking moves and they pulled a goal back in the 65th minute.

Billy Wright had jarred his knee in a challenge and was limping on the touchline as Krizhevsky planted a centre into the Wolves area. With the defence momentarily in disarray without their skipper at the heart of it, Vladimir Ilyin took full advantage by beating Williams with a low shot from the edge of the area.

Ilyin had the ball in the net again in the closing stages as did Genrikh Feodosov with a header but on both occasions the scores were disallowed after hairline offside decisions. The relief of the crowd come the final whistle was evident although few could argue that Wolves weren't worthy of the victory.

Igor Kuprianov, vice-president of the Russian Football Association, commented after the game that he felt that Feodosov's goal should have stood. However, he added: "But we are perfectly satisfied with the result. Wolves played very well." Stan Cullis said of the offside decision: "I was in a good spot and the referee was right."

It wasn't only the result that captured the headlines the next day. A major diplomatic row broke out after the Foreign Office refused to let the Russians broadcast the game to their own radio station. In those days of the Cold War, a diplomat explained: "We agreed to provide facilities for the Russians to broadcast if the Russians agreed not to jam the BBC's overseas commentary. No reply reached us. The facilities were not provided."

Russian commentators, who had spent three days in the town arranging to broadcast, were furious when they arrived at the ground to find that no line had been installed for them. An attaché from the Russian Embassy was called in and he said: "It is unfair. The broadcast was arranged on reciprocal lines, and the BBC was allowed to broadcast from Moscow when Wolves went there." One of his colleagues added: "This makes a very bad impression and it complicates Anglo-Soviet sporting arrangements."

Back in London a Foreign Office spokesman said: "We think that the Russians' jamming of our broadcasts is bad in principle. We take this chance to make our views known." Away from the political shenanigans, the Wolves and Dynamo players toasted each other with lemonade in the dressing rooms.

Wolves: Williams, Stuart, Shorthouse, Slater, Wright, Clamp, Hancocks, Broadbent, Murray, Wilshaw, Mullen.
Dynamo: Yashin, Rodionov, B Kuznetsov, Boykov, Krizhevsky, Sokolov, Shabrov, Feodosov, Y Kuznetsov, Ilyin, Ryzhkin.
Attendance: 55,480.
Referee: AE Ellis.

27

Wolves 5 (Murray 2, Slater penalty, Broadbent, Mullen)
Luton Town 4 (Cullen, Turner 3)
Football League First Division
Wednesday 29th August 1956

WOLVES OPENED the 1956/57 season with a convincing 5-1 win over Manchester City at Molineux as Jimmy Murray helped himself to four goals. But the two away games that followed in a three-day spell both ended in defeat – 1-0 at Luton and 3-2 at Blackpool. Indeed Luton won all three of their opening fixtures and they sat proudly at the top of the First Division table as they made their way to Molineux for the return fixture – a fixture destined to be labelled a classic by those who watched it.

The match was a unique one as it was used for an experiment under the direction of the Football League. Both Wolves and Luton agreed to it being the first game in Britain to be started in daylight and finished underneath the artificial glow of floodlights. Entire games played under lights were still relatively new, but until the Hatters arrived at Molineux there had been no 'half and half' matches.

The kick-off time of 7pm was later than for previous midweek league games but it didn't deter over 46,000 supporters from packing the ground – and how lucky they proved to be. It was determined that there would be a mutual agreement between the clubs as to when the lights would be put on. Watching from the stand was Scottish goalkeeper Malcolm Finlayson who had joined Wolves from Millwall earlier in the day.

For each of the opening three games, Stan Cullis had named the same side but hopes of a fourth were dashed when Bill Shorthouse was ruled out through injury. Into his place and making his first team debut was Claverley-born defender Gerry Harris and his baptism wasn't destined to be a quiet one – anything but.

Wolves attacked the South Bank end on a fine late summer evening and they almost fell behind after just five minutes when Town winger Jim Adam shot against Bert Williams' body when it looked easier to score. But that served to be only a temporary reprieve for Wolves as they conceded two goals inside the next seven minutes.

Both goals were excellent strikes that warranted appreciative applause from the large crowd. The first was a crisply hit drive from Mike Cullen that took a slight deflection off the outstretched foot of Bill Slater on its way past Williams. Then Gordon Turner added the second as he confidently beat the Wolves keeper after running on to a perfectly-weighted through ball.

Two down after 12 minutes, and with the crowd fearing the worst, it took a brilliant save from Williams to prevent a third as he threw himself sideways to keep out another effort from Turner. The save, however, seemed to kick-start Wolves' game and within a minute they had pulled a goal back as Murray leapt high to direct Colin

Wolves' Greatest Games

Booth's centre into the roof of the net. And two minutes later, Murray was fouled as he looked certain to net an equaliser and so that duty was left to Slater who duly despatched the resultant spot-kick.

With both teams throwing everything into attack, more goals were inevitable and it was Peter Broadbent who gave Wolves the lead for the first time when he beat Town keeper Bernard Streten after running on to a through pass from Harry Hooper. However, the lead lasted for barely two minutes as a superb piece of work by Cullen saw him scoot past his marker before crossing for Turner to head beyond the dive of Williams.

But back came Wolves with two goals in the eight minutes leading up to the break. Murray netted the first, burying a low shot from just inside the box, and then, on the stroke of half-time, Hooper's cross was flicked on by Murray to Jimmy Mullen who scored with a shot on the turn. So the interval arrived with both teams warmly applauded as they made their way from the pitch following some classical football that saw the home team 5-3 to the good. And it was while the players took a deserved breather that the historic moment arrived as the lights were switched on.

The second half proved to be nowhere near as prolific with regards to goals, but there was still a plethora of chances for both sides as the fun continued. Wolves enjoyed most of the opportunities without cashing in on one of them, while the only goal of the half went the way of Luton as Turner completed his hat-trick with what was probably the best goal of the nine.

He intercepted a short pass from Eddie Stuart and advanced before firing a rising drive into the home net with Williams standing little chance of saving. It was Turner's second treble in four games. But this match was little short of a thriller and although Wolves took the two points football was the winner with the play of the highest class with no spoiling tactics, end to end attacking and nine goals.

In the following home programme, when Wolves played Everton, the editorial included this passage: "Not since the historic Honved and Spartak games have a crowd been roused to such a pitch of enthusiasm by the sheer breath-taking excitement of the game. Those who saw it will wish it could always be like this and so do we – football at its finest and entertainment at its highest."

Wolves: Williams, Stuart, Harris, Slater, Wright, Flowers, Hooper, Broadbent, Murray, Booth, Mullen.
Luton: Streten, Dunne, Aherne, Pemberton, Kelly, Shanks, Cullen, Turner, Morton, Pearce, Adam.
Attendance: 46,781.
Referee: ES Oxley.

Chelsea 3 (Stubbs, Brabrook, Blunstone)
Wolves 3 (Hooper, Flowers, Murray)
Football League First Division
Saturday 20th September 1956

GENERALLY SPEAKING, over the years games between Wolves and Chelsea have rarely produced tame affairs and, during the 1950s, Wolves enjoyed some comprehensive victories over the Londoners. But there were tight games with eventful finishes – none more so than the one that took place at Stamford Bridge in the autumn of 1956.

After their championship success of 1954, the following year saw Wolves relegated into the runners-up spot by Chelsea. But while Wolves finished in a creditable third place in 1956/57, the reigning champions slumped to a lowly 16th position in the First Division, just four points above the drop zone. And as they prepared to take on Wolves on that September afternoon, Ted Drake's team were again stationed in the lower half of the table having won just three of their opening 12 games.

A week earlier, however, Chelsea had enjoyed a three-goal victory over Everton at Goodison Park while a rampant Wolves side destroyed Portsmouth 6-0 at Molineux. Unsurprisingly, Stan Cullis named an unchanged team.

There was something of a midfield stalemate to begin with until Jim Lewis launched an attack down the right. Billy Wright intercepted the cross that followed and set Jimmy Mullen on a run down the left flank. But Ian McFarlane ran across and he managed to divert the ball back to his goalkeeper, Bill Robertson.

After Bill Slater had stopped Frank Blunstone in his tracks, Wright again broke from defence playing Harry Hooper through. The winger's pace took him past John Sillett and although his left-foot shot beat Robertson, the ball flashed inches wide of the post.

Malcolm Finlayson's goal had an escape after he had turned a hard Lewis shot behind for a corner. Lewis took the flag-kick himself and from it Blunstone's header looked as if it was going to give Chelsea the lead until Eddie Stuart popped up to clear off the line. Chelsea did go ahead in the tenth minute when, despite the close attention of Stuart, Les Stubbs turned the ball home after a low cross from Lewis.

The goal heralded an intense spell of pressure from the home side and Lewis wasn't far off with a header after he had run in from the wing to meet a Blunstone cross. When Wolves did counter, Dennis Wilshaw slipped the ball to Jimmy Murray whose shot was blocked. Murray figured again moments later but his header from Mullen's centre went straight into the arms of Robertson.

A succession of Wolves corners, from both sides, came to nothing and when an opening gave Colin Booth the opportunity to get in a shot, he felt the full force of a defender's tackle before he could do so. Lewis was having a fine game on the Chelsea right and from another of his crosses, Blunstone got in a header that was brilliantly saved by Finlayson. The keeper then had to move smartly to keep out Peter Brabrook's shot after a Lewis free kick.

Seven minutes before the break, Murray missed a good chance when he fired into the arms of Robertson shortly before Chelsea moved into a two-goal lead. Brabrook looked as surprised as anyone when, from 25 yards, he hooked the ball towards the Wolves goal. It looked like the ball was going to sail over the bar but, at the last minute, it dipped and dropped over the outstretched arms of Finlayson. Right on the interval, Brabrook nearly did it again with a flashing drive that flew a foot over the bar.

Two Mullen centres featured as the new half began but Chelsea soon began to dictate the play again with Finlayson the busier keeper although Mullen did shoot into the side netting after running onto a low centre from Hooper. Chelsea were soon back on the attack and Brabrook set up Lewis for a shot that Finlayson parried before Hooper, who had dropped back to help his beleaguered defence, turned the ball behind for a corner.

With the half at its midway point, Blunstone scored Chelsea's third when he rode a double challenge before leaving Finlayson with no chance with a terrific shot. And, just a minute later, he almost did it again, beating the Wolves keeper but being thwarted by Gerry Harris who stuck out a leg and diverted the ball behind.

With 15 minutes remaining, given the dominance that Chelsea had enjoyed, Hooper started the unlikeliest of comebacks when he ran on to Murray's through ball and easily beat Robertson. Then Slater ventured forward and he sent a cross-shot narrowly over the bar and Booth inadvertently got in the way of a Murray shot as the gold and black resurgence gained momentum.

In the 87th minute a Mullen corner led to a second Wolves goal. The ball fell into a crowded goalmouth and in the melee that ensued it was prodded against the post. But Ron Flowers latched onto the rebound and hooked the ball into the net.

By now the home defence were at panic stations and the Chelsea supporters were baying for the final whistle. But they were to be disappointed because, with less than a minute remaining, Hooper sent a crossfield pass to Booth who tapped the ball to Murray and he drove it past Robertson to give Wolves a point that had looked way out of their reach 15 minutes earlier.

Chelsea: Robertson, McFarlane, Sillett, Armstrong, Dicks, Saunders, Lewis, Brabrook, Tindall, Stubbs, Blunstone.
Wolves: Finlayson, Stuart, Harris, Slater, Wright, Flowers, Hooper, Booth, Wilshaw, Murray, Mullen.
Attendance: 43,558.
Referee: J Mitchell.

Wolves 4 (Hooper 3, Mason)
Preston North End 3 (Finney 2, Baxter)
Football League First Division
Saturday, 24th November 1956

WHILE THEIR home form left little to question, away from Molineux things weren't quite so hot for Wolves in the first part of the 1956/57 campaign. Prior to the visit of Preston, Wanderers had lost just once at home but had won only once on their travels. Three-nil defeats at Manchester United and Burnley coming either side of a 5-2 home thrashing of Arsenal showed the inconsistency in Stan Cullis's side prior to the Preston game.

With Colin Booth and Ron Flowers ruled out through injury, in came Bobby Mason, playing in only his second league game, and Eddie Clamp. Also missing was Peter Broadbent with his place taken by Dennis Wilshaw. Wolves and Preston were placed ninth and tenth respectively in the table with both clubs locked on 19 points although the Lancashire side had played one game more.

Wolves defended the hotel end and from the off there was a dangerous moment as Tom Finney burst through the middle but George Showell dashed across to dispossess the legendary winger who had been switched to centre-forward. Showell then instigated a flowing Wolves move involving Bill Slater and Harry Hooper who took a return pass from Mason before shooting across the face of goal.

Hooper and Mason combined again to set up Jimmy Murray but his shot was charged down. Billy Wright used his expertise to take the ball from England team-mate Finney whose roving role up front was causing concern for the home back-line. Preston keeper Fred Else saved well from Murray after more good work from Hooper, before Finney gave the visitors a 27th-minute advantage in their first serious attack.

Tommy Thompson began the move with a smart pass to right-winger Les Dagger, who drew the home defence before crossing low to Finney who was waiting at the far post to slam the ball into the net. Shortly afterwards, Clamp had his work cut out to stop Finney who had his eyes on a second. At the North Bank end, Else saved from Mason after an incisive move involving Slater and Wilshaw. Clamp came to the rescue once more as Thompson raced into the box. Hassled by the left-half, the Preston man drove across the face of Malcolm Finlayson's goal.

The home attack were getting little change from the visiting rearguard and Preston went close to a second goal after a slip by Gerry Harris released Dagger but Wright reacted quickly and he managed to steer the ball back to Finlayson before any damage was done. Just before the break, the Scottish keeper had luck on his side when Sammy Taylor's header rebounded off the bar and into his arms, but the luck didn't last. With seconds of the half remaining, the bounce of a long through ball deceived Wright and Finney ran through, holding off a challenge from the Wolves skipper, before shooting past Finlayson.

Wolves' Greatest Games

With the mist that had descended on the ground getting thicker, the floodlights were switched on but they did little to brighten the mood of the home fans as Preston moved into a 3-0 lead just two minutes after the interval. When the defence failed to deal with a cross from the right, Jim Baxter nipped in to find the net. Wolves just weren't at the races and as discontentment in the crowd filled the air, Ray Evans wasn't far away from a fourth for the Lilywhites with a long-range shot.

However, that was the sign for Wanderers to suddenly snap out of their lethargy. Two Jimmy Mullen corners seemed to give the crowd fresh heart and, with just 25 minutes remaining, Hooper started a comeback of which he was a focal point. The winger went on a solo run and as he moved into the Preston box, he was felled by Joe Walton. Hooper picked himself up and easily beat Else from the spot.

After looking completely at ease, the Preston defence suddenly looked nervous and vulnerable and after a Hooper corner, the ball was headed half clear to Mullen whose shot was blocked. Then Mason barged his way past the double challenge of Evans and Joe Dunn but his shot bounced off the advancing figure of Else. Perhaps the deciding incident of the game came when Dagger shot weakly wide when he had Finlayson's goal at his mercy.

Mason saw his shot blocked by Dunn and then he had the ball taken off his feet by Else who had run from his box to boot clear. However, the young forward played his part in Wolves' second goal ten minutes from the end. Hooper had run into the middle of the field and he took Mason's pass before advancing and smashing a 25-yard drive into the net off the underside of the bar.

Hooper repaid the favour three minutes later as Wanderers drew level when his corner fell to Mason whose first time shot went between the near post and Else. The action wasn't finished and it was left to Hooper to complete his treble and win it for Wolves in the final minute. From the second of consecutive Mullen corners, a half-clearance landed in front of Hooper and he sent a rising drive past Else.

There was still time for a Clamp shot to go behind off a defender and, from the corner, Slater's effort was saved at the foot of the post by Else as an incredible game came to an end.

Wolves: Finlayson, Showell, Harris, Slater, Wright, Clamp, Hooper, Mason, Wilshaw, Murray, Mullen.
Preston: Else, Cunningham, Walton, Docherty, Dunn, Evans, Dagger, Thompson, Finney, Baxter, Taylor.
Attendance: 30,254.
Referee: A Holland.

Wolves 3 (Broadbent, Murray, Wilshaw)
Real Madrid 2 (Marcal 2)
Floodlit friendly
Thursday 17th October 1957

HOLDING A slender two-point lead at the top of the table over arch rivals West Bromwich Albion, surely the last thing that Wolves wanted was to play a prestige friendly against the inaugural European Cup winners, Spanish champions and one of the best teams in the world, Real Madrid, less than 48 hours before a First Division home clash with Chelsea.

However, the challenge for Stan Cullis and his team was obviously one that was too good to resist and Molineux was packed to the gunnels for the Thursday evening visit of the Spanish giants. Wolves were in peak form and in an eight-match run they had dropped just a single point. They had to start the game without skipper Billy Wright, who was away on England duty, with George Showell deputising. Showell was destined to have a terrific game as he shackled the threat of the great Alfredo Di Stefano.

It was Real's second visit to England that year. In April they had faced Manchester United in Spain, winning the European Cup semi-final first leg 3-1. It was a deficit that even the great Busby Babes couldn't recover at Old Trafford in the return. In fact the visitors stretched the aggregate score to 5-1 before Bobby Charlton and Tommy Taylor earned the Reds a draw on the evening. In the final Real beat Reims of France 4-3.

There was no doubting the task facing Wolves as they kicked off attacking the North Bank looking to maintain their unbeaten friendly record under the lights. And they had the best of the possession in the opening minutes although the clearest chance fell to the Spaniards. The diminutive Francisco Gento raced down the left wing to the byline and hooked the ball back into the path of Di Stefano. A goal looked a certainty yet, to the amazement of the crowd, he shot high and wide.

Wolves hit back and twice Dennis Wilshaw drove narrowly wide before the visitors moved into a 13th-minute lead. Jose Joseito took a corner from the right and Ramon Marsal rose to power an unstoppable header into the net off the underside of the bar. The home defence were hard pressed to stop Real increasing their lead as they played some elegant and attractive football in their all white strip which stood out under the new Molineux floodlights which had been first used for a game against Spurs two weeks earlier. The lights were taller and much stronger than the originals that had been installed in 1953.

Eight minutes before the break, Marsal had the ball in the net again, but the referee disallowed the goal for ungentlemanly conduct as Di Stefano was aiming some heated words at Eddie Clamp at the time. Madrid made two substitutions at the start of the second half, which was seven minutes old when Wolves equalised.

Wolves' Greatest Games

Malcolm Finlayson punted the ball downfield for Jimmy Mullen and Peter Broadbent to give chase. One of the Real substitutes, Marcos Marquitos, got in a tangle with his goalkeeper and Broadbent took full advantage of the mix-up to lob the ball into the net.

The goal was the signal for some incessant attacking play from Wolves who pinned the opposition back in their own half. On the hour the pressure paid off and, from one of numerous corners, the home team moved ahead. Norman Deeley took the flag-kick which was met by the head of Murray and duly despatched past Real's Argentinian keeper Rogelio Dominguez with unerring accuracy. Before play resumed, Real captain Jose Zarraga was withdrawn to be replaced by Jesús Ruiz.

It took just ten more minutes before a Spanish equaliser arrived. As Finlayson advanced from his line, Marsal kept his head and slid the ball past the Scottish keeper. But far from retreating into a defensive shell, the goal seemed to spur Wolves to greater efforts and they got their reward nine minutes from time when veteran winger Mullen delivered a low cross that was side-footed home by Wilshaw. Try as they might in the dying minutes, Madrid could find no way past a resolute home defence.

A jubilant Cullis said after the match: "I have seen one of the greatest club teams in the world tonight and Di Stefano is certainly one of the all-time great players. There was a terrific contrast in style. I was very pleased with my lads in the first half, and the Molineux spirit carried us through in the second."

Two days later Wolves disposed of Chelsea, edging a tight contest 2-1 to maintain their lead at the top of the First Division. And a return fixture against Real Madrid was arranged for December that year and Wanderers earned more praise as they put in a commendable performance to earn a 2-2 draw at the Bernabeu with Bobby Mason opening the scoring before Enrique Mateos, from a blatantly looking offside position, scored a controversial equaliser.

Di Stefano put Real 2-1 up in the 70th minute and it was left to Mullen to create the equaliser with a low centre that was deflected into the net by a defender's boot. It speaks volumes for the quality shown by Wolves in the two games that they beat and held a team who were to win the European Cup in five consecutive seasons from its inception in 1956.

Wolves: Finlayson, Stuart, Harris, Clamp, Showell, Flowers, Deeley, Broadbent, Murray, Wilshaw, Mullen.
Real Madrid: Dominguez, Atienza (Marquitos), Lesmes, Santisteban, Santamaria, Zarraga (Ruiz), Joseito, Kopa, Di Stefano, Marcal, Gento (Rial).
Attendance: 55,169.
Referee: M Guigue (France).

Wolves 6 (Farmer 4, Durandt 2)
Chelsea 1 (Greaves)

Wolves won 7-6 on aggregate
FA Youth Cup Final, Thursday 1st May 1958

EVEN THE most optimistic of supporters who turned up at Molineux for the second leg of the 1958 FA Youth Cup Final against Chelsea could not have envisaged that Wolves would come back from the 5-1 deficit inflicted at Stamford Bridge to win the trophy for the first time. But that's what happened.

Wolves had played a major role in the Youth Cup since its inception in 1953 when they reached the final and faced Manchester United. It was a one-sided affair with United romping to a 7-1 victory at Old Trafford in the first leg before the sides shared four goals at Molineux in the return. A year later, in a repeat final, United were triumphant once again although this time things were a little closer. After a four-all draw, Wolves lost out to a single goal in the game at Manchester as United prevailed 5-4 on aggregate.

With Matt Busby and Jimmy Murphy at the helm, United continued to dominate the competition and they kept a vice-like hold on the trophy for the next three years, beating West Bromwich Albion, Chesterfield and West Ham in the respective finals. It wasn't until they met Wolves in the 1958 semi-final, that their winning streak came to an end.

Coached by Bill Shorthouse, the Wolves cubs' path to the last four had begun against West Bromwich at The Hawthorns where Gerry Mannion and Ian Hall were on target in a 2-2 draw. In the replay, Mannion and Brian Perry got two each and Granville Palin and Des Horne the others in a 6-1 victory. Cliff Durandt helped himself to a brace at Villa Park with Les Cocker also hitting the net in a 3-0 win over Aston Villa in the second round before another derby game, this time against Stoke City.

A goal from Perry saved the day against the Potters after they had taken the lead at Molineux. And things looked bleak in the replay as Stoke cruised to a 2-0 half-time lead in front of a 10,000 crowd. However, Wolves hit back through Cocker, Durandt and Mannion to earn a home tie against Leicester City.

The Foxes were outclassed as Wolves swamped them with a nine-goal avalanche. Perry with four and Mannion a hat-trick were the main tormenters of the Filbert Street rookies with Hall and Palin, with a penalty, the other scorers. Next up, in the quarter-final, were Bolton and, for the third time in five ties, Wolves needed a replay to get through.

It finished one apiece at Molineux with Bolton hitting back after Johnny Kirkham had given Wolves an interval advantage, before Perry, Mannion and Durandt were on target in a 3-1 win at Burnden Park. Then it was the turn of the Reds of Manchester. Ted Farmer gave Wolves the lead at Old Trafford and then a fantastic

Wolves' Greatest Games

display by keeper John Cullen restricted United to a Tom Spratt equaliser. Goals from Farmer, Des Horne and Mannion saw Wanderers through to a 3-1 victory in the second leg, and to the final.

Mannion, who had scored nine goals in the cup run, missed the final through injury. The first leg took place at Stamford Bridge and included in the Chelsea team were three men destined to enjoy long and illustrious league careers as well as representing England – Ken Shellito, Barry Bridges and Jimmy Greaves. Things got off to a good start for Wolves as Perry forced home an angled shot to give the visitors an early lead after some excellent work from Durandt.

Greaves equalised in controversial circumstances when the centre that led to his goal appeared to come from beyond the byline. However, protests were ignored and after Durandt had rattled the Chelsea crossbar, Michael Harrison put the Londoners ahead with a shot that slipped through the hands of Cullen shortly before the half-time whistle. The onslaught continued after the break with Michael Block, Harrison and Bridges adding to Wolves' woe as they took the final score to 5-1.

Such an outcome should have meant that Wolves were destined for a third defeat from the three finals that they had reached in the competition. However, with a great fightback against all the odds, they turned things on their head. Despite their team facing a hopeless task, there was still a 17,000 crowd inside Molineux and their loyalty was rewarded as Farmer scored goals in the eighth, 15th, 30th and 40th minutes to level the aggregate score by the interval. All four goals came about through Farmer's razor-sharp finishing in the box, and all were from close range – one of them a header.

Chelsea came into things a little more after the break but the home defence stood firm until eight minutes from the end when Durandt fastened onto Cocker's long clearance to fire Wolves into an overall lead. The South African struck again shortly afterwards before Greaves snatched a consolation for Chelsea. It was too little, too late and Wolves were the unlikely, but fully deserved, winners of the trophy 7-6 on aggregate.

Stan Cullis missed the game as he was on first team duty in Switzerland where his team were playing a friendly against Grasshoppers of Zurich. On hearing the news he said: "Tell them we are proud of them." After the match Chelsea manager Ted Drake was gracious enough to say: "Wolves were marvellous."

They were.

Wolves: Cullen, Kelly, Yates, Kirkham, Palin, Cocker, Read, Hall, Farmer, Durandt, Horne.
Chelsea: Smart, Shellito, Legg, Bradbury, Scott, Long, Block, Cliss, Bridges, Greaves, Harrison.
Attendance: 17,704.
Referee: L Howarth.

Wolves 7 (Deeley 3, Booth 3, Horne)
Portsmouth 0
Football League First Division
Saturday 27th December 1958

WOLVES MADE it a joyful Christmas for their supporters in 1958 with the South Coast followers of Portsmouth left deflated as their side were ripped apart twice in two days by a rampant Molineux team determined to cling on to the league championship trophy. On the last Saturday before Christmas, second-placed Wolves were a point behind frontrunners Bolton. However, while the Trotters were to endure a poor Yuletide as Everton completed the double over them, the Wanderers stars were at their ruthless best.

With Jimmy Murray going through a poor patch of form, Stan Cullis had experimented by playing Peter Broadbent as a centre-forward starting with the 20th December trip to the City Ground when he scored one of Wolves' goals in a 3–1 victory over Nottingham Forest. The multi-talented Broadbent followed that up with a Boxing Day hat-trick at Fratton Park with Norman Deeley and Colin Booth getting in on the act as they added a goal apiece in a 5-3 triumph.

While it came as no surprise that Wolves were unchanged for the return the next afternoon, there were changes for Pompey and among those omitted were English internationals Jimmy Dickinson and Peter Harris. A youthful Derek Dougan was brought in to lead their attack and also included was Reg Cutler – infamous at Molineux for breaking a goalpost and scoring the only goal of a 1957 FA Cup tie against Bournemouth.

In front of a festive North Bank, Pompey keeper Norman Uprichard was called into action inside the first minute when Ron Flowers unleashed one of his long-range specials. Portsmouth forced two corners, the second coming after a misplaced back-pass from Billy Wright eluded Malcolm Finlayson, then Deeley had three separate stabs at goal with Basil Hayward clearing the danger from the scramble that followed the last of the efforts.

Deeley was laid out when he had the wind knocked out of him after one of his own shots was so powerful that it struck a defender and rebounded into his stomach. Portsmouth almost took a shock lead when Sam Chapman found himself in acres of space but he lobbed the ball wide after Finlayson had come out of his goal to narrow the angle. Hayward was spoken to by the referee after an illegal challenge on Booth who would otherwise have been through, and Ron Newman was close to giving Portsmouth the lead when his cross struck the top of the bar.

The fans were starting to get a little restless when Deeley made the breakthrough with an excellent strike. He chested down a pass from Booth and as the ball fell he wasted no time in cracking a volley past Uprichard from just outside the area. Two minutes later Des Horne took the ball to the line before crossing for Bobby Mason

Wolves' Greatest Games

whose header landed on the roof of the net. Just before the break, Harry Harris saw his shot deflected behind by Finlayson for a corner.

Portsmouth missed the chance of equalising five minutes after the break when Chapman completely missed his kick in front of goal. Then Wright executed a scissors kick to relieve the danger after Newman had forced a corner. Wolves were struggling to recreate the form they enjoyed just 24 hours earlier but they did move further ahead after 61 minutes. Broadbent flicked a long through pass into the middle and Booth ran on and slammed the ball past Uprichard.

The keeper earned a merited cheer with an athletic leap to cut out a Broadbent centre, and then he plucked a Deeley lob out of the air after the winger had run unopposed from the centre circle to the 18-yard line. Wolves went three up in the 69th minute after Horne's cross was headed into the air by a defender and Booth made sure that he was in position to nod the ball home as it dropped.

Broadbent was thwarted by Uprichard's outstretched foot after he had run onto Deeley's excellent through ball. However, the keeper was beaten again in the 76th minute after Eddie Stuart ran from defence and crossed for Deeley who made sure with a low shot from near the penalty spot. There was time for Gerry Harris to go close with a cross-shot before Deeley completed his hat-trick in the 78th minute. Booth's shot rebounded off the crossbar and the ball fell invitingly at Deeley's feet and he lashed it into the roof of the net.

However, Booth wasn't to be denied and less than a minute later he too completed a treble – Wolves' third against Pompey in two days. Horne, who had been testing the visiting defence all afternoon with his pinpoint crosses, sent the ball over for Booth to rise and score with a header that went in just underneath the bar that had thwarted him seconds earlier. But Wolves weren't finished just yet.

With six minutes left Horne was rewarded for his efforts when he got onto the scoresheet himself. Taking a short pass from Broadbent, he advanced a few paces before smashing the ball into the back of the net, leaving Uprichard to retrieve for the 12th time in 180 minutes of football.

The win put Wanderers three points clear of West Bromwich Albion who had moved up into second place although the Baggies did have a game in hand on their neighbours. Broadbent was to play just three more games as a centre-forward before reverting to his customary inside-left position.

Wolves: Finlayson, Stuart, G Harris, Slater, Wright, Flowers, Deeley, Mason, Broadbent, Booth, Horne.
Pompey: Uprichard, McGhee, Wilson, Carter, Hayward, Casey, Newman, Chapman, Dougan, H Harris, Cutler.
Attendance: 41,347.
Referee: JP Smyth.

Wolves 6 (Deeley 2, Broadbent 2, Lill, Murray)
Arsenal 1 (Haverty)
Football League First Division
Saturday 7th March 1959

AS THE 1958/59 campaign approached the home straight, there was a three-horse race at the top of the First Division with Wolves heading off the threat of Arsenal on goal average with third-placed Manchester United just a point adrift on the first Saturday of March when the Gunners visited Molineux. Five days earlier, Arsenal's north London neighbours Tottenham Hotspur had left the ground with a point after a one-all draw but there was to be no mistake when Wolves took on their rivals.

There was just one change to the home team with Norman Deeley returning on the left wing in place of Jimmy Mullen after he had missed two games following a bout of flu. For Mullen, the game against Spurs turned out to be his last for the club after a glorious career spanning 23 impeccable years at Molineux. Deeley celebrated his own return by giving Wolves an early incentive in what, in every sense of the phrase, was a top-of-the table showdown.

Arsenal were without four of their best players – Jimmy Bloomfield, Jack Kelsey, Vic Groves and Jackie Henderson, who had moved from Molineux to Highbury in October of that season. Henderson had played just nine games and scored three goals in a brief spell in Wolverhampton following a move from Portsmouth in March, 1958. But, given the power of the Wolves performance that afternoon, it's doubtful if the quartet's presence would have changed the destiny of the points.

Although the pitch was heavy, it didn't prevent a display of fast and flowing football from the members of Stan Cullis's team. From the kick-off Malcolm Finlayson collected a deep centre from Danny Clapton before Billy Wright's free kick led to Wolves taking the lead with 90 seconds gone. Wright played the ball to Deeley who then took a return pass from Micky Lill and sidestepped his marker before shooting past Jim Standen, finding the net just inside the far post. Dave Bowen and David Herd both got in shots as Arsenal looked to get back on level terms but Finlayson easily claimed both efforts.

Deeley carved out an opening for Eddie Clamp but he miskicked on the edge of the area and the chance was gone, then Herd, with a burst of speed, cut through the home defence only for Finlayson to scramble the ball away before the striker could do any real damage. In the 14th minute Wolves moved into a two-goal lead. Jimmy Murray, on the left flank, raced past the challenges of Bill Dodgin and Len Wills before crossing for Peter Broadbent to send a splendid header past Standen.

That second goal was the signal for Wolves to take complete command of the game with little seen of the Arsenal attack. Left-back Dennis Evans, in particular, was having a nightmare in trying to quell the threat of Lill and there were panic

Wolves' Greatest Games

stations in the visitors' defence every time that Wolves attacked. Murray almost got a third when he intercepted Evans' under-hit back-pass but his shot was smothered by Standen.

However, in the next home attack Lill turned the ball home with a left-footed drive after the ball ran to him following a miskick from Murray with Broadbent cutting in from the left to create the opening. There was another chance after Dodgin had fouled Bobby Mason just outside the area but Ron Flowers' powerful free kick bounced clear off a defender. In a rare Arsenal raid, Tommy Docherty hit a shot that swerved inches over the bar.

The second half's first action came in the shape of a long-range shot from John Barnwell that rolled tamely wide of the target. Wolves were soon back on the attack and such was the pressure that the only surprise was that no further goals came until the 63rd minute. Lill's speed took him clear on the left and he took the ball to the line before cutting the cross back, away from Standen, leaving Deeley to tap in for the easiest of finishes.

Four minutes later, Murray made it five with a low shot that went just inside the post after some intricate work along the right wing involving Clamp, Mason and Broadbent. Another four minutes passed and another goal arrived with Broadbent getting in on the act. Murray hooked Lill's corner into the heart of the box and Broadbent just beat Standen to the ball, pushing it over the line past the, by now, demoralised keeper.

Mason was the only home forward not to have registered on the scoresheet and when he did find the net, after a neat header from Clamp ran to him, he was denied what would have been the seventh goal by the linesman's flag. Four minutes from time, the final goal of the afternoon went the way of Arsenal as Joe Haverty grabbed a consolation when he took advantage of a slip by Eddie Stuart and scrambled the ball past Finlayson.

That afternoon, Manchester United beat Everton 2-1 at Old Trafford to stay hot on the heels of Wolves. However, the Molineux team were in no mood to relinquish their title and in the ten games that remained after the demolition of the Gunners, eight were won and the other two drawn with a total of 28 goals scored to take the final tally at the end of the season to 110.

Wolves: Finlayson, Stuart, Harris, Clamp, Wright, Flowers, Lill, Mason, Murray, Broadbent, Deeley.
Arsenal: Standen, Wills, Evans, Docherty, Dodgin, Bowen, Clapton, Ward, Herd, Barnwell, Haverty.
Attendance: 40,480.
Referee: K Dagnall.

Wolves 5 (Broadbent 2, Booth, Clamp, Murray)
Luton Town 0
Football League First Division
Saturday 18th April 1959

ON THE penultimate Saturday of the 1958/59 season, Wolves had all but secured their second consecutive championship, and third of the 1950s. The only threat came from Manchester United who were two points adrift with just two games left to play, one fewer than Wolves. The Molineux team were in terrific form and in no mood to let things slip as Luton Town arrived in Wolverhampton just two weeks before their FA Cup Final meeting with Nottingham Forest at Wembley.

Bobby Mason was ruled out with an eye injury that he had picked up in the victory at Blackpool five days earlier. He was replaced by Colin Booth – otherwise Wolves were unchanged. There was a special moment for Billy Wright as he led the team out. His team-mates hung back and he suddenly found himself alone as players from both sides and the crowd gave him a tremendous ovation in recognition of him becoming the first footballer in the world to win 100 international caps.

Wolves attacked the North Bank end and they were clearly in no mood to take prisoners as they stormed into a two-goal lead after just seven minutes. From a Micky Lill corner there was a chance for Norman Deeley who appealed in vain that his shot had been handled on the line by Brendan McNally. However, the winger had his revenge in the fifth minute when, from his corner, Peter Broadbent sent a swerving header past Luton keeper Ron Baynham into the top left-hand corner of the net.

Two minutes later, Broadbent sent Lill off on a run down the right flank and his pinpoint cross was headed in by Booth. It wasn't until the 15 minute mark that Town posed a threat on Malcolm Finlayson's goal and even then Gordon Turner's effort was mistimed and cleared with ease. Just a minute later Booth was inches away from a third when he fired wide of the far post after being set up by Lill and Deeley. Lill had a chance after he had tricked his way past Seamus Dunne but he was way too high with his final shot.

In rare Luton attacks, Billy Bingham lifted his shot high into the South Bank terraces and Wright intercepted Turner's through pass to Bob Morton. With the game in its 37th minute, Eddie Clamp added a third with a terrific effort. He ran onto a low cross from Deeley and, from 20 yards, sent a grass-high drive just inside the post with Baynham static on his line. As the half drew to a close, both Lill and Booth went close to stretching the advantage.

When play resumed, such was the home dominance that it was more of a case of Wolves v Baynham rather than Wolves v Luton. The keeper pulled off some amazing saves as crosses and shots peppered his goal. He drew deserved applause from the

Wolves' Greatest Games

crowd for one flying leap to keep out a lob from Booth. Ron Flowers grazed an upright with an effort similar to that of Clamp's, then Baynham pulled off a tremendous reflex save to keep out a Broadbent volley. It was unfortunate for the keeper that his first mistake of the game, in the 68th minute, was to cost his side a fourth goal.

He mishandled a driven centre from Jimmy Murray who followed up to steer the loose ball into the net. The pressure continued and after Deeley had sent a header inches wide, Lill, as he had done earlier in the game, shot over the bar from a good position. In the 75th minute, a Finlayson clearance led to Wolves' fifth goal. Murray picked the ball up and from his short cross, Broadbent beat Baynham with a left-foot shot. Lill had another attempt at getting onto the scoresheet and although he managed to keep the ball down, this time he was thwarted by Baynham who stuck out a foot to divert it for a corner. Then, right on time, Bingham failed to net a consolation goal when he was wide of an open goal.

The result meant that Wolves could only be caught by Manchester United on goal average although that was never going to happen. To concede the title to the Old Trafford team, Wolves would have had to have lost their final two fixtures of the campaign, at home to Leicester and away to Everton, by 15 goals in each game and United would have needed to have won their game at Leicester 5-0. In the event, Wolves won theirs 3-0 and 1-0 respectively, while United went down 2-1 at Filbert Street, leaving Wanderers six points clear at the end.

The midweek game against Leicester was to prove significant as it was the last to be played by the legend that was Billy Wright. He missed the final game at Goodison Park through injury but watched his side complete the job from the stands. After 541 appearances, leading the club through their greatest years, he decided at the start of the following season to hang up his boots.

At his funeral in 1994, Gerry Marsden of Gerry and the Pacemakers, talking to the congregation, referred to the skipper as "Sir" Billy, saying he should have been knighted. Never was a truer word spoken and, to the people of Wolverhampton and the club's followers, William Ambrose Wright will always be Sir Billy.

Wolves: Finlayson, Stuart, Harris, Clamp, Wright, Flowers, Lill, Booth, Murray, Broadbent, Deeley.
Town: Baynham, McNally, Dunne, McGuffie, Owen, Pacey, Bingham, Turner, Morton, Cummins, Gregory.
Attendance: 40,981.
Referee: FH Gerrard.

Wolves 3 (Murray, Broadbent, Lill)
Nottingham Forest 1 (Wilson)
FA Charity Shield
Saturday 15th August 1959

IT WAS at the fourth attempt that Wolves finally won the FA Charity Shield, having twice shared the trophy and lost it once. In 1949, at Highbury, they drew 1-1 with Portsmouth before, in 1954, sharing eight goals with West Bromwich at Molineux. Then, in 1958, Bolton proved too strong, winning 4-1 at Burnden Park.

The opposition almost a year later was provided by FA Cup winners Nottingham Forest with Molineux the venue. For the first time, as an experiment, the FA decided to use the Charity Shield as a curtain-raiser for the new season and it turned out to be a great success with an entertaining match being watched by a substantial crowd who had the added bonus of music by the band of the South Staffordshire regiment before the teams took to the field.

The strange thing when the players trotted out was that the familiar sight of Billy Wright was missing. The great man had bowed out and said his farewells the week before in the traditional Colours v Whites practice match having announced his retirement from the game after a glorious career for both club and country.

George Showell had been groomed by Stan Cullis as Wright's replacement and Eddie Stuart took over the captaincy. Gwyn Jones came in for regular left-back Gerry Harris who had been injured in the practice match while Forest gave a debut to left-half Jim Iley, their close-season signing from Spurs.

Forest began strongly and after Tom Wilson had been pulled up by the offside flag, Bernard Kelly sent a shot across the face of goal. It wasn't until the fourth minute that Wolves finally moved forward with Micky Lill twice caught out by the offside trap. When Jimmy Murray did run in on the Forest goal, he was just about to shoot when Bob McKinlay took the ball from him with a last-ditch tackle.

The visitors went closest to scoring in the opening stages after Stuart Imlach raced away down the left wing and crossed for Wilson, who wasn't far off even though he didn't make a proper connection with the ball. The Forest keeper Chick Thomson was called into action when he got down to save a Bobby Mason shot. Two Lill corners followed and from the second Norman Deeley headed across the face of the goal.

In the 20th minute, Deeley sprinted though the middle and drove in a shot that was inches away from the angle with Thomson beaten. Forest responded with an effort from Imlach that Malcolm Finlayson couldn't hold with Stuart having to complete the clearance. Whenever Forest did go on the attack, Showell looked a solid figure in the home defence and his distribution of the ball was anything but wasteful.

Wolves' Greatest Games

Thomson was the busier of the keepers as Wolves began to settle to their task and he did well to hold a fierce effort from Murray before McKinlay wasn't far away from his own post as he cleared a Deeley header. The Forest defence were struggling to contain the speedy Lill and from one of his crosses Deeley got in another header, this time drawing a first class save from Thomson.

In the 37th minute, and against the run of play, Forest took the lead. Deeley, back in his own area, tried to hook clear but miskicked and the ball floated to Wilson who back-headed it into the net. It took Wolves less than a minute to draw level after Iley had fouled Peter Broadbent. The Molineux maestro slipped the free kick into the path of Ron Flowers and he launched the ball into the box where Murray ran in to head past Thomson.

Flowers closed the first-half entertainment with a 20-yard effort that was arrowing towards the bottom corner until Thomson got down to smother the ball. Wolves resumed after the break where they had left off – on top. Mason was twice off target and Deeley twice forced Bill Whare into conceding corners. From the second, taken by Deeley in the 56th minute, Wolves moved ahead. The ball was played out to Lill and when he lobbed it back into the box, Broadbent was there to head home.

Wolves, by now, were really turning it on and after one great build-up involving Broadbent, Murray and Deeley, McKinlay got in a tangle with Thomson and was grateful to get the ball behind for a corner. To relieve the pressure, Forest were more than happy to concede a series of corners and from one of them Murray almost scored a third with a low shot that went across the face of an open goal. When the visitors did break from defence it was through Kelly who was twice just off target.

The man who deserved a goal was Lill and he got his reward nine minutes from the end as he took advantage of hesitancy between McKinlay and Thomson to gain possession, via a rebound, enabling him to run on and tap the ball over the line. There was still time for Deeley to get on the scoresheet but his flying header from Broadbent's cross was inches too high. Following the final whistle, FA chairman Arthur Drewry presented Stuart with the Charity Shield.

Winning that season's FA Cup enabled Wolves to defend the Shield 12 months later against Burnley at Turf Moor. But again the trophy was shared with the game finishing in a 2-2 draw.

Wolves: Finlayson, Stuart, Jones, Clamp, Showell, Flowers, Lill, Mason, Murray, Broadbent, Deeley.
Forest: Thomson, Whare, McDonald, Whitefoot, McKinlay, Iley, Gray, Quigley, Wilson (Knight), Kelly, Imlach.
Attendance: 32,329.
Referee: J Mitchell.

Manchester City 4 (Barlow, McAdams 3)
Wolves 6 (Deeley, Slater 2, Murray 2, Lill)

Football League First Division
Saturday 5th September 1959

YOU COULDN'T really have blamed any Manchester City supporters for having a somewhat intrepid feeling as they made their way to Maine Road to watch their team take on Wolves early on in the 1959/60 season. In the three previous campaigns, games at the venue between the sides had seen Wolves emerge victorious on each occasion with the City defence being breached 11 times in the three games.

There was to be no respite from Stan Cullis's men this time and for home centre-forward Billy McAdams it must have been a bittersweet afternoon because, after all, how many players score a home hat-trick as his team nets four and yet still end up on the losing side – this after being two goals up after just seven minutes?

There were two changes to the Wolves side from the one that had taken a point from a midweek draw at Sheffield Wednesday. Gerry Harris had recovered from injury to replace Gwyn Jones at left-back and Bill Slater made a rare forward-line outing when he came in for Cliff Durandt at inside-left.

Malcolm Finlayson just beat McAdams in a chase for Clive Colbridge's through ball and, from City's next attack, Harris quickly moved in to clear after McAdams had back-heeled Ken Barnes' pass into the path of Colin Barlow. However, Barnes struck in the fourth minute when he rifled a shot into the roof of the net after McAdams had slipped the ball past Harris.

City kept up the early pressure and after George Hannah had blasted the ball high over the bar, they went two up in the seventh minute when Ken Branagan's free kick slipped from Finlayson's grasp and McAdams made the most of the opportunity by nodding the ball home. But, virtually straight from the restart, Norman Deeley halved the deficit when he took a half clearance in his stride before beating Bert Trautmann.

Still in its infancy, the game was turning into a real end-to-end affair with both defences at full stretch. McAdams shot across the face of goal from a good position and Trautmann only just managed to keep out Slater's header. City's cause wasn't helped by some erratic clearances from defence that were snapped up by the Wolves half-back line.

Midway through the half, the industrious Slater levelled matters after Scottish defender Andy Kerr handled the ball to the right of the City box. Micky Lill played a short free kick to Mason and took a return pass before crossing for Slater to convert from inside the six-yard box. Penalty appeals after McAdams went down in the visitors' area were rejected before Jimmy Murray gave Wanderers the lead for the first time after 26 minutes.

Wolves' Greatest Games

Eddie Clamp did the hard work in setting up Murray with a powerful run through the middle of the City defence before slipping the ball to his team-mate who only had Trautmann to beat – and he didn't disappoint. Wolves had recovered from being two down to take the lead and the clock had still to reach the half-hour mark!

Lill's speed took him clear of his marker and although Trautmann missed the cross that followed, there was no-one there to take advantage as Lill had outpaced his own forwards. The home fans vented their wrath on the referee when he once again denied City a penalty after McAdams looked to have been shoved in the back.

However, they were soon cheering after the centre-forward made the score 3-3 five minutes before the break. Deeley missed a sitter, firing over an empty net from close range moments before the centre-forward struck. Hannah took the ball out of defence and advanced upfield before finding McAdams who hit a hard, low shot that Finlayson got his fingers to, but couldn't keep out. The celebratory cheers of the City fans were soon silenced as Lill's pinpoint centre was headed past Trautmann by Murray to give Wolves the advantage at the break.

It took just four minutes of the second half for McAdams to pull City back on level terms and complete his hat-trick. Barnes beat two men before setting up his team-mate who beat Finlayson from close in. Slater looked to have restored Wolves' lead when he netted from Lill's cross but the linesman flagged that the ball had gone behind on its way into the goalmouth.

With both sides piling men forward City had slightly the better of the exchanges but when another goal did arrive, in the 65th minute, it went Wolves' way as Slater notched his second of the afternoon. Kerr was penalised for dangerous kicking near the right-hand corner flag and Lill's free kick was helped on by Ron Flowers into the path of Slater who ran in to side-foot into the net.

Just two minutes later City's resolve was finally broken as Lill made it six. Mason's cross was controlled by Deeley and he laid the ball off perfectly for Lill to leave Trautmann with little chance although he did make a valiant attempt with the shot going between his fingertips and the post.

The only surprise for the final quarter of the game was that there were no more goals, although McAdams almost added a fourth to his tally with a header that just went over and Deeley was unlucky when he nodded against the post with the ball rebounding into Trautmann's arms.

City: Trautmann, Branagan, Kerr, Cheetham, McTavish, Barnes, Barlow, Hannah, McAdams, Hayes, Colbridge.
Wolves: Finlayson, Stuart, Harris, Clamp, Showell, Flowers, Lill, Mason, Murray, Slater, Deeley.
Attendance: 43,650.
Referee: G McCabe.

Wolves 9 (Deeley 4, Flowers, Broadbent, Mason, Clamp, Murray)
Fulham 0
Football League First Division
Wednesday 16th September 1959

WOLVES' UNBEATEN start to the 1959/60 campaign ground to a halt in the sixth game when the new boys of Fulham caused a minor sensation by seeing off the threat of the reigning Football League champions at Craven Cottage.

John Doherty, Maurice Cook and Alf Stokes were on target for the Londoners while all the Molineux side could muster was a solitary strike from Norman Deeley. The game was played on a Wednesday evening and Fulham chairman Tommy Trinder, the comedian, had a great time joking with fellow directors and spectators during and after the game.

However, the weekly Wolverhampton newspaper, the *Chronicle*, sounded a warning which proved prophetic. The report read: "While Tommy Trinder wore a mile-long smile and wisecracked with spectators, Stan Culllis suffered in passionate exasperation. Only drastic changes, if not cheque book action, will give the team the chance of honours this season...so said the pundits yesterday morning. We say wait for next Wednesday. Fulham come to Molineux. Will Trinder be wisecracking then? Or will the wolfish grin be on Cullis's face?"

There was just the one change for the return with Peter Broadbent wearing the number ten shirt in place of Bill Slater while the Cottagers were without centre-half Roy Bentley who had played a major role in their victory the previous week.

It was the diminutive Deeley who began what was to be a rout after just six minutes' play when he sprang the offside trap and confidently beat England Under-21 keeper Tony Macedo. A firm favourite of the Molineux faithful, Deeley along with Broadbent was to make it a night of torture for a visiting defence that was completely outfoxed time after time.

After a rare Fulham attack saw Malcolm Finlayson easily coping with a Stokes shot, the Deeley and Broadbent combination struck once more in the 36th minute with Broadbent pulling the ball back into Deeley's path and the winger making no mistake. And, just a minute later, Ron Flowers scored the third with a shot that would live in the memory of those lucky enough to see it.

He was a good 30 yards out and looked as if he was about to send a pass in the direction of the left wing. But he suddenly drew back his left foot, swivelled with his right, and unleashed a shot that was a blur as it rocketed past Macedo and into the top corner of the net.

Despite non-stop pressure that was interrupted by a fruitless goal attempt by visiting right winger Graham Leggat, the interval arrived with no further additions to the scoreline. But, if the Fulham players thought that they had weathered the storm,

Wolves' Greatest Games

then they were sadly mistaken and with words of 'encouragement' from Stan Cullis ringing in their ears, Wolves set about their task in merciless fashion following the resumption.

Goal number four in the 58th minute was just reward for the industrious and mercurial Broadbent who took a through pass from Jimmy Murray in his stride before guiding the ball inside the far post. A minute later and it was 5-0 and this time it was Bobby Mason's turn to beat Macedo after he connected with Eddie Clamp's hooked centre.

There was no gung-ho approach to Wolves' play. Each attack was skilfully put together with precision and purpose and, urged on by the ecstatic crowd, the onslaught continued and in the 62nd minute Murray got in on the act with a shot on the turn from a position near the penalty spot.

The spot itself was in use in the 68th minute after Mason had been fouled in the box. Deeley took advantage of the situation and calmly slotted the ball past Macedo for his side's fourth goal in a ten-minute spell and to complete a thoroughly deserved hat-trick – not that he was finished just yet!

Clamp grabbed number eight after a surge that took him through the heart of the Fulham defence. The defender's shot packed so much power that although Macedo got a hand to the ball, he couldn't keep it out of the net.

It was left to Deeley to complete the rout three minutes from the end with a low shot that again left the bemused Macedo without a prayer. The crowd desperately wanted ten and it almost arrived in the dying seconds as Mason lifted the ball over the bar from close range after Gerry Harris had driven in a short cross.

It had been breathtaking stuff with the home defence having the quietest of evenings. George Showell, who had been given the runaround by Doherty at Craven Cottage, shadowed his man throughout the game rendering him ineffectual while Finlayson was rarely troubled especially after the interval.

Instead of slinking off, heads bowed, to the dressing room, Fulham showed some remarkable sportsmanship. The visiting players were doubtless demoralised after such a beating and yet they remained on the pitch to applaud the Wolves players off as they made their way down the tunnel.

The Fulham manager, Bedford Jezzard, was magnanimous in defeat as he said: "Wolves played some fantastic football. They were like little tigers. Few teams could have lived with them in this mood."

Wolves: Finlayson, Stuart, Harris, Flowers, Showell, Clamp, Lill, Mason, Murray, Broadbent, Deeley.
Fulham: Macedo, Cohen, Langley, Mullery, Stapleton, Lawler, Leggat, Hill, Doherty, Stokes, Johnson.
Attendance: 41,692.
Referee: GW Pullin.

Chelsea 1 (Tindall)
Wolves 5 (Murray, Flowers, Broadbent, Horne 2)

Football League First Division
Saturday 30th April 1960

AFTER BACK-to-back championship triumphs, Wolves looked to have blown their chances of a third in succession when they lost their final home game of the 1959/60 campaign to Tottenham Hotspur. Going into that final Saturday, the Molineux men still headed the table having a better goal average than Burnley with both teams locked on 52 points and Spurs just one behind.

The problem was that Burnley had a game in hand – the one remaining fixture to be played in the division after the afternoon's games were completed. The Clarets were due to play Manchester City at Maine Road the following Monday evening and, dependent on results, the chances were that everything would hinge on the outcome of that.

Stan Cullis made two changes for his team's game at Chelsea. Out from the Tottenham defeat went Gerry Mannion and Bobby Mason and they were replaced by Barry Stobart and South African Des Horne. The Londoners had been flirting with the relegation area but going into the game, although they were certain to finish in the lower half of the table, their First Division future was guaranteed.

A huge crowd packed into Stamford Bridge and from the start Norman Deeley and Horne forced the home defence back with a series of raids down the respective flanks. Three times in the opening five minutes, Chelsea keeper Reg Matthews was close to being beaten – Stobart with two headers and Ron Flowers with a snapshot from Deeley's centre both going within a whisker of giving Wolves the early advantage.

However, from their first attack, Chelsea took the lead. Deeley's pass bounced off Eddie Clamp into the path of John Brooks who took the ball through the middle of the park before slipping it to Ron Tindall who fired past the advancing Malcolm Finlayson and just inside the post. Despite the setback, Wolves soon settled down and were quickly back on the front foot with Matthews making a fine diving save to turn away Deeley's shot.

The pressure had to pay off and the visitors got the goal they deserved in the 19th minute. Horne, with a brilliant solo run, took the ball to the right of goal before crossing for Jimmy Murray, running in at top speed, to blast the ball past Matthews from just six yards out. Then Stobart was inches away from giving his side the lead with a powerful header from Deeley's cross that beat Matthews as it flashed wide.

Only the woodwork prevented Chelsea from regaining the lead after Peter Brabrook had taken the ball to the byline and hit a low cross that just eluded the incoming Tindall. With Finlayson unable to collect, the ball swerved and hit the far post before rebounding to George Showell who cleared the danger.

Wolves' Greatest Games

The action soon centred on the opposite end of the ground again and Matthews had to make a flying save from Stobart before a flowing piece of football on the right, involving Murray, Stobart and Deeley ended with Clamp shooting narrowly over the bar. On the half-hour mark, Wolves moved ahead. Stobart's through ball was deflected to Peter Broadbent and in turn, his header was bound for the net until John Sillett handled on the line. Flowers sent Matthews the wrong way with the spot-kick.

Finlayson had to move smartly from his line to save from Tindall who had run onto Brabrook's through pass before Wolves moved into a 3-1 lead two minutes before the interval. Horne's corner was headed towards goal by Deeley and when Matthews dropped the ball, Broadbent reacted quickly to hook it into the net and give Wolves a two-goal advantage that was fully deserved.

After play resumed, Chelsea opened the half with a threat from Brooks that was confidently dealt with by Clamp. But the game was effectively put out of the home side's reach in the 54th minute as Horne struck. Deeley crossed from the right and although Broadbent's shot was blocked, the ball dropped for Horne to beat Matthews with a close-quarters volley.

Jimmy Greaves led a strong attack on Finlayson's goal but the danger passed after Brooks ran into an offside position and when Wolves went in search of a fifth goal, Stobart took a return pass from Horne and was just about to shoot when Peter Sillett ran across and cleared. The rout was completed in the 69th minute and once again it was Horne who beat Matthews.

Deeley lifted a deep pass down the right wing into the path of Murray who beat John Mortimore before crossing for Horne to score with a header that went in off the underside of the bar. Stobart was obviously keen to cement a Cup Final place with a goal but Matthews managed to beat away the youngster's fierce drive.

Wolves had already booked their day at Wembley where they were to face Blackburn Rovers the following weekend and Stobart's form, and that of Horne, had certainly given Cullis food for thought ahead of the selection of his team.

But, before all of that, was to come bitter disappointment. Burnley only drew their game with Fulham at Turf Moor, meaning they needed to win at Manchester City which they did, 2-1, leaving Wolves a point adrift in the runners-up spot and with the chance of the double gone.

Chelsea: Matthews, J Sillett, P Sillett, Anderton, Mortimore, Crowther, Brabrook, Brooks, Tindall, Greaves, Blunstone.
Wolves: Finlayson, Showell, Harris, Clamp, Slater, Flowers, Deeley, Stobart, Murray, Broadbent, Horne.
Attendance: 61,567.
Referee: RM Jordan.

Blackburn Rovers 0
Wolves 3 (McGrath OG, Deeley 2)

FA Cup Final, Wembley
Saturday 7th May 1960

WHILE IT has to be admitted that the 1960 FA Cup Final between Wolves and Blackburn wasn't the most memorable spectacle in the world, at least it had the nation's attention. In those heady days the final meant so much more than appears to have done in recent times. The game was always televised live by the only two British television stations and it took place the week after the end of the season on a Saturday with a 3pm start. In short, it was something that all football fans looked forward to.

For Wolves, the long haul to Wembley began in the North East with a difficult third round tie against Newcastle United at St James' Park. The teams had met in a league encounter just over two months earlier at Molineux and goals from Jimmy Murray and Peter Broadbent sent the home supporters away happy. Over 62,000 packed into the Geordie fortress for the FA Cup game, and they were treated to a four-goal thriller.

Wolves dominated the early stages but it was Newcastle who moved ahead in the 18th minute when Ivor Allchurch tapped the ball over the line after Gordon Hughes had helped on Alf McMichael's free kick. Ron Flowers pulled his side level in the 32nd minute with a long-range shot that took a deflection off a defender leaving home keeper Brian Harvey with no chance. Six minutes later, Dick Keith handled in the home area and Eddie Clamp stepped up to despatch the spot-kick.

George Eastham equalised two minutes after the break, turning in a low cross from George Luke. The game was played at a testing tempo throughout and although both sides had chances to win it, none was taken and the replay was scheduled for the following Wednesday evening. The pitch at Molineux was snow-bound but it didn't prevent another absorbing contest.

Just nine minutes had gone when Len White headed in a centre from Hughes to give the visitors a shock advantage. It took Wolves just a minute more to get off the mark themselves. A mistake by George Heslop left Murray with an easy chance and he didn't fail in his task. In the 16th minute, Norman Deeley fired Wanderers into the lead, driving the ball home after taking a through pass from Broadbent.

A rare mistake by Clamp let in Eastham who made it two all, but almost immediately Flowers launched a 30-yard shot that hit the post on its way into the net. Five minutes into the second half, Des Horne cut out a McMichael pass and hit a fourth goal past Harvey to complete the scoring and confirm that it was to be Wolves who would face Second Division side Charlton Athletic at home in the fourth round.

The game with the Addicks was a one-sided affair with Wolves dominating throughout. Yet the Londoners took the lead in the 23rd minute in what was their

Wolves' Greatest Games

first attack of note with Johnny Summers hitting an unstoppable shot past Malcolm Finlayson. Charlton keeper Willie Duff was in inspired form and just he stood between Wolves and a rout.

He was finally beaten two minutes before the interval by Horne who sent a rising drive into the net after good work from Deeley and Murray. Broadbent headed in a cross from Deeley with 11 minutes remaining, before Duff made a superb save in keeping out Clamp's penalty after Broadbent had been fouled by Gordon Jago.

The fifth round saw Wolves travelling to relegation-threatened Luton. Stan Cullis had warned his team: "Let's have no replays" and they duly obliged, although the final score of 4-1 to Wanderers was somewhat flattering as they were pushed all the way by a hard-working Town team. The only goal in the opening half came after just three minutes when Bobby Mason beat Ron Baynham with a cross-shot.

Two minutes into the second half, Gordon Turner equalised with his shot taking a deflection on its way past Geoff Sidebottom who was standing in for the injured Finlayson. Mason restored Wolves' lead with a brilliant diving header from Deeley's cross from the right in the 62nd minute. Two goals in the next quarter of an hour saw a close-range finish by Murray followed by a fluke by Clamp whose lofted centre deceived Baynham and hit the inside of the far post before going in.

The quarter-final paired Wolves with Leicester and the game, at Filbert Street, was spoiled by a series of petty fouls. The visitors moved into an 11th-minute lead when Clamp's centre fell to the unmarked Broadbent who beat Gordon Banks with an angled shot. Clamp was also involved in the second goal which arrived in the 28th minute. His free kick was hooked into the centre by Barry Stobart and City full-back Len Chalmers headed over Banks and into his own net.

The semi-final was an all-West Midlands affair – Wolves v Aston Villa at The Hawthorns. Villa were homing in on the Second Division championship and a crowd of over 55,000 watched a scrappy contest that was decided in the 32nd minute when Deeley scored the only goal of the game. Gerry Mannion opened up a chance for Murray whose cross-shot drew an excellent save from one-time Molineux keeper Nigel Sims. However, he could only knock the ball down and Deeley ran in to volley Wolves into the final.

Five days before the Wembley clash with Blackburn Rovers, Wolves had suffered heartache when Burnley beat Manchester City to take the title and rob Wanderers of a third consecutive championship. So Cullis's men had to be satisfied with the runners-up spot while Rovers had finished in 17th place in the league table just three points above the relegation zone. Wolves were favourites to win the cup but could Blackburn take advantage of a hangover following the league title agony?

Rovers had reached Wembley by beating Sunderland 4-1 and then Blackpool 3-0 in third- and fourth-round replays after 1-1 draws. They then caused a shock in beating Spurs 3-1 at White Hart Lane, and moved into the semi-final after another replay, this time 2-0 against near neighbours Burnley after the first game, at Turf Moor, had finished with the sides sharing six goals. The last-four tie, at Maine Road, ended in a 2-1 win over Sheffield Wednesday.

v Blackburn Rovers, 1960

The weather was sweltering as the teams took to the pitch on the big day. Derek Dougan, who it later transpired had posted a transfer request on the morning of the game, led the Rovers attack while Cullis raised a few eyebrows when he selected the inexperienced Stobart in preference to Mason. Stobart had played in just six senior games.

Wolves defended the tunnel end and after an initial attack from the Lancashire side came to nothing, their goalkeeper, Harry Leyland, took a centre from Deeley. At the other end, Finlayson had to tip a Louis Bimpson cross over the bar. From the corner conceded, Bill Slater failed to clear properly and Flowers ran in to tidy up. The first real chance came in the sixth minute following a flowing five-man move that culminated when Stobart crossed to Horne who was crowded out before he could get a shot in.

Stobart headed high over the bar after a Murray cross, before Clamp cut out a Bryan Douglas pass that was aimed for Ally MacLeod. A centre from Stobart was missed by Horne, Murray and Deeley before Douglas almost made the breakthrough in the 27th minute when he took a pass from Bimpson before firing just wide of Finlayson's near post.

Four minutes later, Broadbent's low cross gave Murray the sort of chance that he usually snapped up, but this time he failed to make proper contact and the ball drifted wide. Murray then supplied the pass for Horne to get in a shot that was fingertipped behind by Leyland. Next it was Finlayson's turn to perform acrobatics as he beat down a Dobing shot before Wolves moved ahead in the 40th minute when Stobart delivered a teasing cross that Mick McGrath turned past his own keeper.

As if that wasn't a bitter enough pill for Rovers to swallow, they suffered a further setback just two minutes later when, after a challenge with Deeley, Dave Whelan suffered a serious leg injury and was carried off on a stretcher with a trip to hospital confirming that the limb was broken. Right on half-time, Deeley's short-range header was taken by Leyland.

Five minutes after the break, Murray slipped the ball past Leyland but his effort was ruled out as Stobart had run into an offside position. Murray also provided the pass to Deeley that left the winger with just Leyland to beat but he shot straight at the keeper. Despite their disadvantage in numbers, Blackburn weren't giving up the ghost as they kept Finlayson on his toes.

However, with 67 minutes gone Deeley shot Wanderers into a two-goal lead after Leyland had made a good save from Murray. From the corner conceded, Horne played a short ball to Flowers whose cross came back off a defender. Flowers returned to Horne and his cross ran through for Deeley to slam it into the net from close range.

Horne missed a great chance to make it three when he was put through after an attempted clearance had rebounded off a defender into his path. He only had Leyland to beat but failed to make proper contact and the ball screwed wide. Flowers found the net but was ruled offside after he had been set up by Clamp. Two minutes from the end though, Blackburn's misery was complete as Leyland missed Stobart's

Wolves' Greatest Games

cross and when Matt Woods knocked the ball towards his own goal, Deeley was there to ram it into the roof of the net.

After he had been presented with the Cup, Slater said: "We are terribly sorry about the injury to Whelan which was a most unfortunate accident. It took the edge off the game, but I felt that we were making progress and just getting on top when it happened. Perhaps this latest occurrence will add weight to the case for substitutes to be allowed in the final. Blackburn played pluckily despite their great handicap."

Deeley added: "I was going through with the ball at my feet when Whelan went to tackle me. We collided and the next thing I knew he was on the ground. I wouldn't have had this happen for all the world."

Whelan's injury and the defeat prompted sections of the Blackburn support to boo the Wolves players as they collected their medals. Their actions were unjust and although the game wasn't a classic, and for half of it Wanderers faced just ten men, Stan Cullis's team were worthy winners of the competition.

Rovers: Leyland, Bray, Whelan, Clayton, Woods, McGrath, Bimpson, Dobing, Dougan, Douglas, MacLeod.
Wolves: Finlayson, Showell, Harris, Clamp, Slater, Flowers, Deeley, Stobart, Murray, Broadbent, Horne.
Attendance: 98,776.
Referee: K Howley.

Wolves 4 (Farmer, Murray 2, Deeley)
Everton 1 (Bingham)
Football League First Division
Saturday 21st January 1961

TED FARMER wrote himself into Molineux folklore when his four goals in the second leg of the 1958 FA Youth Cup Final resulted in an unlikely comeback as he gave a prime example of his predatory skills. Born in Rowley Regis in 1940, he was a regular scorer in the Birmingham League and then the Central League as he waited patiently for over two years for a first team opportunity following the Youth Cup glory.

He had turned professional on leaving school on his 17th birthday and made his mark on his senior debut by scoring twice in a 3-1 victory over Manchester United at Old Trafford in September 1960. By the time Everton arrived at Molineux the following January, he had taken his tally to 20 goals from just 20 league and cup games.

In the First Division, in a spell spanning over three months, Wolves had won ten, drawn two and lost two league games. Surprisingly, given their form, the two defeats resulted in scores of five goals being conceded on each occasion. The last completed game before the arrival of the Toffees was at Leeds Road where Huddersfield inflicted a shock 2-1 FA Cup defeat in a third round replay as Wolves lost their grip on the coveted trophy.

The league game at Blackpool the following weekend was fogged off after just nine minutes. Farmer hadn't played in the cup tie but Stan Cullis brought him back for the abandoned fixture at Bloomfield Road. Wolves lay second in the table with a game in hand to leaders Tottenham Hotspur although they were ten points adrift, while Everton were four points further back in fifth spot.

The national press made a point of commenting that Wolves had no 'big money' buys in the side while the Merseysiders had spent a considerable amount in constructing their team. They were, on the day, without two of their stars – Alex Young and Alec Parker – through injury.

In the early exchanges, Cliff Durandt lofted a long ball into the Everton box that was headed clear by Tommy Jones, and then the South African tried a shot on the turn that lacked power, providing keeper Albert Dunlop with an easy take. Then, with just two minutes gone, Everton moved into the lead. Brian Harris crossed low into the box, the ball reaching Billy Bingham who found himself unmarked in front of goal. The Belfast-born winger steadied himself before shooting past Malcolm Finlayson.

A misdirected back-pass from Eddie Clamp almost gifted the visitors a second goal but Finlayson managed to grab the ball as it was about to cross the line. Farmer fired over the bar from just inside the area but he made no mistake in the seventh

Wolves' Greatest Games

minute as Wolves pulled level. He ran on to Durandt's through ball and dummied Roy Parnell before cracking a low drive past Dunlop. The goal created a unique four-timer for Farmer. It was 21st January, his 21st birthday, 21st senior game and 21st goal.

Jimmy Murray almost gave Wolves the lead with a glancing header following Norman Deeley's free kick, but Dunlop managed to turn the ball away. As Everton retaliated, Roy Vernon and then Frank Wignall shot over the bar. It was Wolves, through Murray, that grabbed the lead with 27 minutes gone. He dispossessed George Sharples and played the ball to Deeley before meeting the return pass from the little winger on the volley. The ball hit the roof of the net before Dunlop could react.

Bobby Collins was obstructed by Clamp in the home area. The Scot took the free kick himself but there was no way through in a congested box and the danger was cleared. Otherwise Wanderers held on quite comfortably to their slight advantage. But after the interval, Everton began to get on top and were looking dangerous when Wolves built a two-goal cushion following a breakaway. Peter Broadbent took the ball down the right and although his first attempt to cross was blocked, he regained possession and sent the ball over to Murray who beat Dunlop with a near-post header.

From being on top, Everton, all of a sudden, looked a dispirited side as Wolves took complete command. It did, however, take a superb save from Finlayson to keep out a quickly-taken free kick from Collins. And their cause wasn't helped when Bingham limped off after he was hurt in a tackle with Johnny Kirkham.

Deeley, by his high standards, hadn't enjoyed the best of seasons with regards to goals and he only had four in his locker prior to the game. But he rounded off the scoring in the 63rd minute with a wonderful strike. He took a pass from Broadbent and advanced on Dunlop's goal. With the Everton defenders expecting him to lay a pass out to one of the wings, he suddenly let fly from 30 yards with a shot that was so powerful, although Dunlop got both hands to the ball he couldn't prevent it from going into the net.

That evening Farmer celebrated his birthday, and the victory, with his team-mates in the Six Ashes at Bobbington. But the glittering career that beckoned was to be a short-lived one as he was injured during a practice match in 1964 and he never recovered and was forced to hang up his boots just two years later. He scored over 300 goals as a Wolves player in the first, second, third, fourth and amateur teams.

Wolves: Finlayson, Stuart, Showell, Kirkham, Slater, Clamp, Deeley, Murray, Farmer, Broadbent, Durandt.
Everton: Dunlop, Parnell, Jones, Gabriel, Labone, Sharples, Bingham, Collins, Wignall, Vernon, Harris.
Attendance: 31,119.
Referee: GW Pullin.

Wolves 3 (Wharton, McParland, Crowe)
Tottenham Hotspur 1 (White)
Football League First Division
Saturday 3rd February 1962

DOUBLE WINNERS Tottenham Hotspur arrived at Molineux on a winter's afternoon in 1962, no doubt with their eyes on a repeat performance after the 4-0 Molineux mauling they inflicted on Wolves 16 months earlier. Spurs had become the first team since Aston Villa in 1897 to win both the title and the FA Cup.

The Londoners' manager, the great Bill Nicholson, will have been satisfied with his team's showing up to the visit to Molineux. They went into the game lying in second place in the top flight just two points behind Burnley although the Clarets did have two games in hand. Their last fixture had been in the FA Cup where Danny Blanchflower and co made short work of Plymouth at Home Park, beating the Second Division team by 5-1 on the same afternoon as Wolves exited the competition following a 2-1 home defeat at the hands of West Bromwich. Ironically, Spurs and Albion were paired together in the fifth round.

While Tottenham were chasing further honours at the top of the table, Wolves were enduring a season of struggle, easily the worst since before the war, and going into the game they lay just four places and two points off the bottom. Stan Cullis had boosted his squad by signing inside-right Chris Crowe from Blackburn Rovers, and Peter McParland, a left-winger from neighbouring Aston Villa with the pair costing around £60,000 in total.

Cullis made three changes to the team who had lost to the Baggies. Johnny Kirkham came in for Fred Goodwin and McParland and Crowe made their debuts with Barry Stobart and Cliff Durandt dropping out. In the opening minutes Bill Slater and Ron Flowers collided in trying to clear a long through ball and Cliff Jones quickly tried to take advantage but he shot straight at Fred Davies in the Wanderers goal.

Spurs' Scottish keeper Bill Brown saved bravely at the feet of Peter Broadbent who was racing through on goal before Crowe earned vocal appreciation from the home support when he sprinted through the middle before passing to Terry Wharton who had run into an offside position. Crowe was making more of an early impression than McParland who was being closely shadowed by Peter Baker.

Jimmy Greaves had his first chance of the afternoon when Terry Medwin headed a cross down to him, but his shot was blocked just before Wolves moved into a 16th-minute lead. McParland fell under a challenge but he regained his feet and sent over a centre that Wharton headed powerfully into the roof of the net. Wolves seemed to have adopted a shoot-on-sight strategy and they could have moved further ahead but for the agility of Brown.

Wolves' Greatest Games

The Spurs forwards were hardly getting a look-in and it was against the run of play that they pulled level in the 23rd minute. John White took a short pass from Les Allen and, as the home defence backed off, he hit a great shot that flew over the head of Davies. Moments later, the visitors suffered a setback when Allen was injured in a challenge with Crowe and, after treatment, he moved out onto the wing, limping heavily, while Medwin moved into the centre of the attack.

Despite this setback, Spurs were starting to gain the upper hand and were looking the more likely to take the lead until McParland made it a scoring debut in the 33rd minute. Wharton repaid his new team-mate's part in the opening goal by providing a fine centre from the right that the diving McParland headed into the net. Brown got both hands to the ball but he couldn't keep it out.

Within a minute McParland almost struck again, but this time his low shot on the turn scraped the outside of a post. Just before the break, Eddie Stuart and Jones collided in a no-quarters-asked challenge that left both of them in need of treatment before they could carry on. Allen was still hobbling badly when the game resumed after the interval as Spurs began the half strongly. There were loud penalty appeals when Jones went down under a challenge but the referee waved play on. Greaves wasn't going to let the matter drop though and he talked himself into the book.

When Wolves went in search of another goal, Maurice Norman saved his side by taking the ball off Broadbent's foot after Flowers had floated a cross into the area. A further goal did arrive in the 53rd minute with Crowe, not to be outdone by his fellow new signing, side-footing the ball home after a through pass from Wharton.

In the final third of the game, the best chances fell to Wolves with Jimmy Murray just failing to connect to another Wharton cross with a diving header, and Broadbent seeing his drive pushed onto the post by Brown who then snapped up the rebound. The nearest Tottenham came to pulling one back was when Dave Mackay fired narrowly wide shortly before the end.

Despite the morale-boosting win, the remainder of the season saw more inconsistency in the Wolves team that led to an 18th-placed finish – the worst in the top flight since 1933. Tottenham, on the other hand, retained the FA Cup and finished third in the First Division, just five points short of another double.

Wolves: Davies, Stuart, Thomson, Kirkham, Slater, Flowers, Wharton, Crowe, Murray, Broadbent, McParland.
Spurs: Brown, Baker, Henry, Blanchflower, Norman, Mackay, Medwin, White, Allen, Greaves, Jones.
Attendance: 45,687.
Referee: HP Hackney.

Wolves 8 (Farmer 4, Murray 2, Wharton, Hinton)
Manchester City 1 (Showell OG)
Football League First Division
Saturday 18th August 1962

SIX OF the team who had played in the final game of what, for Wolves, was a disappointing 1961/62 season, made it into the starting 11 for the first game of the following campaign when Manchester City opened the proceedings at Molineux. After his team finished a lowly 18th, their worst position in 29 years of top flight football, Stan Cullis had not brought in any 'new blood', relying instead on a more youthful-looking side for the start of the new term.

True, for that first game he still included the likes of Jimmy Murray, George Showell and Ron Flowers to add some experience. But Fred Goodwin and Dave Woodfield had played just three games between them and there was no place for Peter Broadbent, Peter McParland and Cliff Durandt with the latter not destined to play in Cullis's first team again. City, too, gave youth its chance with 16-year-old Glyn Pardoe leading their attack. And, on the left wing was a man who was to become a familiar figure at Molineux where he was to play the bulk of his career, Dave Wagstaffe.

Flowers, skippering the side for the first time, defended the North Bank end but it was the visitors who were first to show as Neil Young set up Dave Shawcross who lifted his shot high over the bar from the edge of the 18-yard box. In their second attack, after just two minutes, Wolves took the lead in spectacular fashion. Chris Crowe's speed took him clear of his marker and from his centre, Ted Farmer, with a horizontal leap, bulleted a header past Bert Trautmann.

Slips by Crowe presented chances for Peter Dobing and Joe Hayes with Woodfield and Flowers, respectively, clearing the danger. After the lively Farmer had fired wide despite the attention of two defenders, Wolves went two up in the 17th minute. A long clearance fell to Alan Hinton on the left and his low cross ran perfectly for Murray to side-foot the ball past Trautmann.

Bill Leivers got in a tangle with the German keeper a few moments later and Trautmann had to dribble the ball virtually to the halfway line before he found the space to clear. In the home goal, Fred Davies made a great save to keep out an effort from Hayes who had broken clear through the middle. Hayes was severely testing the home defence and after he was unlucky to see his firm header come back off the bar, he was thwarted by Davies once more who saved with his foot at the expense of a corner.

The 27th-minute flag-kick, however, proved to be a profitable one for City. It was taken by Wagstaffe and Davies looked to have the ball covered but an obvious lack of communication saw Showell heading into his own net. Two minutes later it was Wolves' turn to hit the woodwork with Terry Wharton lashing a shot against the underside of the bar with the rebound falling just out of Murray's reach. Then there was a scramble in the City goalmouth after Crowe's cross had hit Trautmann's chest and bounced into the middle of a congested box before Leivers unceremoniously booted the ball into the crowd.

Four minutes before the break, Farmer grabbed his second goal to put Wolves 3-1 to the good. Hinton's cross bounced back to the striker who ghosted past his marker before burying a cross shot past Trautmann from close in. City started the new half on the front foot and won three successive corners. But they were soon undone as Wolves hit them with three more goals in a four-minute spell.

The first, in the 49th minute, came from the tireless Wharton who drove the ball into the roof of the net after Crowe had seen two attempts in quick succession come back off defenders. Then Farmer's grit and determination saw him complete his hat-trick as he brushed aside two challenges to get to the ball after Wharton's cross had been deflected on to the post by a defender.

The score quickly moved on to 6-1 after Farmer had robbed Leivers of the ball and fed it to Hinton whose first-time shot flew past Trautmann and went just inside the far post from 20 yards out. As the goals suggested, it was all Wolves by now and once again the woodwork saved City as another terrific effort from Farmer bounced to safety off the crossbar with Trautmann well beaten.

But the breathless crowd didn't have to wait much longer for the seventh goal which arrived in the 57th minute. Farmer sent Hinton on a run down the left flank and his floated centre ran perfectly for Murray who had the simplest of tasks in netting. Some sympathy had to be directed towards the veteran Trautmann who had been afforded virtually no cover by his defenders.

Despite the game being well out of their reach, whenever they got forward the City attack tried hard to put some respectability on the scoreboard. But, when they did get through, Davies was in no mood to be beaten and he pulled off a tremendous point-blank save to deny Hayes before Farmer struck again ten minutes from the end.

With the 39-year-old Trautmann appealing in vain for the offside flag, Farmer calmly waited for a deep centre to drop before hooking the ball into the net to complete a memorable personal afternoon with four goals scored and involvement in two of the others.

Wolves: Davies, Showell, Thomson, Goodwin, Woodfield, Flowers, Wharton, Crowe, Farmer, Murray, Hinton.
City: Trautmann, Kennedy, Betts, Benson, Leivers, Shawcross, Young, Dobing, Pardoe, Hayes, Wagstaffe.
Attendance: 26,986.
Referee: RE Smith.

Wolves 7 (Stobart 2, Hinton 2, Wharton 3)
West Bromwich Albion 0
Football League First Division
Saturday 16th March 1963

ON BOXING DAY 1962, Wolves supporters were denied a late Christmas present by the weather. The home side mastered the icy conditions much more so than their arch rivals, West Bromwich Albion, and they took a deserved 2-0 lead into the break with Chris Crowe and Alan Hinton the scorers. However, the snow got heavier during the interval and the loudspeaker announcement that the game had been abandoned was greeted with boos by the disappointed home fans although, in fairness, the referee was left with little option.

The winter of 1962/63 saw one of the most persistent cold snaps on record and in a 15-week period from the beginning of December until the Baggies made their second trip to Molineux that season in mid-March, Wolves had managed to stage and complete just one home game – a goalless draw against Sheffield United. The weather began to relent at the beginning of March and prior to the visit of Albion Wolves had enjoyed a 4-3 victory over Birmingham City at St Andrew's which prompted Stan Cullis to name an unchanged team.

Albion, who had beaten Ipswich Town 6-1 seven days earlier, were without centre-forward Derek Kevan who had served the Baggies for nine years but was the subject of a shock transfer to Chelsea during the week before the Wolves game. He watched from the stands and witnessed his former colleagues getting trounced in what was to be the biggest margin of victory for Wolves in games between the clubs.

Wolves attacked the North Bank end and full-back George Showell immediately moved forward to support winger Terry Wharton to put the visiting defence under early pressure. A Don Howe free kick was headed behind by Showell for what proved to be a fruitless corner and home keeper Fred Davies then competently dealt with a cross from Ken Foggo before Wolves moved into a ninth-minute lead.

Barry Stobart skilfully controlled a centre from Crowe before driving home a left-footed shot past the advancing Tony Millington from near the penalty spot. There was a chance for Bobby Hope to make a rapid response when a clearance rebounded into his path but he hesitated and the home defence cleared their lines. Then Ron Fenton blasted a shot over the bar after Foggo had turned the ball into the home area.

After a spell of Wolves pressure, Albion had the opportunity of pulling level when Hope's perfect through ball gave Keith Smith a clear sight of the goal but, like Fenton, he fired over. Crowe hit a rocket of a shot across the face of Millington's goal and it took a marvellous one-handed save from Davies to keep out a Ron Bradley effort that looked destined for the back of the net.

Wolves' Greatest Games

Albion had enjoyed chances but failed to take them and they were made to pay in the 25th minute as Stobart struck again. Wharton headed the ball forward to Peter Broadbent who cut in along the byline before picking out the unmarked Stobart who had all the time in the world to beat Millington which he did, effortlessly, from close in.

The Baggies appeared to be missing the experience of Kevan and there seemed to be an uncertainty about their attacking moves. Hope fired wide from a good position and then Fenton was way off the mark with a header. Dave Woodfield, with a spectacular overhead kick, cleared a Clive Clark centre from virtually off the line before Howe's foul on Hinton led to a Wolves attack that ended with Stobart missing a hat-trick chance when he was wide of the far post.

A typical burst of speed from Ron Flowers saw the wing-half advance on Millington's goal before unleashing a tremendous shot that drew a save from the keeper that was equally as good as Davies's minutes earlier. It was a case of déjà vu at the break with the score identical to that of the abandoned game.

Albion started strongly after the restart and the first opportunity saw Davies fingertipping a 30-yard Graham Williams free kick over the bar. Then Hope, Fenton and Bobby Cram all had goal attempts that were off target. When Wolves finally got going again, Stobart set up Hinton but he ballooned his shot a good way up the South Bank. Hinton then took a crossfield pass from Wharton before driving a cross through Albion's six-yard box with no-one able to get a touch.

It was Hinton who got Wolves' third goal with 66 minutes gone. Stobart and Crowe combined to set up the chance and Hinton's connection was perfect with Millington hardly moving as the ball flew past him. Two minutes later the keeper just got down to Stobart's low cross as Wharton closed in. Albion hit back with an effort from Clark that Davies saved in mid-air.

Wharton put the game beyond Albion's reach in the 69th minute when he ran through the middle and drew Millington from his line before stroking the ball home. The winger made in 5-0 in the 81st minute with a simple tap-in after Millington had failed to hold on to a fierce effort from Crowe.

With three minutes to go, Hinton became the third home player to grab a brace from the game when he turned a low centre from Stobart over the line. Not to be outdone, Wharton completed his hat-trick in the dying seconds when he ran in to head home following a Hinton centre.

Wolves: Davies, Showell, Thomson, Kirkham, Woodfield, Flowers, Wharton, Crowe, Stobart, Broadbent, Hinton.
Albion: Millington, Howe, Williams, Cram, Jones, Bradley, Foggo, Fenton, Smith, Hope, Clark.
Attendance: 22,618.
Referee: K Dagnall.

Wolves 4 (Crawford 2, Knowles, Harris)
West Ham 3 (Brabrook, Harris OG, Byrne penalty)
Football League First Division
Monday 14th September 1964

THE DAY after Wolves had achieved their first win of the season will go down as probably the most infamous in the history of Wolverhampton Wanderers. Tuesday 15th September was the date that playing and managerial legend Stan Cullis was sacked. The result of the game against West Ham very quickly became irrelevant as not only the town, but the whole of English football, reeled in shock that such a thing could happen.

Cullis had only returned to the club for the game against the Hammers after a month-long spell of sick leave. But he had recovered from the viral infection that had laid him low and had been given the all-clear by the doctors. He needed to be back because his team were in trouble. After seven games they were marooned at the bottom of the table with just the solitary point collected from a home draw with Leicester City.

Seven days before West Ham arrived at Molineux, in the reverse fixture at Upton Park, the home side rattled in five goals without a response. Then, in the weekend's game at Blackburn, there followed a 4-1 drubbing for Wanderers. Cullis made four changes on his albeit brief return to the helm, bringing Fred Davies back in goal in place of Jim Barron, Fred Goodwin for the injured Ron Flowers, Ray Crawford for John Galley and the veteran Peter Broadbent for Jimmy Melia – at the time, the club's most expensive signing.

In the opening seconds Terry Wharton went on a diagonal run and his low centre went through the legs of Peter Knowles and just outside the far post. Then Hammers keeper Jim Standen fell on a Broadbent shot as, urged on by the lowest of the four home gates they had played in front of that season, Wolves made a bright start to the game.

Just three minutes had passed by when they moved ahead. Wharton fired over a corner and Crawford sent a downward header under the dive of Standen and into the net. The Hammers were obviously taken aback by the force exerted by the home forwards and it took good saves from Standen to prevent further goals with shots from Bobby Thomson and Knowles being pushed around the post.

The main West Ham threat, in their occasional raids, came from Johnny Byrne and when he found himself through on goal he tried a lob that was easily gathered by Davies. In the 27th minute, Wharton shook the visitors' crossbar after the Hammers defence had been carved open by George Showell and Knowles.

Wolves fully deserved a second goal and it arrived seven minutes later. Davies's hefty clearance was headed on by Crawford to Knowles whose shot was so powerful that it went in off Standen's body with the keeper unable to move his hands in time.

Wolves' Greatest Games

The goal seemed to kick-start West Ham into life and Davies had to scramble away a low shot from Byrne while Martin Peters headed a fraction wide. But five minutes before the break Davies was beaten when Peter Brabrook tapped the ball in at the near post after Byrne had slipped a short cross to him.

The goal seemed to knock the confidence out of the home team and in the minutes leading up to, and after the interval, West Ham realised the situation and very quickly got on top. And while there was a touch of fortune about the goal, they drew level six minutes into the second half. Gerry Harris charged across the goalmouth to intercept a Brabrook cross but he succeeded only in bundling the ball into his own net.

But, for the crestfallen Claverley-born defender, there was to be a happy ending. He had to wait, though, because in the 65th minute West Ham turned the game on its head by taking the lead. Seconds after Brabrook had hit the bar with Davies beaten, Bobby Woodruff had cause for complaint when he was adjudged to have fouled Geoff Hurst in the box. But the decision stood and Byrne made no mistake from the spot.

Urged on by their partisan supporters, Wolves regained the initiative and their fighting spirit and only the agility of Standen prevented powerful efforts from Broadbent and Knowles from finding the net. But the keeper was beaten in the 78th minute after Harris had raced down the wing and crossed for Crawford to bag his second of the game after Standen had parried the ball.

Standen had done much to keep his team in the game but it was his mistake, two minutes from the end, that gifted Harris, and Wolves, the winner. The defender was fully 40 yards out from goal when he hit a speculative shot that the keeper appeared to have covered. But the ball squirmed out of his grasp and trickled over the line to send the crowd wild with delight.

The delight evaporated the next day and a feeling of shock, disbelief and anger descended on the town as people took in the terse board statement which read: "The Wolves Board of Directors have informed their manager Stanley Cullis they wish to be released from their contract arrangements with him. This he has consented to do."

Protests from supporters demanding his reinstatement fell on deaf ears. The man who had brought glory to the club as a player and, more especially, a manager was gone for good.

Wolves: Davies, Thomson, Harris, Goodwin, Showell, Woodruff, Thompson, Knowles, Crawford, Broadbent, Wharton.
West Ham: Standen, Bond, Burkett, Bovington, Peters, Moore, Sealey, Boyce, Byrne, Hurst, Brabrook.
Attendance: 19,435.
Referee: F Schofield.

Wolves 8 (Woodruff 2, Wagstaffe, McIlmoyle 2, Flowers, Holsgrove 2)
Portsmouth 2 (Wilson OG, Hiron)
Football League Second Division
Saturday 27th November 1965

INSIDE-FORWARD Bobby Woodruff played for five Football League clubs during his career and each of them benefited from one of the longest throws in football history. If Woodruff had to take a throw-in adjacent to the opposition's penalty area he could, with ease, launch the ball into the heart of the six-yard box and in some cases to the far side of it.

An industrious player, he lost his place in Wolves' first team following the 9-3 debacle at Southampton just nine games into the club's first campaign in the second tier of English football since 1932. But the disaster at The Dell heralded a change of fortunes with the next nine games leading up to the visit of Pompey realising five wins and four draws.

Transfer-listed Woodruff was recalled against Portsmouth at the expense of leading scorer Peter Knowles and before the game he asked to be removed from the list. His wish was granted and he celebrated by opening the scoring after just two minutes. Right-winger Terry Wharton skipped past the challenge of John Gordon and his cross saw Woodruff bullet a header past the helpless John Milkins in Pompey's goal.

Dave Wagstaffe, Wharton's fellow winger on the opposite flank, added a second just five minutes later. His initial cross was returned to him in the shape of a half clearance. This time he seized on the chance to send a volley into the roof of the net from the narrowest of angles with his unfavoured right foot.

It wasn't all smiles for Woodruff that afternoon for in his team's next attack, following Wagstaffe's strike, he collided with Milkins and had to leave the field with blood pouring from a head wound. While he was off the field having treatment, Hugh McIlmoyle struck to put Wanderers three up with just 11 minutes gone. The Scot was some distance from goal when he gained possession and he sent a perfect chip over the heads of the defence and over Milkins with the ball dropping gently just under the bar.

Despite being a man down, Wolves continued to go forward and John Holsgrove went close following a Wharton corner but he just failed to get enough purchase on the ball to convert. The bandaged Woodruff returned to the fray in the 19th minute and he immediately played his part in the build-up to the fourth goal. The creative Wagstaffe teed the ball up for Ron Flowers and he struck a ferocious effort from fully 30 yards out that hit the back of the net while Milkins was still diving.

Little had been seen of Portsmouth as an attacking force but Dennis Edwards spurned the opportunity of reducing the arrears when he headed tamely wide with just home keeper Fred Davies to beat. Wolves replied with a fifth goal on the half-hour mark and it was Woodruff who was once again on target. He ran onto a through pass from Wharton and hit a low drive that Milkins got a hand to but was unable to prevent from trickling over the line.

Four minutes before the break, Holsgrove scored his first goal for the club following his summer transfer from Crystal Palace. Ernie Hunt delivered a short cross and the lanky defender side-footed the ball over the line from close quarters. Six up at half-time – it had been tremendous stuff and even the snow that began to fall during the interval did little to quell the buzz of the crowd.

The snow got heavier by the time the new half began and the wind was blowing it straight into the faces of the marauding Wolves team. But it didn't stop them and one superb inter-passing move ended with a shot from Wharton flying just inches wide with Milkins a spectator.

Harry Harris's afternoon came to a premature end when he was injured and replaced by Cliff Portwood after 55 minutes just before Holsgrove got his second of the game when he dived almost to ground level to head home a corner from Wharton. Within a minute Portsmouth finally got on the scoresheet – albeit with an own goal. Ray Hiron's shot didn't look to carry any danger but the ball hit Joe Wilson and ricocheted into the net.

It took a brilliant save by Milkins to keep out a McIlmoyle header and then Wagstaffe shot wide following a scramble in the Portsmouth box. The home support, with their side six up at the break, must have had their thoughts of double figures but those hopes were fading and a quarter of an hour from the end the visitors grabbed a second consolation as Hiron struck a terrific shot that went just inside Davies's near post.

Woodruff fluffed the chance of a hat-trick when he miskicked in front of goal but, with the last move of an eventful contest, McIlmoyle scored his second and his side's eighth goal. Milkins managed to knock down the centre-forward's header but the predatory McIlmoyle quickly latched onto the loose ball and slammed it into the net for his ninth goal of the season.

The two points secured from the win meant that Wolves maintained fourth place in the Second Division table, two behind leaders Coventry City. And the eight goals took the season's tally to 53 – easily the best of the four English divisions.

Wolves: Davies, Wilson, Thomson, Flowers, Woodfield, Holsgrove, Wharton, Hunt, McIlmoyle, Woodruff, Wagstaffe.
Unused sub: Harris.
Portsmouth: Milkins, Lunniss, Tindall, Campbell, Harris (Portwood), Gordon, Lewis, McCann, Hiron, Edwards, Barton.
Attendance: 17,199.
Referee: G McCabe.

46 Wolves 1 (Wharton)
Everton 1 (Ball penalty)
FA Cup fourth round
Saturday 18th February 1967

IN THE good old days when the FA Cup draw took place on the radio on a Monday lunchtime, Wolves supporters must have been licking their lips in anticipation when the Molineux side were given a fourth round home tie against the FA Cup holders, Everton. And yet Ronnie Allen's men were a little lucky still to be involved in the draw after they had been just a couple of minutes from exiting the competition in the previous round.

In their second season in the Second Division, following the relegation of 1965, promotion-chasing Wolves had met third tier side Oldham Athletic at Boundary Park in the third round and with just two minutes remaining, the Latics held a two-goal lead. But goals from Bobby Thomson and Mike Bailey in the dying seconds earned a replay that saw Wolves cruise home 4-1 to earn the prestigious Everton tie.

Allen named the side who had beaten Charlton at The Valley seven days earlier while Everton welcomed back from injury the seasoned Brian Labone at centre-half. Bailey elected to defend the North Bank end as the visitors made some early inroads on the home defence with David Woodfield at the heart of it working hard to snuff out any real threats.

Everton included two of England's World Cup-winning side – Alan Ball and Ray Wilson. And the industrious Ball began a move that saw Alex Young releasing Jimmy Gabriel on a run to goal with Woodfield just getting back to get a boot in and divert the ball back to goalkeeper Fred Davies. Then an inswinging corner from Ball flew dangerously across the face of the Wolves goal.

Terry Wharton shot over the bar with Wanderers' first goal attempt of note and then when Ernie Hunt crossed to Bob Hatton, the young striker's header was half cleared to skipper Bailey who sent a first time volley wide of the target. Everton responded with a probing run by Johnny Morrissey but Ball fired wide after taking a pass from the winger.

The magical footwork of Peter Knowles had the home fans roaring in appreciation as he set Hatton up for a shot that Everton custodian Gordon West parried before recovering to clear. Then the keeper performed acrobatics with a one-handed flying save to keep out a vicious left-footed drive from Bailey who had sidestepped his marker on the edge of the area after taking a pass from Knowles.

Wilson sliced a shot wide after he had ventured forwards in support of a run from his international colleague, Ball, but with Hatton causing the experienced Labone all sorts of problems the underdogs were growing in confidence and a deafening roar signalled the breakthrough for the home side in the 29th minute. And it was all down to the wing trickery of Dave Wagstaffe who completely outfoxed Tommy Wright before crossing for Hatton to power a header against the post. Before West or any of his defence could react, Wharton raced in to force the rebound home.

It took a desperate last ditch tackle from John Hurst to stop Hunt who had broken clear and looked odds-on to add a second shortly afterwards, and then Knowles had to receive treatment after he was sandwiched between two defenders. Everton twice went close to pulling level with Davies saving well from Jimmy Husband and John Holsgrove clearing off the line from Young.

In the 39th minute a brilliant save from West denied Wolves a second. Wagstaffe delivered another telling cross and Hunt ran in to bullet a header that had 'goal' written all over it. But West somehow twisted in mid-air as he dived to turn the ball over the bar. Though disappointed, Wolves supporters showed their appreciation by warmly applauding West's agility and lightning reactions. Just before the break, Knowles sent a rising drive just a foot over the bar.

Everton began the second half strongly and after a period of intense pressure, Knowles cleared off the line from Gabriel and then Davies leapt through the air to turn away a shot from Young who had pounced on the clearance. Knowles was hurt again in the incident and he limped off to be replaced by Hugh McIlmoyle who celebrated his introduction with a hooked shot that was just too high.

Davies was hurt and had to receive attention before continuing after he had bravely saved at the feet of Gabriel and, after Ball had been booked for felling Wagstaffe, the Wolves keeper was in action again with a fine save as he kept out a snap-shot from Wright. But he was finally beaten in the 79th minute by a Ball penalty. The ginger haired midfield dynamo burst into the area and flew through the air after Woodfield had run across to challenge. The contact seemed to be shoulder to shoulder but the referee immediately pointed to the spot and Ball netted with an unstoppable penalty kick.

There was, however, no white flag hoisted by the valiant Wolves team and four minutes from the end it looked as if Hunt had snatched a winning goal as he met a Wagstaffe cross but, with the ball seemingly on its way into the top corner, West appeared as if from nowhere to make yet another tremendous save. So a pulsating cup tie ended all square in front of an emotionally drained crowd. And there the dream ended with Everton taking the replay by 3-1 three days later.

Wolves: Davies, Taylor, Thomson, Bailey, Woodfield, Holsgrove, Wharton, Hunt, Hatton, Knowles (McIlmoyle), Wagstaffe.
Everton: West, Wright, Wilson, Hurst, Labone, Harvey, Young, Ball, Gabriel, Husband, Morrissey.
Unused sub: Brown.
Attendance: 53,439.
Referee: G McCabe.

Portsmouth 2 (Portwood 2)
Wolves 3 (Bailey, Knowles, Hunt)
Football League Second Division
Saturday 25th February 1967

WOLVES TRAVELLED to the South Coast looking to lift the gloom after a midweek mauling at the hands of Everton in an FA Cup fourth round replay at Goodison Park. After a creditable draw against the reigning league champions at Molineux, Ronnie Allen's team were clearly second best at Goodison as they fell to a 3-1 defeat in front of a crowd of 60,000.

For the trip to Portsmouth, Allen made two changes with teenager Phil Parkes replacing Fred Davies in goal and the veteran Dave Burnside leading the attack in place of Bob Hatton who was named as substitute. Second-placed Wolves were hoping at the very least to keep pace with leaders Coventry City who held a four-point advantage although Wanderers did have the benefit of a game in hand.

After three-quarters of the match, things were looking ominous for the men in all gold after Pompey had opened up a two-goal lead. Yet things had started quite brightly for the visitors with John Milkins much the busier keeper in the opening stages. He had to be at his best to save a first-time effort from Mike Bailey and, after Portsmouth had responded with a header from Ray Pointer that Parkes smothered on the line, Burnside and Peter Knowles created an opening for Terry Wharton whose fierce cross-shot was beaten away by Milkins.

Portsmouth took the lead in the 15th minute after Parkes had diverted a Ray Hiron drive on to the post. The ball rebounded to Hiron and although Parkes had recovered his feet to close down the striker, he played the ball across goal to Cliff Portwood who had the easiest of tasks in side-footing it into the empty net.

The goal inspired Portsmouth and just a minute after Portwood's strike it took a good save from Parkes to keep out another header from the dangerous Pointer. However, the keeper was beaten again after 27 minutes and once more it was Portwood who inflicted the damage. Nick Jennings fired a free kick into the box and Harry Harris was stationed at the far post to nod the ball down for Portwood to hook home from close quarters. The goals clearly took the spark out of Wolves and little was seen of them as an attacking force for the rest of the half. Knowles was spoken to after a spat with Jennings and the only time that Milkins had cause for concern was when Wharton shot into the side netting.

As in the first period, Wolves made a good start when the game resumed although the home defence looked capable of quelling any attacking threats. In fact it was Portsmouth who almost added to their lead and, but for Parkes, Portwood may have been taking the match ball home with him.

Wharton's miskick went straight to him and he only had Parkes to beat. But the keeper made a superb save to knock down a rising drive and John Holsgrove was on hand to clear the danger at the expense of a corner. Then a through ball from Bailey gave Burnside the chance of cutting the deficit but Milkins managed to deflect his shot over the bar with his legs.

Wolves were starting to warm to the task and were making inroads on the home defence and Knowles wasn't far off as he fired inches wide of the far post. With 20 minutes remaining, skipper Bailey gave his team hope as he raced onto Burnside's long through ball and lashed a shot past Milkins for his fourth goal of the season.

After having looked fairly comfortable following Portwood's two-goal salvo, the Pompey defence suddenly began to look nervous and Bailey almost did it again five minutes later with Ernie Hunt this time setting things up and the outstretched leg of Milkins, to the relief of the home support, diverting the ball away.

The game was held up briefly as the referee, Ray Johnson, received treatment for cramp. But he recovered in time to point to the centre circle after Knowles had headed Wolves on level terms following a well delivered centre from Bailey in the 79th minute. Enthusiasm got the better of Knowles who celebrated by kicking the ball out of the ground – an action that later earned him a bill for the ball from Pompey officials.

With the bit well and truly between their teeth, Wolves went flat out for a winner and it arrived eight minutes from time albeit in controversial circumstances. As Hunt headed a Dave Wagstaffe cross into the net, Milkins was lying prostrate on the floor along with David Woodfield after the pair had collided. Milkins was unable to continue and his place in goal for the remaining few minutes was taken by full-back Ron Tindall.

It was all too much for one irate Portsmouth supporter who ran onto the field but was held by a policeman before he could reach any of the players. The game was the fiftieth in the league between the sides and it's doubtful if any of the other 49 had produced such a dramatic finale. The news wasn't all good for Wolves supporters, however, as Coventry edged a five-goal game of their own, at home to Carlisle. The 3-2 win maintained their four-point lead at the top.

Portsmouth: Milkins (Wilson), Pack, Tindall, Gordon, Radcliffe, Harris, Portwood, Hiron, Pointer, Kellard, Jennings.
Wolves: Parkes, Taylor, Thomson, Bailey, Woodfield, Holsgrove, Wharton, Hunt, Burnside, Knowles, Wagstaffe.
Unused sub: Hatton.
Attendance: 23,144.
Referee: RL Johnson.

48 Wolves 4 (Dougan 3, Knowles)
Hull City 0
Football League Second Division
Saturday 25th March 1967

DEREK DOUGAN was a showman – a character who had virtually everything in his locker. Brilliant in the air, agile if somewhat awkward on the floor, controversial, flamboyant, he was a man who enjoyed entertaining the watching masses as much as he did putting the ball in the net. And when he was signed by Ronnie Allen to put the cap on the closing stages of the 1966/67 promotion campaign, it was looked upon as a major coup by the manager who paid Leicester City just £50,000 for his services.

It spoke volumes for the regard that Dougan was held in by supporters, that on his home debut for Wolves, against Hull City, the South Bank contained many Leicester fans who chose to come and watch the Ulsterman play for his new club rather than turn up for the Foxes' home fixture against Tottenham Hotspur. There were also fans from another of his former clubs, Peterborough United, in the crowd that afternoon. They weren't to be disappointed and neither were all the Wanderers supporters in the biggest league gate of the campaign at that stage, 5,000 above the norm.

Dougan's debut seven days earlier was a sedate affair against Plymouth Argyle at Home Park with Peter Knowles getting the only goal of the game as the new man up front found himself tightly shackled by home centre-half Andy Nelson. The Tigers of Hull weren't so lucky. Their cause wasn't helped by the loss through injury of influential left-winger Ian Butler. To add a little spice to the occasion, the *Match of the Day* cameras were perched high up in the Waterloo Road Stand.

Wolves were second in the table, two points adrift of leaders Coventry but with a game in hand, while Hull were just above the halfway mark, still holding out hopes of making up ground on the top two. But, by ten to five that evening, after being run ragged by Dougan, those hopes had all but evaporated.

Kicking towards the South Bank, Wolves soon started to make inroads on the visitors' defence with the wing play of Terry Wharton and Dave Wagstaffe proving a real problem. Hull's first threat was cleared by David Woodfield who was then in action at the other end after Wagstaffe had won, and taken, a corner on the left – the defender's header being cleared from in front of goal by Dennis Butler.

Dougan gave an early indication of his heading ability when he tested Iain McKechnie as Wolves laid siege to his goal and it was only down to the grit and determination of the City keeper and his defence that they survived such a testing opening with the home side forcing six corners inside the first ten minutes. When Hull did eventually venture forward, Phil Parkes had little trouble in fielding a long-range Ken Wagstaff shot before City won their first corner after 30 minutes.

Wolves' Greatest Games

A snap-shot from Knowles saw McKechnie fingertipping the ball over the bar before the crowd erupted as Dougan broke through in the 37th minute. Bobby Thomson moved upfield in support of his attack and when McKechnie pushed his shot aside after Wagstaffe's low cross, Dougan was there to tap in the loose ball despite the presence of two defenders. Shortly before the break, there could have been more goals but Woodfield's header went wide and a defender got in the way of Wharton's goal-bound drive.

After taking such a battering in the opening 45 minutes, the visitors made a strong start to the new half and after forcing two corners they went close to levelling when Chris Simkin's lob skimmed the bar with Parkes beaten. Then lanky defender John Holsgrove used his height to good advantage as he cleared two dangerous crosses as City continued to grow in confidence.

Ernie Hunt, who was the victim of some heavy challenges throughout the game, eventually limped off to be replaced by veteran midfielder Dave Burnside seconds before Dougan struck again on the hour mark. He showed complete coolness as he homed in on Wharton's accurate through pass and with McKechnie racing towards him to narrow his options, Dougan delicately chipped the ball over the keeper and into the empty net. Knowles celebrated by gleefully swinging from the crossbar in front of the celebrating North Bank.

But the crowd went wild as Dougan showed the more colourful side of his game in the 73rd minute when he completed his hat-trick. Wagstaffe and Wharton had swapped wings and when Dougan missed the latter's low cross, he had to wait for Wagstaffe to return the ball from the right side after he had beaten two defenders and cut inside to the line. Wharton headed his fellow winger's centre back into the heart of the goalmouth for Dougan to flick the ball over his own head and, as it dropped, to volley it into the roof of the net from close quarters. He later admitted "there was a touch of Irish luck" with the way that the ball had dropped for him.

It was left to Knowles to complete the fun when, with six minutes left, he met Wharton's cross with a header that just eluded the diving McKechnie. Dougan's treble was the opening gambit of the nine goals he scored in his 11 games from signing until the end of the season. And they were the first of the 123 he netted in a career at Molineux that was to last for eight seasons.

Wolves: Parkes, Taylor, Thomson, Bailey, Woodfield, Holsgrove, Wharton, Hunt (Burnside), Dougan, Knowles, Wagstaffe.
Hull: McKechnie, Davidson, D Butler, Greenwood, Milner, Simpkin, Henderson, Wagstaff, Chilton, Jarvis, Long.
Unused sub: Wilkinson.
Attendance: 30,991.
Referee: D Laing.

Wolves 4 (Wharton penalty, Dougan 2, Burnside)
Bury 1 (Jones)

Football League Second Division
Saturday 27th April 1967

A 13-GAME unbeaten run in the league took Wolves to the very threshold of a return to the top flight after their two-season sojourn in the Second Division. A total of 23 points from a possible 26 in the run-in saw Wolves going into the game with Bury holding a one-point advantage over second-placed Coventry City. The game was very much a top versus bottom affair with the Lancashire side at the bottom of the league and staring relegation in the face.

With regular centre-half David Woodfield ruled out by a thigh injury that he had picked up in the victory at Preston a week earlier, Graham Hawkins came into the team and the other change saw Terry Wharton returning in place of Peter Knowles who was named as the home substitute.

Wolves, defending the Bushbury end of the ground, forced two early Dave Wagstaffe corners and when full-back Gerry Taylor supported his attack he crossed and Wharton's back header just eluded the incoming Derek Dougan. Bury's first attack involved Bobby Collins and Paul Aimson but Phil Parkes was alert to the danger and after he had caught the ball his quick throw out to Wagstaffe led to Wolves taking a 12th-minute lead.

The winger found Dougan who, in turn, pushed the ball forward to Ernie Hunt who was stationed to the left of the Bury goal. As he was lining up a shot he had his legs unceremoniously taken from under him by Jim Kerr and the referee immediately pointed to the spot. Although Shakers keeper Neil Ramsbottom guessed correctly as he dived to his right, he stood little chance as Wharton's penalty was a combination of power and accuracy.

However, Ramsbottom did make a fine save moments later after Dave Burnside had missed his kick at goal following a Wagstaffe pass. The ball ran through to Mike Bailey and from 20 yards he hit a drive that had the keeper at full stretch as he turned the ball behind. With 18 minutes gone, Wolves doubled their lead with Dougan registering his sixth goal for the club with a neat piece of control as he took Wagstaffe's cross before easily beating Ramsbottom.

Despite this latest setback, Bury made light of their precarious league position and Parkes had trouble in controlling a long-range shot from Collins with the ball going behind for a corner. Then Kerr went on a fine run before finding Greg Farrell who was preparing to shoot when Taylor ran across and kicked the ball away from the right-winger's boot.

Collins then laid a free kick into the path of Alec Lindsay, who hit a searing shot that was only just off target. It was yet another warning to the home defenders that there was still a job to do and the point was brought home when George Jones

Wolves' Greatest Games

reduced the arrears six minutes before the break. A Bury corner wasn't cleared and when the ball bobbled to Jones, he hooked it into the net.

As the interval approached, Burnside let fly and scraped the bar and Wagstaffe was robbed by a fine tackle by John Bain. Wagstaffe would otherwise have been clean through. Ronnie Allen would no doubt have tried to hammer the message home to his players to not relax but just three minutes after the game restarted, Bury should have been level. Collins chipped the ball to Alex Dawson who was in acres of space but completely miskicked.

At this stage Wolves were looking unconvincing and it took a smart stop from Parkes to prevent a Farrell equaliser, the keeper beating the ball down before diving on top of it. A third goal eased the nerves of crowd and players alike. Burnside was the man on the mark after Hunt had headed a Wagstaffe cross back into his path. He finished with a low shot that flew past Ramsbottom.

Taylor, who had earlier received treatment after picking up a knock, was unable to continue and he was replaced by Peter Knowles whose new short haircut raised a few comments from the crowd as he took to the field. He was soon involved in two attacks as, with the advantage of a two-goal cushion, the Wanderers players began to relax and play the fluent football that had taken them to the top of the table.

Dougan wrapped things up with the best goal of the game after he ran on to a Wagstaffe pass just outside the centre circle in the Bury half. The Ulsterman raced towards goal, holding off Brian Turner's challenge before hitting a shot that beat Ramsbottom and crashed against the underside of the bar before nestling in the back of the net.

Dawson missed his second 'sitter' of the afternoon when he fired wide of an open goal and then Ramsbottom made a superb save to keep out an equally good header from Knowles. In the final minute, Knowles did find the net but his effort was ruled out for an infringement. It didn't, however, quell the enthusiastic crowd who raced onto the pitch and waited in front of the directors' box for the players to make an appearance.

With tracksuits donned, they did so along with manager Ronnie Allen who said: "Thank you, all you people, for your support. We are proud of you and hope that you will give us the same backing next season when I'm sure we'll continue to give you a good show."

Wolves: Parkes, Taylor (Knowles), Thomson, Bailey, Hawkins, Holsgrove, Wharton, Hunt, Dougan, Burnside, Wagstaffe.
Bury: Ramsbottom, Bain, Tinney, Kerr, Turner, Lindsay, Farrell, Jones, Dawson, Collins, Aimson.
Unused sub: Owen.
Attendance: 30,863.
Referee: JE Thacker.

Aberdeen 5 (Smith, Munro 3 (two penalties), Storrie)
Wolves 6 (Knowles, Burnside 3, Dougan, Thomson)

After extra time and sudden death, USA Tournament, Los Angeles Coliseum
Friday 14th July 1967

IN THE summer of 1967, marking their return to top flight football, Wolves accepted an invitation to take part in a prestigious tournament in America. The United States Soccer Association ran the competition which involved 12 clubs from around the world each adopting and being based at an American or Canadian city.

There were two six-team divisions with each side playing ten games. Wolves, as Los Angeles Wolves, were in the Western Division along with ADO The Hague of Holland (San Francisco), Cagliari of Italy (Chicago), Bangu of Brazil (Houston), Sunderland (Vancouver) and Dundee United (Dallas). The Eastern Division consisted of Aberdeen (Washington), Stoke (Cleveland), Hibernian (Toronto), Glentoran (Detroit), Cerro of Uruguay (New York) and Shamrock Rovers (Boston).

Wolves began with a 1-1 draw with Bangu in Houston with Dave Woodfield heading a late equaliser. Next was a 'home' game against Cerro and again Wolves fell behind but goals from Ernie Hunt and Dave Burnside gave them victory. A goalless draw with Stoke in Cleveland was followed by a 2-1 win over Hibernian in Toronto. Bobby Thomson gave Wolves an interval lead and although the Scots hit back with a penalty, Derek Dougan netted the winner.

Sunderland were the visitors to Los Angeles for the fifth game and at the break the score stood at one-all with Hunt the home scorer. In a one-sided second period, Pat Buckley with two, Dougan and Peter Knowles took the final score to 5-1. Glentoran were then overpowered by 4-1 at The Coliseum with Thomson, Dougan, Hunt and Knowles the scorers.

Two more draws followed; against Aberdeen in Washington, with Burnside cancelling out Jimmy Simpson's goal before he and Frank Munro were sent off after a tussle. Terry Wharton's penalty levelled the scores in a draw against Shamrock Rovers. Then came Wolves' first defeat when they went down in a bad tempered affair against ADO in San Francisco. Hunt and Dougan were both dismissed as was one of the Dutch players while Dave Wagstaffe and Buckley needed hospital treatment after some questionable tackling. Hunt was dismissed for retaliation after an awful challenge and Dougan for putting his hand on the referee's shoulder after the official had refused an obvious penalty.

Three days later Wolves met ADO again, this time in Los Angeles and they exacted revenge with a 2-0 win. Wharton got the first and then Fred Davies headed in a Wharton centre. Because of depleted options through injuries, goalkeeper

Wolves' Greatest Games

Davies played as a striker when he came on as a substitute. A two-all draw with Cagliari confirmed Wolves would be one of the finalists with the Italians equalising twice after goals from Dougan and Hunt.

Knowles was the next player to suffer a sending-off by an over-zealous referee in the 2-2 draw with Dundee United. Wolves had come from a goal down to take the lead through Knowles and Thomson with the Scottish side drawing level against the ten men in stoppage time. Then Wolves were ordered to replay their game against Aberdeen who had claimed the illegal use of a substitute. The Dons strode to a 3-0 victory which cemented their place at the top of the Eastern Division and a place in the final against Wolves.

What a game the final was! After three minutes Thomson hooked the ball towards the Aberdeen box. It was headed on by Dougan to Knowles who calmly side-footed past Bobby Clark. Jens Petersen's cross-shot was half cleared by Woodfield as far as Jim Storrie. He didn't make a proper connection with his shot but the ball ran through to Jim Smith who turned before slotting the ball home for the equaliser. Shortly afterwards, Smith was sent off for a foul on Wagstaffe.

After 63 minutes Aberdeen took the lead after Gerry Taylor fouled Pat Wilson as he ran into the area. Frank Munro assumed spot kick duties to score but it took less than two minutes for Burnside to level matters. Wagstaffe's long ball was headed on by Dougan to Knowles on the left. He crossed and Hunt chested the ball down and turned and laid a short pass into the heart of the goalmouth for Burnside to run in and convert. Almost immediately, Aberdeen regained the lead. A long ball was pumped out of defence into the Wolves box and Dave Johnston headed down to Martin Buchan whose short pass ran to Storrie and he scored with ease. Just as quickly, Wolves levelled again as Wagstaffe's centre was headed out by Petersen and Burnside, from the edge of the box, ran in to deliver a terrific header that dipped just under the bar. The crowd had been treated to four goals in as many minutes.

Burnside completed his hat-trick after Thomson fed Dougan on the left and the striker cut inside before pulling it back for the veteran to convert from six yards. It wasn't over though and Munro's header took the game into extra time. After 112 minutes, a good ball by Hunt put Wharton through on the wing and his centre was brilliantly controlled by Dougan before he lashed the ball into the roof of the net.

A Wharton penalty was saved by Clark before, in the dying seconds, John Holsgrove fouled Wilson in the box and Munro completed his treble from the spot to take the game into sudden death of which ten minutes had gone when Ally Shewan turned a Thomson cross into his own net to give Wolves an incredible 6-5 victory.

Aberdeen: Clark, Whyte, Shewan, Munro, McMillan, Petersen, Storrie, Smith, Johnston, Buchan, Wilson.
Wolves: Parkes, Taylor, Thomson, Holsgrove, Woodfield, Burnside, Wharton, Hunt, Dougan, Knowles, Wagstaffe.
Attendance: 17,824.
Referee: R Giebner.

Wolves 3 (Hunt, Bailey, Burnside)
West Bromwich Albion 3 (Foggo, Kaye, Brown)
Football League First Division
Wednesday 23rd August 1967

CLASHES BETWEEN Wolves and West Bromwich Albion can usually be relied upon to provide those watching with an added bit of spice and controversy and never was that more so than when they met in August 1967 on a balmy summer's evening. Molineux was jam-packed with over 50,000 inside to see the first South Staffordshire derby in over two-and-a-half years.

Wolves had just returned to the top flight after a two-season sojourn and had celebrated with an opening day victory over Fulham at Craven Cottage with goals from Derek Dougan and Mike Bailey paving the way to a 2-1 triumph. On the same afternoon, an early Bobby Tambling strike gave Chelsea the points when they met Albion at The Hawthorns.

Ronnie Allen kept faith in the 11 who had won on the banks of the Thames with Peter Knowles named as substitute. The game was just six minutes old when Albion had the opportunity of taking the lead after Dave Woodfield was adjudged to have fouled Jeff Astle. The pair had already tangled in the opening exchanges and home protests about the decision went unheard. However, Phil Parkes, born just a short distance from Albion's ground, came to the rescue as he brilliantly saved the normally accurate Brown's spot-kick.

Wolves took the lead in the 31st minute after the first mystifying decision of the evening. Terry Wharton's shot just cleared the bar but the referee immediately signalled a corner when it was fairly obvious that no Albion man had touched the ball. Dave Wagstaffe took the flag kick and it was nodded on by Dougan to Ernie Hunt who, from six yards out, flicked the ball past Baggies keeper John Osborne.

For the remainder of the half Wolves defended well and looked the more likely to find the net and, fortunate though the goal was, they fully deserved their slight advantage come half-time. Whatever Albion boss Jimmy Hagan said to his men during the interval, it certainly had the desired effect as they began the second period on the front foot.

Parkes was at full stretch as he turned a drive from Brown around the post, but the 19-year-old was at fault as Albion drew level in the 51st minute. Astle fed Ken Foggo on the right and his cross appeared to catch Parkes in two minds and the ball went into the net off the keeper's body for the equaliser.

Play became somewhat scrappy as both sides vied for control of the game but, after 65 minutes, it was skipper Bailey who had the home fans celebrating wildly with a superb strike. The former Charlton man was fully 30 yards from goal when he took a pass from Wagstaffe and unleashed a low shot that flew past Osborne and into the bottom corner of the net.

Wolves' Greatest Games

Eight minutes later former Baggies inside-forward Dave Burnside looked to have sealed victory for Wanderers when he scored an almost identical goal to that of Bailey's with Wagstaffe, once again, taking a hand as he slipped a free kick into the path of his team-mate. If the Wolves supporters that made up the vast majority of the huge crowd thought that the job was done, they were sadly mistaken as two highly controversial incidents saw their side robbed of a point and reduced to ten men in a dramatic climax to the game.

There were seven minutes remaining when John Talbut crossed for John Kaye to get in a powerful header that struck the underside of the bar and bounced down before being cleared. The Albion players appealed that the ball had crossed the line but the referee allowed play to carry on and Wolves had taken it to the other end of the field before he spotted the linesman flagging and, after consulting him, he allowed the goal to stand.

As it was in the days before a television camera was focused on the goal line, we will never know if that linesman, a Mr Orpin of Cardiff, made the correct call. However, if the Molineux fans were grieved by that decision, they were positively enraged by what took place in the final minute.

Graham Williams crossed from the left and as Parkes left his line to punch the ball clear, he was clattered by Clive Clark. And, to make matters worse, Brown ran in at the back post and blatantly thumped the ball into the net. A foul on the keeper or handball? However, referee Jim Carr of Sheffield failed to spot either offence and he signalled the goal.

Parkes, perhaps understandably, was incensed and he gave chase to the official, appearing to jostle him when he eventually caught up with him. His actions and words were too much for Mr Carr who immediately sent the keeper off and Wagstaffe donned the keeper's jersey for the final few seconds. The mood of the crowd was decidedly ugly as the final whistle sounded and Mr Carr needed a police escort for company as he left the pitch.

Speaking to the press shortly after the incident, Ronnie Allen, no stranger to the blue and white stripes of Albion, said: "Parkes claimed that Brown punched the last goal in. No wonder he went wild." There was certainly plenty to talk about in pubs throughout the West Midlands before closing time that night!

Wolves: Parkes, Taylor, Thomson, Bailey, Woodfield, Holsgrove, Wharton, Hunt, Dougan, Burnside, Wagstaffe.
Unused sub: Knowles.
Albion: Osborne, Fraser, Williams, Howshall, Colquhoun, Talbut, Foggo, Astle, Kaye, Brown, Clark.
Unused sub: Clarke.
Attendance: 52,438.
Referee: JE Carr.

Wolves 5 (Knowles 2, Wignall, Dougan 2)
Newcastle United 0
Football League First Division
Saturday 23rd November 1968

RONNIE ALLEN, the man who led Wolves back from the Second Division to the top flight, and masterminded the signings of Derek Dougan and Mike Bailey, was dismissed by Wolves just 16 months after their elevation. In the first season back in the First Division, the team had finished 17th, five points above the relegation trapdoor.

A slow start to the next campaign came to a head when Liverpool, with the teenage striker Alun Evans they had signed from Wolves leading their line, came to Molineux and lashed six goals past home keeper Alan Boswell without reply. Whether or not that was the beginning of Allen's demise, remains conjecture. Certainly the results after that rout improved with three wins and three draws coming from the next eight league games. However, on the back of away draws at Nottingham Forest and Burnley, with a home win over West Ham in between, came the shock news that Allen had been shown the door. His successor was Bill McGarry, a strict disciplinarian in the mould of Major Frank Buckley. An uncompromising wing-half back in his playing days with Port Vale, with Allen as a team-mate, Huddersfield Town and Bournemouth, he was capped four times by England.

His managerial career began at Bournemouth as a player-manager, before he moved to Watford and then Ipswich Town. It was in his fourth year at Portman Road that he led the Suffolk side to promotion – a year after Wolves. There was heavy press speculation that the Molineux board wanted McGarry as successor to Stan Cullis in 1964. Now, it looked like they had finally got their man. Accompanying him from East Anglia was his number two of almost six years, Sammy Chung.

For his first game at the helm, Newcastle United were in opposition at Molineux and they were sitting in mid-table just a point and two positions higher than Wolves. Coach Gerry Summers, who had been put in temporary charge, selected the team and he made just one change with skipper Mike Bailey having recovered from injury returning for Mike Kenning who was named as the substitute. Bailey took over his usual right-half spot while Frank Wignall, who had deputised at Burnley, reverted to the forward line and wore the number seven shirt.

As if to impress their new boss, the home side started the game in a brisk fashion and keeper Iam McFaul was a busy man in the first few minutes until Newcastle broke from defence and Keith Dyson tested Phil Parkes with a low drive. The Wolves keeper then kept out headers from Wyn Davies and Bryan 'Pop' Robson before his side moved into a 12th-minute lead. Dougan back-headed a long through ball into the path of Peter Knowles who rounded two defenders before shooting home with McFaul four or five yards behind him watching on his knees.

Wolves' Greatest Games

The Geordies weren't far off an equaliser from Davies whose header, following a corner, clipped the angle of post and bar. However, Wolves' attacks had much more conviction about them and it was only a surprise that they had to wait until two minutes before the break before they added to their tally. Bobby Thomson, who was having a terrific game in defence, raced down the left flank and delivered a cross that went behind three Newcastle men straight into the path of Wignall who smashed an unstoppable drive past McFaul.

McGarry's men kept the pressure on after the restart and three minutes into the new half Dougan made it three with a copybook header from Dave Wagstaffe's corner after McFaul had turned over a header from Knowles. Shell-shocked, the visitors tried to hit back through Davies but, once again, he found Parkes in peak form as the keeper made another fine save from a firm header.

After 52 minutes Knowles scored his second of the game with the type of effort that made him such an idol of the supporters. Wagstaffe sent in a waist-high cross and Knowles, with his back to goal, executed a perfect scissors kick that beat McFaul and nestled in the corner of the net with Bailey poised on the goal-line had the ball looked like it was going to drift wide. He wasn't needed!

Credit to Newcastle who never gave up the fight against, it appeared that afternoon, insurmountable odds. Their manager, Joe Harvey, tried several times to reshuffle his players all to no avail although he couldn't have wished for a harder worker than Robson, who never stopped running. A Dave Elliott shot was deflected wide and another header from Davies that was cleared by the confident home defence. These were the nearest that the Tynesiders came to reducing the deficit.

Wignall received a healthy round of applause when he was replaced by Kenning in the 72nd minute, and four minutes later Dougan rounded off the scoring. With a typical burst of speed, and no little skill, Wagstaffe ran along the byline and pulled the ball back for Dougan who made no mistake from ten yards, beating McFaul and Dave Craig who were both stationed on the line.

When McGarry arrived at Wolves he told a reporter: "If Wolves are impatient for success and burning with ambition, then it's just fine by me. As I see it, a manager must burn with ambition. Deep inside me I want to win every game in every league."

The Stoke-born hard-man couldn't have wished for a better start from his new charges.

Wolves: Parkes, Palmer, Thomson, Bailey, Woodfield, Holsgrove, Wignall (Kenning), Knowles, Dougan, Wilson, Wagstaffe.
Newcastle: McFaul, Craig, Clark, Gibb, Burton, Moncur, Scott, Robson, Davies, Elliott, Dyson.
Unused sub: Winstanley.
Attendance: 25,425.
Referee: RV Spittle.

Wolves 3 (Curran 2, Dougan)
Nottingham Forest 3 (Newton 2, Rees)
Football League First Division
Saturday 6th September 1969

THE MIDLANDS derby game between Wolves and Nottingham Forest, in the early stages of the 1969/70 campaign, was something of an added attraction to the main event which saw Molineux idol Peter Knowles playing his final game before retiring to concentrate on his newly-found Jehovah's Witness faith when he was just 24 days short of his 24th birthday.

Knowles had the world, quite literally, at his feet. He remains one of the most gifted players ever to have done service with Wolverhampton Wanderers and his announcement that the Forest game was to be his last was met with a mixture of despair and disbelief from club officials and supporters alike. His Beatle-like looks made him the focus of attention for the female support in the crowd, while the menfolk marvelled at his work on the pitch.

Certainly he could be impudent, brash, and petulant, but he could also bamboozle opposition defenders as he completely wrong-footed them with a drop of the shoulder, a shimmy or a piece of footwork that would leave those watching open-mouthed. Wolves had won the opening four games of the campaign and Knowles scored a goal in each of the first three. He had also played every minute of the eight league encounters and one League Cup tie leading up to Forest's visit.

The North Bank choir soon made themselves heard after the kick-off as they chanted "we want goals, give it to Knowles". Their idol responded with a flash of speed that took him past Henry Newton before striking a 25-yard drive that was saved by visiting keeper Alan Hill. In the eighth minute, Frank Munro floated a free kick into the Forest area and Derek Dougan leapt above his marker to power a header that beat Hill but came back off the upright.

Dougan should have opened the scoring when he sprinted clear of the Forest defence and collected a low cross from Hugh Curran. Hill raced from his line to confront the Irish striker who lifted his shot high over the bar. But there was no easing up of the pressure on Hill's goal and Dougan atoned for his miss by setting up the opening goal for Curran. Derek Parkin pumped a long ball into the box and Dougan rose superbly to nod down for Curran to crack the ball past Hill.

Curran almost made it two a minute later with a diving header from Dave Wagstaffe's centre that flashed inches wide. Then Terry Hennessey bravely got his head in the way of a Knowles volley which drew more chants from the crowd of "please don't leave us Peter Knowles" to the tune of 'Guide Me Oh Thou Great Redeemer'.

Five minutes before the break Knowles opened up the way for Dougan to notch Wolves' second. From inside his own half, the England Under-23 international deliv-

Wolves' Greatest Games

ered a defence-splitting pass to Curran on the right and his cross was nodded down by the unmarked Dougan who then ran the ball over the line. The way that Knowles celebrated with Dougan, the pair of them leaping up and down in the air with their legs behind them, certainly didn't indicate that this was a man about to quit the game.

In the five minutes after the interval, Wolves could easily have doubled their tally. Curran slid in on a Dougan cross but his shot went into the side netting, then, in the next attack, the Scot headed against the bar after a centre from Wagstaffe. Curran was in dynamic form and when he did beat Hill with a low shot, Hennessey raced across to clear off the line. However, the former Norwich man wasn't to be denied and he put Wolves three up in the 52nd minute with Knowles again involved as his cross was headed on by Dougan to Curran who had the easiest of tasks in finding the net.

Mike Bailey, with an amazing shot from near the right-hand corner flag, had Hill scrambling to save at his near post and with Wolves three goals up and dominating, it's doubtful if you could have got a price on Forest taking something from the game – but they did! The fightback started in the 61st minute when Newton hooked the ball home in a crowded box after a cross from Barry Lyons.

The goal seemed to take the rhythm out of Wolves' play and in the 67th minute, Ronnie Rees volleyed past Phil Parkes from the edge of the box. Knowles twice went close to marking his farewell with a goal with a rising drive that flashed just wide and, after he had been set up by Dougan, another shot that went inches the wrong side of the post.

In the 79th minute Newton stunned the crowd into silence when he took advantage of a mix-up between Parkes and Parkin to slam the ball home. It could have been worse as Rees broke through in the last minute and looked odds-on to get an unlikely winner only to lift the ball over the bar. At the final whistle, Knowles sprinted off as a few fans ran on towards him.

In the matchday programme, manager Bill McGarry wrote: "His [Knowles] training gear will be laid out on Monday morning and I will expect him to be here." However, McGarry, and the football public of Wolverhampton that idolised him, were left disappointed as the training gear lay untouched as Knowles stood by his convictions and never played another first class game.

Wolves: Parkes, Wilson, Parkin, Bailey, Holsgrove, Munro, McCalliog, Knowles, Dougan, Curran, Wagstaffe.
Unused sub: Walker.
Forest: Hill, Hindley, Winfield, Chapman, Hennessey, Newton, Rees, Lyons, Collier, Barnwell, Hilley.
Unused sub: O'Kane.
Attendance: 33,166.
Referee: R Darlington.

54

Wolves 3 (Wagstaffe, Curran 2)
Chelsea 0
Football League First Division
Saturday 13th December 1969

CHELSEA WERE the 'in' team of the 1960s. The area of London that housed Stamford Bridge was regarded by the younger generation as the fashion capital of the country and likewise the football team were crammed with characters who were feted for the glamorous soccer that they played. The players were very much a part of the swinging sixties in the British game.

Shortly before Christmas 1969, Chelsea arrived at Molineux on the back of an 11-game unbeaten run and they sat in sixth place in the First Division table – one point and one position above Wolves. Their goalkeeper was Peter Bonetti who, three days earlier, had kept a clean sheet for England against Portugal at Wembley. Wolves were without injured skipper Mike Bailey and Canadian Les Wilson dropped back from the forward line to cover for him while Frank Munro came in to lead the attack. The other change saw Bernard Shaw preferred at right-back to Gerry Taylor.

After a Dave Wagstaffe cross in the opening seconds was cleared, Chelsea began to dominate the early possession to such an extent that Wagstaffe had to drop into defence to help out and young striker Bertie Lutton cleared for a corner from inside his own box.

Peter Houseman lifted the flag kick into the box and David Webb got in a header that Phil Parkes could only knock down before he gathered the ball at the second attempt. A John Holsgrove tackle on Ian Hutchinson gave Chelsea a free kick in a dangerous position but the Wolves defensive wall did its job when Alan Hudson took the kick. Another attack from the visitors saw the ball bouncing around in Parkes' goalmouth before Dave Woodfield eased the tension with a run from defence before releasing Wagstaffe on the left.

Although that forward venture came to nothing, it was as if it gave the home players belief in themselves and, for the first time, Wolves began to get the upper hand. Lutton won a free kick just outside the area and when Wagstaffe tapped the ball into Derek Parkin's path, the full-back hit a low shot that took a deflection on its way through to Bonetti who had to change direction to make the save. The keeper then had to back pedal to take a deceptive cross from Wagstaffe.

Parkin figured in the next Wolves attack when he unleashed a tremendous effort that flew inches over the bar. The confidence in the home team seemed to grow visibly as play progressed and this was transferred to the crowd who were getting ever louder in their support. It took three Chelsea players to stop a Wagstaffe run and then Hugh Curran was crowded out before he could get a shot in after Shaw had pushed the ball to him.

Wolves' Greatest Games

Five minutes before the break, it was Wagstaffe who broke the deadlock with his second goal of the season. The winger had moved over to the right side when he suddenly cut inside as Shaw distracted the Chelsea defence with a dummy run towards the byline. Wagstaffe took the ball to the edge of the area and found the net with a left-footed rising drive with Bonetti static on his line.

Two minutes later, Wagstaffe turned into the provider as Wolves doubled their lead. He sent over a perfect corner from the left and Curran ran in to bullet a downwards header that was too good for Bonetti. Given the slow start that they had made, it was hard to imagine that Wanderers would go in to the interval having kept a clean sheet and two goals to the good but the scoreline was fully merited given the way that Bill McGarry's men had turned things around.

They started the second period from where they had left off the first and after Shaw had tested Bonetti with a 22-yard shot, Curran made it 3-0 in the 51st minute. And again it was from a Wagstaffe corner that the burly striker profited as he drove the ball home after he was afforded the space by a leaden-footed Chelsea defence.

To their credit, the Londoners tried to hit back and it took a goal-line clearance by Woodfield to clear after John Hollins' lob had beaten Parkes. But Wolves were soon back on the attack and Wagstaffe was just off the mark after Wilson had been fouled on the edge of the box. Eddie McCreadie was then booked for a heavy challenge on Lutton.

Wolves conceded a succession of corners and, from one of them, Hollins hit a long-range shot that was well saved by Parkes. On 69 minutes Wagstaffe was inches away from his second of the game when he hammered a 25-yard shot that grazed the top of the upright. Then back came Chelsea and Parkes was at his finest when he foiled Hutchinson who had looked odds on to score.

Both Woodfield and Wilson cleared off the line as the match moved into its closing stages and Chelsea tried desperately to get something from it. But it was Wolves who went close again with five minutes remaining as Munro met Wagstaffe's cross with a fine header that drew a brilliant save from Bonetti. The two points from the win saw Wolves leapfrog their opponents in the league table.

But Wanderers won only two of their remaining 18 league games, while Chelsea went on to win the FA Cup, beating Leeds in a replay at Old Trafford.

Wolves: Parkes, Shaw, Parkin, Wilson, Holsgrove, Woodfield, McCalliog, Lutton, Munro, Curran, Wagstaffe.
Unused sub: McAlle.
Chelsea: Bonetti, Webb, McCreadie, Hollins, Dempsey, Harris, Cooke, Hudson, Osgood, Hutchinson, Houseman.
Unused sub: Hinton.
Attendance: 26,775.
Referee: V James.

Wolves 3 (Gould 3)
Manchester United 2 (Gowling, Kidd)
Football League First Division
Saturday 3rd October 1970

WOLVES PAID Arsenal £50,000 for the services of Bobby Gould in the summer of 1970, and he was to repay the faith shown in him by scoring 22 league and cup goals in his first season as he helped the club to a fourth-place finish in the First Division. Undoubtedly, his undying memory of his time at Wolves will have been the treble he hit against Manchester United at Molineux.

While United were without Ian Ure, Pat Crerand and Denis Law for the game, they still included the likes of Bobby Charlton, Brian Kidd and the genius that was George Best. Wolves, on the other hand, were missing the injured Hugh Curran but they still packed plenty of punch up front with Derek Dougan partnering Gould and John Richards in reserve as the substitute.

After losing four of their opening five matches, Wolves had clicked into gear and they had won two and drawn two of their games leading into the United fixture. The week before the game Wanderers had won 3-2 against Burnley. Manager Bill McGarry made just one change for the visit of United, switching Dougan and Richards with the Northern Ireland striker having been on the bench at Turf Moor.

With United in town, it was no surprise that the biggest crowd of the season up to that point were inside Molineux on a blustery but dry afternoon. Wolves attacked the North Bank end and were ahead after just two minutes. Frank Munro cleared a United raid finding Bernard Shaw who made progress down the right before pushing the ball through to Gould. The striker stumbled and the opportunity looked to have gone. However, Steve James missed the chance to clear, allowing Gould to recover his footing and drill the ball past United keeper Jimmy Rimmer.

A minute later a Munro clearance was headed on by Gould to Dougan on the right but his low cross was cut out by Rimmer. United replied with a shot from Kidd that was saved by Phil Parkes and a weaving run from Best whose low ball into the area was cut out by John McAlle. Best then left two defenders in his wake as he crossed for Charlton to get in a header that was superbly kept out by Parkes.

United continued to threaten and after Charlton was just off target with a trademark long-range effort, the equaliser arrived in the 11th minute. It was all thanks to the World Cup winner who slammed a shot against the bar leaving Alan Gowling with the simple task of heading the rebound into the net from close range.

Best, Kidd and Charlton got shots in on Parkes' goal as United looked for a second but after withstanding the pressure Wolves regained the initiative as Gould struck again. Dave Wagstaffe picked up a defensive clearance and sent Dougan away on the left. He pushed a great ball towards the far post that left Rimmer stranded and Gould ran in to slam it into the net from close in.

Wolves' Greatest Games

The home goal was then subjected to another heavy spell of United pressure but once more the defence stood their ground and when Jim McCalliog broke away to force a corner, his kick caused chaos in the United box with Wagstaffe, Kenny Hibbitt and Gould all having goal attempts blocked or charged down before Wagstaffe finally fired over the bar.

United started strongly after the interval and would have levelled for a second time had Derek Parkin not been stationed on the line to clear from Gowling after a left-wing corner. Then Willie Morgan just failed to get a toe to Charlton's low driven cross. While United's efforts were to no avail, Gould then struck again to complete his hat-trick.

McCalliog was the orchestrator as he cleverly beat John Fitzpatrick before hitting a low ball into the middle where Gould was waiting to tap it over the line. With the home fans still celebrating, Wagstaffe set up McCalliog for a shot that Rimmer turned aside with the ball only just missing the upright as it went behind.

Dougan fired a cross-shot wide of the far post and Morgan almost broke through the home defence but was thwarted by Munro's challenge. In the 62nd minute, Kidd reduced the arrears. He forced the ball home after Charlton's free kick, following a foul by Parkin, hadn't been cleared from the Wolves area.

Wagstaffe tested Rimmer with a shot on the run and when Charlton took a return pass from Best he was inches away from giving United an equaliser. Shaw went even closer for Wolves after Richards had replaced Dougan in the 73rd minute. The substitute immediately laid the ball through for the full-back who ran into the United box and hit a shot that beat Rimmer but bounced back off the crossbar.

Gould looked to be on for his fourth goal as he streaked clear but as Rimmer advanced he fired wide of the post. An unhappy afternoon for Coseley-born James ended when he was carried off on a stretcher after he was hurt just before the finish of the game.

As for Gould, after his profitable opening term at Molineux, his second season lasted for just five games before he was transferred to West Bromwich. He was to return to Molineux in 1975 for a two-year stint and his total contribution in the 1970s for the club was 31 goals from 93 appearances.

Wolves: Parkes, Shaw, Parkin, Bailey, Munro, McAlle, McCalliog, Hibbitt, Gould, Dougan (Richards), Wagstaffe.
United: Rimmer, Watson, Burns, Fitzpatrick, James (Sartori), Sadler, Morgan, Gowling, Charlton, Kidd, Best.
Attendance: 38,629.
Referee: A Dimond.

West Bromwich Albion 2 (McVitie, Brown)
Wolves 4 (Curran 2, Bailey, Gould)

Football League First Division
Saturday 20th March 1971

THE 100TH league meeting between Wolves and West Bromwich Albion took place at The Hawthorns and it turned out to be one of the best, especially if you were a supporter of the gold and black half of the divide. Going into the game Wolves led by 39 wins to 37 and the Molineux club also held a slight goal advantage having scored 175 times against Albion's 168.

With Derek Dougan ruled out of the game with a calf strain, Hugh Curran returned in his place and the craggy Scot wasn't to let anybody down that afternoon. The pitch was heavy after persistent morning rain but by the time the kick-off arrived, the sun was shining brightly. Albion defended the Birmingham Road end of the ground and the early moments saw both sides twice getting caught out by the respective offside traps – Tony Brown and Jeff Astle for the Baggies, and Kenny Hibbitt and Bobby Gould for Wolves.

Alan Merrick cleared the first Dave Wagstaffe cross of the afternoon and then Graham Lovett fouled the winger who took the free kick finding Bernard Shaw but he drove his shot wide. Ray Wilson's lofted through pass spelled danger for Wolves which was relieved when Astle was penalised for a foul on Phil Parkes as the pair jumped for the ball.

Brown found some space for himself in the Wolves box but he failed to make proper contact with the ball allowing Parkes a comfortable save. Thanks to the midfield prompting of Mike Bailey the visitors were starting to edge the attacking play and it took a great save from Jim Cumbes to prevent what would have been a fluke opening goal from Jim McCalliog.

Merrick got plenty behind an attempted clearance in his own box only for the ball to hit the Scottish midfielder on the head and rebound back towards goal. The ball looked as if was going to drop under the bar but Cumbes earned applause from all corners of the ground as he leapt backwards and with one hand turned it over the bar.

The game was 31 minutes old when Albion moved into the lead. Bobby Hope dispossessed Bailey and fed George McVitie who skipped past John McAlle's challenge before firing past Parkes. Wolves hit back with two raids from Wagstaffe and from the second Curran went full length to head into the side netting. Shaw forced a corner after running half the length of the pitch and when that came to nothing Albion went in search of a second goal and had McAlle not made a last-ditch tackle on Brown it would almost certainly have come.

As the interval approached a series of petty fouls broke up the rhythm of the game as Albion began to take control. But it was to be a different story after the

Wolves' Greatest Games

resumption. Wagstaffe, who was at his best, almost did the trick with a run that left his marker for dead and a shot that whistled a foot wide with Cumbes in no position to save.

Curran and Hibbitt put the home defence under pressure after some neat interplay before Wolves drew level in the 53rd minute. Unsurprisingly, it was Wagstaffe who was at the heart of the move with a run followed by a pass inside to Curran whose shot went just inside the near post. Before play resumed Bill McGarry sent Mike O'Grady on in place of Hibbitt.

McAlle came to the rescue once more when he headed clear from under the bar after Hope had spotted Parkes off his line and sent in a precision lob. From being a whisker away from going ahead, Albion suddenly found themselves behind for the first time and again it was Curran who was on target. From a right-wing corner by Wagstaffe the ball was cleared but only as far as Shaw who crossed for Curran to score with a downward header.

The cheers of the Wolves fans in the Smethwick End were soon stifled as the Baggies equalised just two minutes later. Brown collected a neat flick from Astle before driving the ball under the body of the diving Parkes. Then, another two minutes saw another goal and this time it was Wolves' turn to celebrate.

Bailey did the trick with a superb solo run that took him through the heart of the Albion defence and into the area before he unleashed a ferocious cross-shot that gave Cumbes no chance of saving. The game was being played at a terrific pace and virtually from the restart Brown beat Parkes to a cross but hooked the ball narrowly wide of the goal.

Things inevitably became a little fractious in the white hot atmosphere and, after a tremendous scramble in the home area, Gould and John Kaye were lectured by the referee after a brief tussle. There were to be no last-minute nerves for Wolves as Gould's 79th-minute goal gave them a two-goal advantage.

Needless to say, Wagstaffe was behind it meaning that he had been involved in three of the four goals. His cross found Curran and although Cumbes did well to keep out the striker's shot, the ball rolled back perfectly for Gould who tapped in from close quarters. The win lifted Wolves up above Chelsea into third place in the table behind leaders Leeds and Arsenal.

Albion: Cumbes, Kaye, Wilson, Lovett, Wile, Merrick, McVitie, Brown, Astle, Hope, Hartford.
Unused sub: Suggett.
Wolves: Parkes, Shaw, Parkin, Bailey, Munro, McAlle, McCalliog, Hibbitt (O'Grady), Gould, Curran, Wagstaffe.
Attendance: 35,716.
Referee: D Giffard.

Heart of Midlothian 1 (Ford)
Wolves 3 (Bailey, Curran 2)
Texaco Cup final first leg
Wednesday 14th April 1971

Wolves 0
Heart of Midlothian 1 (Fleming)
Texaco Cup final second leg
Monday 3rd May 1971

THE TEXACO CUP, as the name suggests, was a sponsored competition that had its inauguration in 1970 with six English, six Scottish, two Northern Irish and two Irish clubs invited to take part. Wolves were one of the English contingent who accepted and they were, not without some difficulty, to become the first winners of the trophy.

It was at Molineux that Wanderers tended to struggle having won each of the four away legs leading up to Mike Bailey hoisting the cup in the Waterloo Road Stand. It all began in September 1970 at Dundee. Bobby Gould and Jim McCalliog gave the visitors a 2-0 advantage at Dens Park before Gordon Wallace pulled a goal back. The second leg turned out to be a tame goalless draw.

Next on the agenda for Wolves was Greenock Morton and a comfortable 3-0 win at Cappielow Park, courtesy of a brace from Gould and a Derek Dougan header. It meant that one foot was planted in the semi-final of the competition. But again, there was a stutter at Molineux as Gerry Sweeney and Ian Campbell took Morton to within one goal of levelling the tie before substitute Hugh Curran eased the tension with a header 20 minutes from time.

The last four draw paired Wolves with the part-timers of Derry City and the Ulster team's resolve at Brandywell wasn't broken until the 82nd minute when Gould headed in a John Richards cross for the only goal of the game. The return was scheduled to take place before Christmas but a frozen pitch meant a deferment until well into the month of March. When the game did take place, goals from Derek Parkin, Curran, Mike O'Grady and Gould saw Wolves home with a comfortable 5-0 aggregate.

Waiting patiently in the final were Heart of Midlothian who staged the first leg at Tynecastle. The Scots took just seven minutes to move into the lead as Jim Townsend's centre was deflected by John McAlle into the path of Don Ford who ran in to head past Phil Parkes. Wanderers pulled level ten minutes later when Dave Wagstaffe beat two men in as many yards before laying the ball off for Bailey, who drove the ball past home keeper Jim Cruickshank.

Two goals from Curran, in the 28th and 31st minutes, put Wolves very much in the ascendant. O'Grady played a part in each of the strikes with Curran putting away a half-chance after taking a short pass from his team-mate, and then following up to

Wolves' Greatest Games

score after Cruickshank was only able to push out a fierce cross-shot from O'Grady.

Bailey, who was almost ruled out of the game with a back injury he had picked up against Manchester United at Old Trafford two days earlier, played a true captain's role as he marshalled his defence to thwart any Hearts attempts to get back into the game although it took a fine save from Parkes, in the last minute, to divert a George Fleming shot against a post.

Wolves made three changes for the second leg, with Bernard Shaw, Kenny Hibbitt and Dougan replacing Gerry Taylor, O'Grady and Curran respectively while Hearts made two – Tommy Veitch for Jim Brown and Davie Laing for Eric Carruthers. For the 28,000 crowd who turned up to hopefully see the first addition to the Molineux trophy cabinet in 11 years, the game turned out to be a massive anti-climax.

For the first ten minutes Wolves were well on top and it looked like it would be just a matter of time before they added to their 3-1 advantage. After that the game belonged almost exclusively to the visitors and were it not for some wasted chances the maroon-clad Scots could easily have achieved a sensational result.

The only goal of the game came in the 25th minute when some slack defensive work presented Fleming with an easy chance which he accepted, slotting a low shot past Parkes from just inside the area. The home defence then had their work cut out in preventing Hearts from getting the goal that would have evened up the aggregate score.

There were the odd moments of respite for a crowd that was getting more restless as the game went on. O'Grady, on as a substitute for Hibbitt, tested Cruickshank with a well struck shot and the keeper made an even better save just before the end when he kept out a firm header from Dougan after a cross from Wagstaffe.

Carl D Hall, managing director and chief executive of Texaco Ltd, presented Bailey with the golden trophy to bring a disappointing, though successful, conclusion to a season that had seen Wolves finish fourth in the First Division – their best finish since the near double season of 1959/60.

First leg
Hearts: Cruickshank, Sneddon, Kay, Thomson, Anderson, Brown, Fleming, Townsend, Ford, Wood, Carruthers (Young).
Wolves: Parkes, Taylor, Parkin, Bailey, Munro, McAlle, McCalliog, O'Grady, Gould (Dougan), Curran, Wagstaffe.
Attendance: 26,057.
Referee: T Wharton.

Second leg
Wolves: Parkes, Shaw, Parkin, Bailey, Munro, McAlle, McCalliog, Hibbitt (O'Grady), Gould, Dougan, Wagstaffe.
Hearts: Cruickshank, Sneddon, Kay, Thomson, Anderson, Veitch, Townsend, Laing, Ford, Wood, Fleming.
Unused sub: Carruthers.
Attendance: 28,462.
Referee: R Tinkler.

Newcastle keeper Jimmy Lawrence clears from George Hedley in the 1908 FA Cup Final at Crystal Palace.

Inspirational skipper Billy Wright heads clear from Leicester's Jack Lee in the 1949 FA Cup Final.

Manchester United's keeper, Reg Allen, punches clear this time. But he was to concede six goals in this October, 1952, encounter at Molineux.

Roy Swinbourne is surrounded by Honved defenders. He was to have the last laugh, though, as he scored two in the epic 3-2 floodlit friendly against the Hungarian giants.

The clock has hardly moved past three o'clock as Johnny Hancocks fires Wolves into a second minute lead against Huddersfield Town in the winter of 1955.

Barry Stobart is just waiting for a slip as Blackburn keeper Harry Leyland collects under the watchful eye of centre-half Matt Woods in the 1960 FA Cup Final.

Bert Trautmann dives in vain as Jimmy Murray scores Wolves' second goal in the opening day of the season rout of Manchester City in 1962.

Bernard Shaw guides the ball back towards his goalkeeper to help quell the Juventus threat in the 1972 UEFA Cup quarter-final.

The final against Tottenham Hotspur was to end in bitter disappointment for Wolves who were deemed unlucky by most neutral pundits. Jimmy McCalliog is seen here in first-leg action with Spurs keeper Pat Jennings.

There were just nine minutes remaining when John Richards hit the winner in the 1974 League Cup Final against Manchester City.

Andy Gray is about to tap home the only goal of the game in the 1980 League Cup defeat of Brian Clough's Nottingham Forest.

Andy Thompson looks to be in a determined mood as he passes Burnley's Andy Farrell in the 1988 Sherpa Van Trophy Final at Wembley.

Don Goodman's penalty hits the roof of the net to put the seal on the amazing FA Cup shoot-out comeback against Sheffield Wednesday in 1995.

Kenny Miller wheels away in triumph after he had scored Wolves' third goal in the 2003 play-off final at the Millennium Stadium. Also seen, against a backdrop of dejected Sheffield United supporters, is Shaun Newton who supplied the cross for the goal.

Jonathan Spector reverts to underhand tactics in an attempt to stop Kevin Doyle during the impressive 3-1 win over West Ham at Upton Park in March, 2010.

Partly hidden, George Elokobi powers home an equalising header against Manchester United. Kevin Doyle got the winning goal shortly afterwards as Wolves ended United's season-long unbeaten run in February, 2011.

Richard Stearman finds the net against Spurs in the thrilling 3-3 draw at Molineux in March, 2011. The goal was disallowed for a foul on the keeper but replays showed it was the wrong decision as Heurelho Gomes had his arms around Stearman who still managed to hit the ball home.

Wolves 5 (Wagstaffe, Hibbitt, Dougan 2, McCalliog penalty)
Arsenal 1 (Kennedy)
Football League First Division
Saturday 20th November 1971

T HE *MATCH OF THE DAY* cameras were at Molineux for the mid-table clash between Wolves and double winners Arsenal on a bitterly cold November afternoon. Sleet had been swirling around the ground prior to kick-off which could have had an acclimatising effect on Bill McGarry's team who were facing a trip to icy East Germany in the days that followed for a Uefa Cup tie with Carl Zeiss Jena.

McGarry named the same players who had come from behind to beat high-flying Derby County seven days earlier with a John Richards brace, his first goals of the campaign, putting paid to the Rams. Arsenal had been struggling to replicate the form that had seen them win the league championship and beat Liverpool in the FA Cup Final at Wembley. The Gunners had lost seven of their 16 games and they sat just a point above Wolves in the table.

There was a cheer from the crowd as Pickwick-like referee Roger Kirkpatrick sprinted across the field doubtless in response to comments made by Derek Dougan questioning the fitness of referees. Arsenal were the first to threaten with George Graham playing Sammy Nelson clean through after just two minutes. He advanced on Phil Parkes' goal and looked certain to score but he sliced his left-foot shot high up into the North Bank.

Two Dave Wagstaffe crosses and one from Jim McCalliog kept the Arsenal defence busy while the home rearguard got in a tangle in trying to clear their lines and John McAlle had to put the ball behind to relieve the pressure. Peter Storey was twice rebuked by the referee after he had fouled Kenny Hibbitt and then Wagstaffe.

Wolves had Bernard Shaw to thank for keeping things on level terms as he headed off the line from John Roberts before George Armstrong hit a cross cum shot that flew dangerously in front of Parkes' goal. Then Storey was spoken to for a third time after a brief spat with Frank Munro who was also lectured by Kirkpatrick.

Bob Wilson was almost caught out by a Wagstaffe cross that bounced just wide of the far post, and then the keeper saved on his line after a Hibbitt shot took a deflection off Graham. The home crowd were silenced in the 37th minute as Ray Kennedy gave the visitors the lead with a super strike. Parkes dived in vain as the Arsenal striker unleashed a shot from fully 30 yards out that rocketed into the top left-hand corner of the net.

Wagstaffe took exception to a challenge from Pat Rice and both were spoken to by the referee who had shown a degree of leniency in keeping his notebook in his pocket during a feisty opening half. Whatever manager McGarry said to his troops during the break certainly had the desired effect although nobody could have prophesied what was to come in the next 45 minutes.

Wolves' Greatest Games

From the restart, the pressure on the Arsenal defence was relentless as the snow fell attractively in the glow of the floodlights as darkness descended. Dougan took the supporters' minds off the weather with a fierce drive that crashed into the side netting before the crowd howled in anger after their side was denied a penalty when Roberts used both hands to pull back Richards as he ran on to a Dougan flick.

Wagstaffe, with his first of the season, fired Wolves level with a goal equally as good as that of Kennedy. It was from a similar distance although from a slightly tighter angle after he had dispossessed Nelson. The winger's left-footed rising drive hit the back of the net with Wilson still in mid-air.

The keeper had to receive attention after his valiant but fruitless attempt to save, and when he had regained his feet he had to punch the ball away after another heavy home attack. However, the pressure had to pay off and it did in the 64th minute.

This time it was Hibbitt who joined Kennedy and Wagstaffe in the spectacular goal stakes. The midfielder beat Wilson all ends up with a venomous strike from around 20 yards after he had run onto Wagstaffe's crossfield pass. With the cheers still ringing out, Dougan made it three. He was forced wide to the left of goal but he hit a cross-shot as he fell and the ball crept past Wilson and went just inside the far post.

Wilson had to dive at the feet of Richards to prevent the youngster from making it three in as many minutes. However, a fourth goal wasn't long in coming and it was from the spot that McCalliog put the game out of Arsenal's reach with Wilson well beaten after the kick had been awarded following Roberts's foul on Dougan. McCalliog completely out-foxed the keeper by pausing in his run-up to the ball before guiding it into the net

Dougan rounded off the scoring in the 73rd minute following a Wagstaffe corner. The Northern Irish international side-footed the ball through the legs of the unfortunate Wilson in front of a delighted North Bank.

That afternoon, Ted McDougall hit eight goals as Bournemouth beat Margate 11-0 in an FA Cup first round tie. McDougall was believed to have been a £100,000 target for Wolves although he ended up moving to Manchester United. Also that day, Everton hit eight without reply against Southampton at Goodison Park but, at 10.05pm it was Wanderers who grabbed the headlines as they entertained the viewers with a five-star display.

Wolves: Parkes, Shaw, Parkin, Bailey, Munro, McAlle, McCalliog, Hibbitt, Richards, Dougan, Wagstaffe.
Unused sub: Eastoe.
Arsenal: Wilson, Rice, Nelson, Storey, Roberts, McLintock, Armstrong, George, Radford, Kennedy, Graham.
Unused sub: McNab.
Attendance: 28,851.
Referee: RB Kirkpatrick.

Manchester United 1 (McIlroy)
Wolves 3 (Dougan, Richards, McCalliog penalty)

Football League First Division
Saturday 8th January 1972

WOLVES WERE in awesome form when they travelled up to Old Trafford to take on league leaders Manchester United. Bill McGarry fielded an unchanged side for the 11th consecutive game for the trip and a run of six wins and two draws had hoisted the team to within six points of the leaders prior to kick-off. Added to that were home and away victories over East Germany's Carl Zeiss Jena in the Uefa Cup to earn a quarter-final place in the competition.

United had lost just three of 23 league fixtures, and Leeds were the only team to have left Old Trafford with a win under their belts. On the eve of the game, Reds manager Frank O'Farrell had sent shockwaves around the city by dropping United icon George Best. In his place O'Farrell named the 17-year-old Sammy McIlroy who, like Best, was Belfast-born.

Wolves defended the Stretford End and twice in the opening minutes had the chance to grab an early foothold in the game. Dave Wagstaffe forced a corner, the first of two in quick succession, and from the second Denis Law, who had been forced to drop back to assist his defence, cleared upfield. Phil Parkes was forced into a full-length save by Willie Morgan's fierce ground shot but Wolves were quickly back on the offensive and after a Wagstaffe centre was pushed out by United keeper Alex Stepney, John Richards drove the ball back towards goal and David Sadler had to boot clear from in front of the near post.

Parkes had to be alert after a low shot from Frank Burns took a double deflection off Law and Bernard Shaw but Stepney was the busier keeper, smothering a byline cross from Derek Dougan and then denying the striker with a point blank reflex save to turn the ball over the bar. The Wolves team grew more and more confident and they were putting together some moves that had the home defence struggling to cope. And so the lead they took in the 20th minute was more than deserved.

Paul Edwards and Tony Dunne collided with one another as they tried to quell the threat of Richards and the ball ran to Wagstaffe on the left. His centre was met by Kenny Hibbitt on the far side of the box and he chipped the ball back across for Dougan to head home just inside the near post. All that United could muster by way of response was a shot by Law that was way too high, and another by Brian Kidd that lacked the power to trouble Parkes.

Derek Parkin's foul on McIlroy presented Bobby Charlton with a free kick opportunity but his effort was both high and wide. Wolves, however, were looking dangerous every time they attacked and a mistake by Stepney almost resulted in a second Dougan goal. The keeper failed to deal with the striker's cross from the right as the ball bounced off his shoulder and only just wide of the far post. But, with 29 minutes gone, Wanderers did increase their lead.

Frank Munro lofted a deep free kick on to the head of Dougan who nodded down perfectly for Richards to run in and beat Stepney with ease. Munro then went about his defensive duties by halting Morgan's run towards goal. The visiting rear-guard were cool and collected in dealing with the few threats that came its way while United's defenders looked nervous every time Wolves attacked – a fact highlighted by Burns who hastily headed a Wagstaffe cross behind for a corner when he had all the time in the world to clear.

The second half opened with Wolves going close to adding to their tally. More United panic saw Edwards kicking the ball virtually from the hands of Stepney. Wagstaffe collected and Munro, from the tightest of angles, drove narrowly over the bar. But six minutes into the half, McGarry's men suffered their first setback of the game when they lost the services of Dougan who went down, with no-one near him, clasping a leg. After treatment he limped off to be replaced by Hugh Curran.

Further hold-ups followed as first Hibbitt and then Dunne required treatment before Shaw moved smartly across to clear after Law had set up a shooting opportunity for Kidd. Parkes dived to save a well-struck effort from McIlroy and Stepney then had to smother a Curran shot after the Scot had cut in from the right. After Wolves' first-half domination, the game was a lot more open now and both keepers were called upon to make splendid saves with Parkes deflecting a Charlton shot over the bar with his foot as he fell in the opposite direction, and Stepney getting a hand to a Richards hooked half-volley that seemed destined for the back of the net.

Fifteen minutes from time Jim McCalliog put the issue beyond doubt when he beat Stepney from the spot after Dunne was adjudged to have fouled Curran. Parkes was tested by Charlton once more with the ball going behind for a corner off the keeper's heels and four minutes from time, United's persistence was finally rewarded when McIlroy took a pass from the World Cup winner and drove the ball home.

There was no doubt that Wolves were worthy winners of the contest as they maintained their sixth place in the First Division table. The defeat was the second of seven in succession suffered by United which effectively ended their title challenge.

United: Stepney, Dunne, Burns, Gowling (Sartori), Edwards, Sadler, Morgan, Kidd, Charlton, Law, McIlroy.
Wolves: Parkes, Shaw, Parkin, Bailey, Munro, McAlle, McCalliog, Hibbitt, Richards, Dougan (Curran), Wagstaffe.
Attendance: 46,781.
Referee: H Davey.

60

Wolves 2 (Munro, Dougan)
Leeds United 1 (Bremner)
Football League First Division
Monday 8th May 1972

JUST 50 hours after he collected the FA Cup from Her Majesty The Queen at Wembley, Billy Bremner led the Leeds team out at Molineux knowing that a draw with Wolves would be sufficient to give the Yorkshire side the double. United's involvement in the FA Cup and Wolves' in the Uefa Cup meant that the game was played after most teams had packed their bags for the summer holidays.

Brian Clough's Derby County, their campaign over, headed the First Division on 58 points while Leeds and Liverpool were both just a point and two points adrift respectively, and both with better goal averages than the Rams. On the same Monday evening, Arsenal, the beaten finalists at Wembley, faced Liverpool at Highbury with the Merseysiders hoping that Leeds would slip up and that a victory over the Gunners would see them steal in and take the title honours.

Despite the close proximity of the Wembley euphoria, Leeds were still odds-on to make light of a Wolves team who had failed to register a point in five consecutive home league games and had also lost the first leg of the Uefa Cup Final at Molineux. Ignoring recent form, manager Bill McGarry kept faith with the 11 who had lost in the league to Sheffield United and to Spurs in the first all-English European final.

Leeds boss Don Revie had to make one change from his Wembley team. Mick Jones was out after suffering a dislocated elbow on the big day. Revie decided to play Bremner as a centre-forward and Mick Bates in midfield. Although Bremner did get on the scoresheet, Revie's move was doomed to failure as Frank Munro, at the heart of the home defence, kept a firm check on the fiery Scot.

Rumours were rife around the town that members of the Wolves playing staff had been offered bribes to throw the game and, when one of his men reported this to McGarry, he gave a warning to his squad after calling them together in the centre circle at the Castlecroft training ground following the morning-of-the-game session. He told the players that if he ever heard of any of them taking a bribe, then they would never play for the club again.

Unsurprisingly, Molineux was packed to capacity for the clash and the first opening fell to Bremner who slipped as he attempted an overhead kick. Leeds' appeals for a penalty after Phil Parkes had collided with Allan Clarke in the home box were more out of hope than conviction. However, the visitors did seem to have a justifiable case in the 25th minute as they continued to control the attacking play.

After Bremner's shot was blocked, the ball ran to Clarke whose cross appeared to be handled by full-back Bernard Shaw. It looked to be an obvious penalty but to the relief of the home fans and astonishment of the Leeds players, the whistle didn't sound and play continued. Shortly afterwards, Parkes had to dive full length to save a powerful drive from Peter Lorimer.

After absorbing pressure for most of the half, Wolves moved ahead two minutes before the break. Dave Wagstaffe laid a corner back into the path of Shaw whose attempt at a shot skewed through the area. Johnny Giles sliced an attempted clearance straight to Munro and he steered the ball between the near post and Paul Reaney who was stationed on the line.

Despite the setback, Leeds were immediately back on the offensive once the second period commenced and a Lorimer free kick caused much consternation for the home defence before the ball was scrambled away. Twice Parkes had to save shots from Clarke and the keeper also did well to keep out an effort from Giles. But it wasn't all Leeds attack and David Harvey was called into action to deny Kenny Hibbitt.

He was beaten, though, after 67 minutes, when Danny Hegan's accurate pass, from deep inside his own half, picked out John Richards. He spotted fellow striker Derek Dougan to his right and found him with a brilliantly-timed flick. Harvey had left his line but Dougan took aim and rolled the ball past the Scot and into the middle of the goal from 15 yards.

Revie immediately withdrew the struggling Clarke, replacing him with Terry Yorath and pushing Bremner and big Jackie Charlton forward. The tactic had an instant reward after Giles had found Paul Madeley on the left. His cross was met by Bremner who rocketed a first-time volley into the roof of the net.

United abandoned any thoughts of defence and they nearly paid the price when Richards lobbed the ball against the bar from just inside the box and then Wagstaffe's shot was headed off the line by Madeley. Leeds, though, had nothing to lose by this stage and they were almost rewarded in the dying seconds when Charlton pushed over a cross to Yorath and his header drifted over Parkes.

Gerry Taylor was the man who broke Leeds' hearts as he popped up to head clear off the line. Moments later the final whistle blew and the dejected United players trooped from the pitch with their dream of a double gone.

Liverpool had been held to a goalless draw by Arsenal so the title was Derby's. Triumphant Rams manager Clough said: "It is incredible. I do not believe in miracles, but one has occurred tonight. I believe they played four-and-a-half minutes of injury time at Molineux – it seemed like four-and-a-half years to me."

Wolves: Parkes, Shaw, Taylor, Hegan, Munro, McAlle, McCalliog, Hibbitt, Richards, Dougan, Wagstaffe.
Unused sub: Bailey.
Leeds: Harvey, Reaney, Madeley, Bremner, Charlton, Hunter, Lorimer, Clarke (Yorath), Bates, Giles, Gray.
Attendance: 53,379.
Referee: WJ Gow.

Wolves 1 (McCalliog)
Tottenham Hotspur 2 (Chivers 2)
Uefa Cup Final first leg
Wednesday 3rd May 1972

Tottenham Hotspur 1 (Mullery)
Wolves 1 (Wagstaffe)
Uefa Cup Final second leg
Wednesday 17th May 1972

AFTER THEIR exploits against continental opposition in the 1950s and early 1960s, it wasn't until 1972 that Wolves at last made it through to the final of a major European competition. However, having beaten some of the best in getting through to what was the first all-English major European trophy final, Wanderers fell at the last hurdle against Tottenham Hotspur.

The path in reaching the two-legged final stages involved five home and away ties against some of the finest clubs in Europe. It all began with a home game against Portugal's student team, Academica Coimbra. Wolves' first goal in the competition was claimed by John McAlle in the 28th minute with a close-range finish after a Dave Wagstaffe corner. McAlle had opened his account for the club a week earlier in a League Cup tie at Manchester City.

The Portuguese seemed content to try to restrict Wolves' score with the apparent aim of leaving themselves an achievable target in the return leg. Their task was made all the more difficult when John Richards scored with a 61st-minute cross-shot before Derek Dougan wrapped things up nine minutes from the end when he ran on to a through pass before slamming the ball home. The Academica players protested long and hard that the Irishman was offside but the referee ignored their appeals.

The return game wasn't a pretty spectacle as Wolves cruised through to the second round. Manuel Antonio scored what was to be Academica's only goal of the tie with a shot that went in off the post. It took Dougan just eight minutes to level matters when the bounce of Phil Parkes's clearance deceived two defenders and left the striker with just the keeper to beat which he did with ease.

Six minutes after the break, Danny Hegan was sent off for retaliation after he had clearly been kicked by Victor Campos. A monotonous offside trap and some x-rated tackling were the tactics adopted by Academica but they failed in their task as McAlle volleyed home a cross-shot for his third goal in three weeks. In 508 appearances for Wolves, they were his only goals. Dougan went on to complete his hat-trick by heading in a Wagstaffe cross on 71 minutes and then driving home a Parkes clearance in the dying seconds to give Wanderers a 7-1 aggregate win.

An identical score saw Wolves through to the third round after they had met the Dutch side ADO Den Haag. An excellent first-half display by Parkes had kept his side in the game in the opening leg in Holland. Wolves moved ahead on the hour

Wolves' Greatest Games

when Kees Weimar failed to control a loose ball and was made to pay by Dougan who raced in and found the net. Despite struggling with a leg injury, Jim McCalliog got the second after 76 minutes when he was set up by Richards, and Dougan opened the way for Kenny Hibbitt to grab a third eight minutes from time. Seconds later, Bernard Shaw handled in the box and Harry Hestad converted the spot-kick.

The second leg contained a unique hat-trick of own goals. After seven minutes Dougan opened the scoring having taken a pass from Hugh Curran. Four minutes after the break, Weimar headed a Curran cross into his own net and further Dutch calamities saw Aad Mansveld slicing a Dougan cross past his own keeper and then Theo Van Den Burch chested McCalliog's centre into his own goal.

The third round draw provided a stiffer test in the form of East German amateurs Carl Zeiss Jena. The small crowd in Jena was mainly comprised of army personnel who watched in near silence in the freezing conditions. The game was decided in the 12th minute when Richards headed a McCalliog cross towards goal. German keeper Hans-Ulrich Grapenthin managed to knock the ball away but only as far as Richards who tucked the rebound away.

The second leg was something of a stroll as an early goal took the sting out of the Germans. Dougan headed down Derek Parkin's floated cross to Hibbitt who smashed the ball home after eight minutes. Ten minutes before the break, Dougan glanced home a header from Hibbitt's corner, and the lanky striker then became Wolves' highest scorer in European competition when he took advantage of a half-clearance to shoot past Grapenthin.

The quarter-final opposition couldn't have been much more of a test, the mighty Juventus. Yet playing against such a powerful side seemed to bring the best out of Wolves. Pietro Anastasi opened the scoring in front of a partisan crowd in Turin after Giuseppe Furino's cross was deflected to him off a defender after 37 minutes. Wanderers fully deserved the equaliser that came their way midway through the second half. Dougan's header was cleared by Furino but only as far as McCalliog who hammered a right-footed shot home from 20 yards. Manager Bill McGarry was sent to the stands shortly afterwards for coaching from the touchline.

Wolves dominated the first half of the return and they should have been ahead before Hegan's delightful lob from 25 yards found the net six minutes before the interval. And six minutes after the break Dougan headed in from a Wagstaffe corner to put Wolves 3-1 up on aggregate. There were a few nervy moments after West German World Cup star Helmut Haller scored from the spot after Munro had handled five minutes from time, but the Molineux men held on to record a notable triumph.

The semi-final draw paired Wolves with the Hungarians of Ferencvaros. Goalkeeper Parkes proved to be the hero of the hour in both games. The crowd that attended the first leg in Budapest's NEP Stadium watched the two teams share four goals and for the opening 25 minutes, during which time they took the lead, Wolves were the better side. Eighteen minutes had gone when McAlle pumped a long ball through to Dougan who back-heeled into the path of Richards. The striker wheeled

v Tottenham Hotspur, 1972

into the area before shooting past home keeper Bela Voros for his first goal in ten games.

Two goals in a four-minute spell, however, gave Ferencvaros an interval advantage. Shaw conceded a penalty when he needlessly handled and Istvan Szoke drilled the kick past Parkes. Then Szoke provided the centre from which Florian Albert side-footed home. There was a big danger of things slipping away in the 74th minute when Shaw again handled in the box, this time to keep out a Laszlo Balint header. Parkes earned himself a few slaps on the back from his colleagues as he stuck out a leg to deflect away Szoke's kick. Five minutes later, Munro scrambled the ball home from Wagstaffe's corner to earn parity on the night.

For the return, with Wagstaffe and Shaw suspended, Alan Sunderland played at full-back and Steve Daley wide on the left. It took the duo just 25 seconds to put Wolves ahead as, from Sunderland's deep cross, Voros could only palm the ball down to Daley who guided it home with the outside of his right foot. Ferencvaros hit back hard and after Albert had a goal ruled out for offside, Parkes had to turn a fierce drive from Laszlo Branikovits onto the bar.

Just before the interval, Munro made it two as his header from a McCalliog cross was helped into the net by Voros. However, when Lajos Ku scored with an angled shot a minute into the second period, it was very much a case of all to play for. After Shaw's double handling offences in the first leg, this time it was his replacement Sunderland who handled to give Szoke the chance of levelling the tie with around 20 minutes remaining. Again he shot to Parkes's right, and again the keeper stuck out his left leg to save the day. The Hungarians threw themselves forward in the hope of getting an equaliser that would have taken the game into extra time, but it was Dougan who came nearest to scoring when he fired against the bar.

Spurs beat AC Milan on aggregate in the other semi-final to set up the all-English clash with the first leg played at Molineux. Wolves dominated the game and yet they lost out to a double from England centre-forward Martin Chivers. The opening 45 minutes was decidedly scrappy with most of the action taking place in midfield. The game was refereed by Russian Tofik Bakhramov who, as a linesman, was the official who signalled that Geoff Hurst's shot that hit the underside of the crossbar and bounced down had, indeed, crossed the line in the 1966 World Cup final. His main duty in the first half at Molineux were to caution Shaw and Joe Kinnear for fouls on Ralph Coates and Wagstaffe respectively.

Nine minutes after the break, Cyril Knowles deflected a Richards shot off the line and from the corner conceded, Hibbitt's rising drive was also cleared, this time by Phil Beal, with Pat Jennings beaten. Jennings then had to save from Beal who almost headed into his own net. Against the run of play, after 56 minutes, Spurs took the lead when Mike England's deep free kick caught Parkes in two minds and Chivers headed past the stranded keeper.

Wolves equalised ten minutes later after Alan Mullery was penalised for handling on the edge of his area. While he was arguing, and with the Spurs defence in disarray, Hegan quickly pushed the free kick to McCalliog who fired through a defender's legs

Wolves' Greatest Games

and into the net off Jennings. It was all Wolves and after Jennings dived full length to prevent a John Pratt own goal, Dougan struck a shot that flew narrowly wide. Three minutes from time, though, Chivers ruined the party when he cut in from the left and unleashed a 25-yard piledriver that rocketed into the net.

Spurs took their advantage to 3-1 after 29 minutes of the second leg when Mullery knocked himself out as he headed a Martin Peters cross past Parkes. However, the goal seemed to inspire Wolves and ten minutes before the break, Wagstaffe scored what was regarded by many as the goal of the season – a left-footed drive from the edge of the box that flew into the top-right corner. Try as they might, Wolves just couldn't conjure up the equaliser they deserved. Jennings tipped a Dougan header over and he could only block a Richards shot with Kinnear on hand to clear.

As the Spurs team paraded the trophy at the end, the dejected Wolves players were doubtless pondering that justice hadn't been done. McGarry said: "Spurs won this match up at Molineux, but I still can't work out how you can be the best side in both games and still lose."

As if to confirm the point, Spurs boss Bill Nicolson added: "You've got to give Wolves a lot of credit. We never really had control of this match." However, the one thing Spurs did have was the cup.

First leg
Wolves: Parkes, Shaw, Taylor, Hegan, Munro, McAlle, McCalliog, Hibbitt, Richards, Dougan, Wagstaffe.
Unused subs: Parkin, Arnold, Daley, Curran, Eastoe.
Spurs: Jennings, Kinnear, Knowles, Mullery, England, Beal, Gilzean, Perryman, Chivers, Peters, Coates.
Unused subs: Evans, Daines, Naylor, Pratt, Pearce.
Attendance: 38,362.
Referee: T Bakhramov (Soviet Union).

Second leg
Spurs: Jennings, Kinnear, Knowles, Mullery, England, Beal, Gilzean, Perryman, Chivers, Peters, Coates.
Unused subs: Evans, Daines, Naylor, Pratt, Pearce.
Wolves: Parkes, Shaw, Taylor, Hegan, Munro, McAlle, McCalliog, Hibbitt (Bailey), Richards, Dougan (Curran), Wagstaffe.
Unused subs: Parkin, Arnold, Daley.
Attendance: 54,303.
Referee: L Van Ravens (Netherlands).

Wolves 5 (Richards 3, Dougan, Hegan)
Stoke City 3 (Hurst penalty, Greenhoff, Bloor)

Football League First Division
Saturday 30th September 1972

A HAUL of 33 league goals in the 1971/72 campaign had boosted John Richards's chances of a full England call-up. Richards was the darling of the terraces at Molineux and the supporters that had watched him terrorise the finest of defences in the First Division, were in no doubt that their man deserved to be wearing a shirt with the three lions replacing the leaping wolf on his domestic attire.

The opening weeks of the 1972/73 season saw him making a prolific start to league matters and he scored seven times in the first ten games along with another three in League Cup and Texaco Cup ties. Following the visit of Stoke City to Molineux for a Staffordshire derby, the hat-trick that he scored against the Potters took him to an average of just one short of a goal a game.

City arrived having endured an unspectacular beginning that year with just seven points from ten games leaving them sitting only a point off bottom place whereas Wolves lay in fifth place just two points off the top.

Bill McGarry made two changes to his line-up following a midweek goalless draw at Kilmarnock in the Texaco Cup – Frank Munro came back in for Brian Owen at centre-half, and Dave Wagstaffe replaced Steve Kindon on the left wing with the former Burnley man named as substitute.

Leading Stoke's attack was World Cup hero Geoff Hurst, who was still only 30 years old and capable of inflicting damage to the opposition as Wolves soon found out on that Saturday afternoon. Just three minutes had gone when Bernard Shaw found himself adjacent to his own penalty area. The left-back under-hit his pass to goalkeeper Phil Parkes and Hurst nipped in to intercept.

The former West Ham man was just two or three yards from goal when Shaw, in trying to atone for his lapse, felled him for a blatant penalty. Pretty lethal in open play, Hurst had a reputation for being one of the best spot-kick takers around as he used a mixture of power and accuracy and it proved to be no exception to the rule when he blasted the ball past Parkes.

The goal only served to wake Wolves and it took just ten minutes for them to draw level after a goal that was engineered by the enigmatic Danny Hegan. He put Kenny Hibbitt in possession on the right and then sprinted forwards to take a return pass. Hegan then looked up and squared an accurate pass that fell invitingly for Richards to slam the ball past City goalkeeper John Farmer.

Shortly afterwards the home fans were howling for a penalty for their own team after a powerful shot from Wagstaffe had been punched out by Farmer. As Richards tore in to latch on to the loose ball, he went down under a challenge but the referee ignored the protests of both players and supporters.

Wolves' Greatest Games

However, his decision only delayed the inevitable because Wolves, by now, had built up such a head of steam that a second goal had to come and it duly arrived with the half at its midway point. Munro took the ball to the byline to the right of the Stoke goal and his short cross fell to Derek Dougan who casually flicked it into the net with the outside of his foot.

Just a minute later, Stoke were back on level terms after a well-constructed counter attack involving John Mahoney and Terry Conroy whose cross to the far post was punched out by Parkes. But the ball dropped for Jimmy Robertson to set up a chance for Jimmy Greenhoff that wasn't wasted.

Just before the interval both goals had lucky escapes. Farmer had to tip over a rising drive from Mike Bailey and from the corner conceded Alan Bloor cleared Dougan's header off the line. Then Hurst broke free down the middle drawing Parkes from his line before lobbing the ball over the keeper and against the face of the crossbar from where it was scrambled clear.

The second period opened with a Hegan drive that swerved a yard wide, and a tremendous save from Farmer who somehow kept out a Dougan header after a cross from Wagstaffe. After 66 minutes, Wolves did get a third goal. The build-up was classic and the execution, by Richards, ruthless.

Munro, who was having a fine game in defence, lifted a pass from the centre circle to the left wing into the path of Wagstaffe who sent John Marsh the wrong way with a cut inside the defender before setting up Richards who ran on for two or three paces before drilling a low shot past Farmer.

Stoke wouldn't lie down and die and they levelled once more with 15 minutes remaining as Alan Bloor forced the ball home after Greenhoff lifted a free kick into the area. Back came Wolves and on 82 minutes Hegan just beat Farmer in a chase to Wagstaffe's through ball before flicking the ball into the net in front of the North Bank.

In the last minute Richards completed his treble when he intercepted Micky Pejic's back-pass and slid the ball under Farmer. Richards did finally win an England cap eight months later and although he played a part in the build-up of both England goals in a 2-1 victory over Northern Ireland at Goodison Park, playing in an unfamiliar midfield role, it turned out to be his only full honour for his country.

Wolves: Parkes, Shaw, Taylor, Bailey, Munro, McAlle, Hegan, Hibbitt, Richards, Dougan, Wagstaffe.
Unused sub: Kindon.
Stoke: Farmer, Marsh, Pejic, Skeels, Smith, Bloor, Robertson, Greenhoff, Hurst, Mahoney, Conroy.
Unused sub: Jump.
Attendance: 24,133.
Referee: P Walters.

Wolves 2 (Richards, Hibbitt penalty)
Coventry City 0
FA Cup quarter-final
Saturday 17th March 1973

IN THE two mid-1960s seasons that Wolves spent in the Second Division, Coventry City became something of a bogey side both at Molineux and at Highfield Road. The Sky Blues won all four encounters between the teams and it wasn't until after the two were promoted together in 1967 that Wolves finally enjoyed some success against their Midland rivals.

Games between the clubs were always keenly contested and when they were drawn together in the sixth round of the FA Cup, the tie drew a 50,000 crowd that paid record receipts to watch the contest. There was drama before the proceedings had even kicked off. Terrace idol Derek Dougan was warming up when he caught the full force of a Steve Kindon shot on the back of the head.

Kindon, who had been named as substitute for the game, packed one of the hardest shots in the game and The Doog was, for want of a better phrase, 'out of it' as he slumped to the floor. Trainer Sammy Chung raced on to administer treatment while manager Bill McGarry made an earlier than planned trip from his seat in the stands to the pitch to assess the damage to his player while poor Kindon looked a worried man as he sat on the bench, head bowed.

However, all was well that ended well and Dougan regained his feet and took his place as the game began before playing a major role in Wolves taking the lead after just seven minutes. Attacking the South Bank end, the home team had started in determined fashion and their early pressure was rewarded when Frank Munro headed the ball into the City half where it was nodded on by Dougan with uncanny precision in front of John Richards, who beat Bobby Parker for speed before shooting low past Bill Glazier.

In their next attack, Jim McCalliog suddenly pulled up with what looked like a thigh injury. He tried, without success, to run it off and was replaced by Kindon after 13 minutes. The setback didn't really knock Wolves out of their stride and although Willie Carr was an influential figure in midfield for the Sky Blues, the home back-line were standing firm. Coventry's defence, on the other hand, looked to be panic-stricken whenever Wolves pushed forward.

Kenny Hibbitt rolled a free kick to Gerry Taylor whose drive was powerful enough but too close to Glazier, who then was fortunate to survive after Hibbitt himself had a goal attempt. The midfielder hit a tremendous shot from 20 yards that the keeper stopped but failed to control. As the ball ran loose it looked like Richards was about to get his second goal but Parker got back just in time to clear for a corner.

A long clearance from Phil Parkes skidded off a defender's head and dropped nicely for Dougan whose long-range dipping volley was a yard too high. Dougan,

Wolves' Greatest Games

showing no signs of problems from his earlier misfortune, found the net in the 34th minute when he headed in after a Hibbitt corner. However, the score was ruled out after the referee spotted an apparent push although no-one was quite sure who the culprit was.

It wasn't until five minutes before the break that the Wolves goal finally came under any kind of real threat. Tom Hutchison crossed from the left and the ball looked destined for the head of Colin Stein until Taylor nipped in to intercept and head behind. The corner was cleared and the final chance of the half fell to Brian Alderson who was well wide from 20 yards.

Wolves deserved a second goal and it came from the spot four minutes after the restart. Richards raced into the box and he was sandwiched between Mick Coop and Chris Cattlin for a clear foul. The referee didn't hesitate as he pointed to the spot and Hibbitt had little difficulty in beating Glazier.

City substitute Mick McGuire almost halved the deficit with a fine shot that flew inches wide of the post, but generally speaking the game had lost a lot of its zip as Wanderers seemed content to sit on their lead with the visitors rarely making any threatening overtures. Indeed Richards was the victim of a marginal offside decision as he beat Glazier at the midway point of the half.

Glazier's next action saw him saving a low shot from Derek Parkin and then, 15 minutes from time, Hibbitt played Dougan through on goal. With the City defence AWOL, the Ulsterman drew Glazier from his line and slipped the ball past him only to watch it roll agonisingly wide of the post. Richards, who had been at his best in the game, somewhat blotted his copybook when he volleyed over the bar from just six yards out with only Glazier to beat.

But in the end, the better team had won and earned the right to face Leeds United in the semi-final. The Coventry result meant that all four of Wolves' cup ties that year had taken place at Molineux and not a goal had been conceded with the games against Manchester United, Bristol City and Millwall all ending 1-0 before the visit of Coventry. The only goal conceded in that year's campaign fell to Billy Bremner as Wolves lost out to Leeds at Maine Road in a game where they deserved at least the chance of a replay.

Wolves: Parkes, Taylor, Parkin, Shaw, Munro, McAlle, McCalliog (Kindon), Hibbitt, Richards, Dougan, Wagstaffe.
City: Glazier, Coop, Cattlin, Smith (McGuire), Barry, Parker, Mortimer, Alderson, Stein, Carr, Hutchison.
Attendance: 50,106.
Referee: J Homewood.

64

Arsenal 1 (Hornsby)
Wolves 3 (McCalliog, Dougan 2)
FA Cup third-place play-off
Saturday 18th August 1973

IN MARCH 1970, Manchester United and Watford, that year's losing FA Cup semi-finalists, met at Highbury, in a newly devised fixture to determine third place in the competition. United won 2-0 and the following year, Stoke beat Everton 3-2 in front of just over 5,000 spectators at Selhurst Park in another end-of-season affair. The powers that be then decided to make the fixture a pre-season game with one of the clubs involved hosting the game. In 1972, Birmingham prevailed in a penalty shoot-out after a goalless draw with Stoke at St Andrew's with a much healthier attendance of over 25,000.

The winter of 1973 had been a bittersweet one for Wolves who finished in a creditable fifth position in the First Division but suffered the heartbreak of twice missing out on a trip to Wembley after losing to a goal in the last minute of extra time to Spurs in the two-legged League Cup semi-final, and an unlucky single-goal defeat against Leeds United at Maine Road in the FA Cup.

With Arsenal, somewhat surprisingly, losing to Second Division side Sunderland at the same stage of the competition, it meant that the Gunners and Wolves were earmarked for an August showdown at Highbury for a game that, if nothing else, would have provided both sides with a useful workout before the league campaign that began the following week.

Arsenal were suffering from injury and suspension problems and were missing regulars Pat Rice, Charlie George, Peter Storey, George Armstrong and Eddie Kelly, and manager Bertie Mee brought in teenagers Brian Hornsby, Brendon Batson and David Price. Bill McGarry, on the other hand, was able to field one of his strongest sides for the game which was played in baking sunshine.

The early chances went to the home side and, in particular, to Hornsby. Brian Chambers sent John Radford on a run down the right flank and Hornby met his cross with a first time shot that was brilliantly saved by Phil Parkes who turned the ball around the post.

Hornby was even closer after he had controlled a pass from Ray Kennedy and hit a low shot on the turn that hit the base of the post. Wolves' first chance went the way of Derek Dougan but, with only Bob Wilson to beat, the striker's shot lacked power, allowing the keeper to dive and save.

Dougan had justifiable appeals for a penalty rejected when he appeared to be shoved in the back by a defender but the referee, for some reason, gave an indirect free kick. Jim McCalliog touched the ball to Dave Wagstaffe who hit a fierce shot that had Wilson athletically saving at the expense of a corner. A quick throw-in by Wagstaffe led to Wolves moving ahead in the 16th minute. McCalliog took possession and after he had dummied his way past Price, he cut in and beat Wilson at the near post with a low, right-foot drive.

Kennedy headed wide after a Batson cross but the home defence were all at sea after some skilful work by Dougan who set up Richards. He drew Wilson from his line and pushed the ball past him as he advanced but his effort rolled agonisingly wide of the gaping net. However, a second goal wasn't far away and it arrived ten minutes before the interval. Danny Hegan and Derek Parkin combined in midfield before the full-back laid a perfect long through ball into the path of Dougan who hit a tremendous shot into the roof of the net with his right foot.

Alan Ball, with his infectious enthusiasm, was doing his best to motivate the youngsters in the Arsenal side but they looked demoralised in the August sun after the two strikes from Wanderers. However, the Gunners did pull one back five minutes after the break after two probing raids by Richards had come to nothing. Derek Jefferson failed to deal with a bouncing ball and Hornsby nipped in to slot his effort past the advancing Parkes and into the corner of the net.

The goal seemed to finally liven up the Arsenal attack and Parkes twice in the space of a minute kept out shots that could easily have levelled matters. First he turned a 20-yard drive from Radford over the bar and then, after the corner had been played back to Price on the edge of the area, the midfielder ran in and cracked a shot that drew another excellent save from the keeper.

Wolves, with an hour gone, regained their two-goal advantage with Dougan collecting his second of the contest. John Richards crossed from the right and when McCalliog's shot was blocked by Peter Simpson, the ball spun in front of Batson who was unable to control it to gift Dougan a chance that he didn't spurn as he converted from close in.

Hornsby, who was Arsenal's best player on what was his debut, threaded a pass through which left Radford in the clear but Parkes had spotted the danger and claimed the ball at the striker's feet. However, that was to be the last worthwhile chance for the Londoners as Wolves held out quite comfortably for the win. The third-place play-off lasted for just one more season, with Burnley beating Leicester at Filbert Street in front of another small crowd, before the format was scrapped.

Arsenal: Wilson, Batson, McNab, Price, Blockley, Simpson, Chambers, Ball, Radford, Kennedy, Hornsby.
Unused sub: Powling.
Wolves: Parkes, Palmer, Parkin, Hegan, Jefferson, Taylor, McCalliog, Sunderland, Richards, Dougan (Hibbitt), Wagstaffe.
Attendance: 21,033.
Referee: J Hunting.

Manchester City 1 (Bell)
Wolves 2 (Hibbitt, Richards)
League Cup Final
Wembley
Saturday 2nd March 1974

THE SPARTAN surroundings of the Shay Stadium must have seemed a million miles away from the illustrious trappings of Wembley when Wolves travelled to meet Halifax Town on a Monday evening in October 1973 for a League Cup second round tie. After the previous season's double despair as Wolves lost out in the semi-final stage of both the FA Cup and the League Cup, the Molineux faithful must have thought the chance of a trip to the twin towers was to remain on the wish list.

Yet not only were Wanderers destined to lift the trophy, but they also beat one of the top clubs in the country in one of the most entertaining finals for many a year. But on that murky Monday evening in Yorkshire it took the experience of Derek Dougan to soothe the nerves as Halifax, watched by 8,222, their highest crowd in two years, were piling on the pressure looking to cancel out Alan Sunderland's 36th-minute opener for Wolves after he beat the offside trap and lobbed the keeper from 20 yards.

Town had already spurned the chance of levelling six minutes after the break when one-time Molineux reserve Fred Kemp fired wide with a penalty. There was 20 minutes left when Dougan moved on to a cross from substitute Steve Daley and coolly hit a left-footed drive into the bottom corner of the net. In the 82nd minute John Richards wrapped things up with a close-range finish.

Next came another away draw, this time against a Tranmere side who had beaten Arsenal at Highbury in the second round of the competition. Rovers moved into a 31st-minute lead through Eddie Loyden who headed past Phil Parkes after a corner from Russell Allen, the son of former Molineux manager Ronnie. Sunderland levelled matters four minutes before the break when he took a Dougan pass in his stride and ran for 15 yards before beating home keeper Dick Johnson.

Bill McGarry's men had to fight hard for the right to a replay and they didn't have things all their own way at Molineux after Dougan had opened the scoring in the 53rd minute. Allen equalised 20 minutes later, moments before a partial floodlight failure. The referee allowed play to continue and full power was restored shortly before Barry Powell's 86th-minute winner to give Wolves a home tie against Exeter City.

The game against the Fourth Division side was played on a midweek afternoon because of the power crisis that was a result of the miners' strike. The attendance of 7,623 was the lowest since the war and those that couldn't make the game missed Wolves strolling through to the last eight of the cup following a 5-1 win. Kenny Hibbitt, with a shot from eight yards, opened the scoring a minute before the break.

Wolves' Greatest Games

Dougan made it two, hitting an angled drive under the body of Exeter keeper Allen Clarke in the 65th minute, before a minute later, Dick Plumb headed in Brian Joy's free kick to halve the deficit. Three goals in the final 17 minutes confirmed Wolves' dominance with the first going to Richards who cleverly flicked Mike Bailey's pass home off the inside of the post. Hibbitt got his second of the game when he converted Powell's cross and Richards finished things off with a sharp header from Hibbitt's corner.

The quarter-final was again at Molineux and again played on a midweek afternoon albeit against much tougher opposition – Liverpool. The only goal of the game came two minutes after the break when Richards intercepted Tommy Smith's intended pass to Larry Lloyd, and homed in on goal before driving the ball into the roof of the net past the advancing Ray Clemence.

Now just Norwich City stood between Wanderers and a place at Wembley. The first leg, at Carrow Road, was a tense, tight affair with the first goal going in favour of the Canaries through Ian Mellor who fired a low shot from 25 yards past Parkes. The equaliser came 12 minutes from the end when Bailey pushed forward and, from 30 yards, unleashed a shot that Kevin Keelan in the home goal was unable to hold allowing Richards to hammer the loose ball high into the net. In the final minute Dave Stringer had to clear a long-range lob from Geoff Palmer off the line after the defender had spotted Keelan off his line.

The only goal of the second leg came in the 48th minute on a murky, wet Saturday afternoon and it was Richards, with his 18th goal of the season, who did the trick. Dougan flicked a long through ball on to his strike partner and Richards beat Stringer before hitting a powerful right-footed cross-shot past Keelan. At the end, even the normally reserved McGarry ran back out and punched the air in front of a delirious North Bank. After 14 years, Wolves were back at Wembley, to face Manchester City.

Parkes, after playing in every round, unluckily missed out on the final after damaging ankle ligaments in training just two days after the semi-final victory over Norwich. Sceptics doubted that his replacement, Gary Pierce, would be able to hold his nerve in the white hot atmosphere of Wembley but his man-of-the-match performance, on what was his 23rd birthday, was instrumental in Wolves' success.

The teams took to the field in tracksuits, City's matching the springtime sky and Wanderers resplendent in black tops and gold trousers. Bailey won the toss and set his men to defend the end of the ground that was a sea of gold and black.

In the opening seconds the free kick awarded after Rodney Marsh's foul on Sunderland came to nothing and in City's first attack, Frank Munro robbed Marsh and got the ball back to give Pierce an early touch of the ball. Tommy Booth cleared a Palmer cross as Wolves settled into their task and Munro intervened after Colin Bell's neat pass found Francis Lee.

Sunderland almost gave his team the lead in the tenth minute with a fluke. Dougan headed Dave Wagstaffe's cross down to him and his shot struck a defender

v Manchester City, 1974

and was looping under the bar until Scottish keeper Keith McRae fell backwards and tipped the ball over the bar. From Wagstaffe's corner, Munro headed straight at the keeper.

From a Hibbitt corner Sunderland went as close as he could have to breaking through. This time it was Dougan who nodded the ball down to Sunderland whose shot took a deflection before striking the face of the far post and bouncing away to be cleared.

Bailey over-hit a through ball intended for Richards and when Bell tried to find Mike Summerbee deep inside the Wolves box, Derek Parkin was there to intercept and clear. Pierce had to make his first real save of the game when he dived to take a Summerbee header after Willie Donachie had fired in a free kick from the left.

Wolves were soon back on the attack and McRae had to punch clear a Sunderland cross before Bailey went on a run that saw him dispossessed as he was about to enter the City box. Summerbee reacted angrily to a John McAlle challenge a yard to the left of the Wolves area. From the free kick, taken by Summerbee, McAlle headed back to the City man whose second ball into the goalmouth saw Pierce palming clear with Munro booting the loose ball upfield.

Bailey figured again with a shot that went straight to McRae after Wagstaffe had gone on a 40-yard run before feeding his skipper. On the half-hour mark, Sunderland miskicked when he took a return pass from Richards. Parkin had to receive treatment after he had been caught by Summerbee, and at the same time Tony Towers was attended by the City trainer. Both players were soon able to resume.

Pierce turned a Marsh header round the post then Richards shot narrowly wide after he had been closed down by McRae. At the other end Lee's 30-yard drive swerved wide of the target. Just two minutes before the interval, Wolves moved ahead after a spectacular goal from Hibbitt. Sunderland, in the right-hand corner of the pitch, pushed the ball back for Palmer to cross and Hibbitt with a flying leap volleyed home. The midfielder later admitted that he had mishit the ball.

The second period began with Bailey clearing a Summerbee corner and, as City began to press forward, Towers shot high over the bar. Then Palmer had to clear off the line from Marsh and when the ball was returned into the box, Lee was only just too high with a header. With the game approaching the hour mark, City drew level. Marsh's route to goal looked to be blocked by Bailey and Palmer but he found the space to chip the ball over and when it fell to the unmarked Bell he had time to pick his spot before firing past Pierce.

The goal put some extra zest into City's attacking play and Pierce pulled off a fine save from Marsh who tried to side-foot the ball into the net after he had taken a low cross from Glyn Pardoe. Wolves were far from finished and Sunderland headed over a Wagstaffe centre and Mike Doyle cleared a Richards effort off the line although the referee had blown for a foul against the striker.

In the space of a minute, Pierce made two tremendous saves. He back-pedalled and turned over a chip from Lee and, from Summerbee's corner, the keeper threw himself through the air to push away Bell's header. He then cut out a low cross from

Wolves' Greatest Games

Summerbee before watching a Denis Law header go over following a Summerbee free kick.

Wagstaffe pushed the ball past Donachie but then pulled up with a muscle injury and while he was being treated Bell struck the bar with a rising drive. Powell replaced Wagstaffe but unknown to the crowd he had been warming up to replace Richards who was suffering from a pelvic injury. It was a sequence of events that proved highly beneficial to Wolves.

Towers headed behind a Hibbitt cross and when the Wolves man took the corner, Booth headed away as Munro jumped for the ball. It went out to Sunderland on the far side of the box. He pushed it back to Bailey who threaded the ball back to the young midfielder whose low cross clipped the heels of Marsh before running to Richards, who drove a low shot into the corner of the net from 12 yards.

The six minutes that remained must have seemed like an eternity to the fans behind McRae's goal and Booth, with a deflected header, and Lee with a low shot, went close to taking the game to a replay which would have been played at Stoke on the following Thursday.

Referee Dave Wallace's final whistle was the signal for members of the Wolves team to break down in tears of joy while manager McGarry ran straight to Pierce and warmly shook the keeper's hand after his match-winning performance.

City: McRae, Pardoe, Donachie, Doyle, Booth, Towers, Summerbee, Bell, Lee, Law, Marsh.
Unused sub: Carrodus.
Wolves: Pierce, Palmer, Parkin, Bailey, Munro, McAlle, Hibbitt, Sunderland, Richards, Dougan, Wagstaffe (Powell).
Attendance: 97,886.
Referee: E Wallace.

66 Wolves 4 (Hibbitt 4, one penalty)
Newcastle United 2 (Tudor 2)
Football League First Division
Saturday 24th August 1974

THE £5,000 that Ronnie Allen paid to Bradford Park Avenue for the services of Kenny Hibbitt in November 1968 must rate as one of the best bargain buys in the history of Wolves. The 17-year-old had played in just 15 league games for the Yorkshire club before his move south and he didn't get much time to get to know his new boss as Allen was dismissed just two days after the transfer.

Bill McGarry, Allen's successor, must have been a relieved man to name an unchanged side for the visit of Newcastle following the midweek goalless draw with Liverpool at Molineux as a sickness bug had swept through the club. The virus seemed to target the younger members of the playing staff and that morning's Midland Intermediate game against West Bromwich at Castlecroft had to be postponed with eight of the team laid low. McGarry himself had been forced to take a day off in the week but had recovered to oversee the fixture against the Geordies.

Like Wolves, the visitors had won one and drawn the other of their opening two games aand in their line-up was Kenny Hibbitt's brother, Terry. Wolves made all the early running but were shaken when Newcastle moved into the lead with seven minutes gone. Mick Burns beat Derek Parkin to the right of the home area before taking the ball to the byline and working his way in. He pushed the ball into the path of John Tudor who had little difficulty in beating Phil Parkes.

Wanderers were a whisker away from equalising four minutes later after Mike Bailey and Geoff Palmer combined to set up John Richards whose fierce drive was deflected into the side netting by a defender. A typical barnstorming run down the wing from Steve Kindon ended with a cross that Glenn Keeley had to head behind and from Hibbitt's corner Alan Sunderland failed to make a connection in the melee that followed.

Hibbitt restored parity in the 21st minute. Richards did the spade-work by laying off a perfect through ball which was lashed home by Hibbitt from just inside the area. And just four minutes later, after Irving Nattrass had felled Richards in the box, Hibbitt sent Iam McFaul the wrong way from the spot to give his side the lead. Wolves fully deserved the advantage and they went in search of more goals as they put the Newcastle defence under relentless pressure with England centre-forward Malcolm Macdonald scarcely getting a look-in.

Barry Powell was inches too high with a superb volley and Keeley bravely stuck his head in the way of a Sunderland shot, deflecting the ball away for another corner. Kindon was a constant torment to the Newcastle rearguard on the left wing with his power and pace. Bailey wasn't far off a third goal after he had worked an opening for himself but his effort went just the wrong side of the post. Then, with the referee

Wolves' Greatest Games

about to blow the whistle for the break, Newcastle almost grabbed an equaliser. Terry Hibbitt flighted a great through pass into the home area and Burns, who had joined United during the previous month, lobbed the ball over the advancing Parkes and over the bar.

The furious pace that the game was being played at was maintained at the start of the new half with Wolves, again, having the better of things. Richards was close when he turned and volleyed over after Powell had nodded the ball down to him. Revelling in his work, Richards then set up Sunderland but his shot lacked the power needed to beat McFaul who dived to save. In a rare Newcastle attack, Parkes had to race from his area to boot the ball upfield before Macdonald could take possession in what would have been a one on one situation.

But, just as Newcastle looked as if they were going to ease the initiative away from Wolves, Hibbitt struck again to complete his first hat-trick for the club. The game was 66 minutes old when he hit a low 20-yard shot that beat McFaul but came back off the base of the post. Sunderland pounced on the rebound but his attempt to force the ball home was thwarted by Keeley who booted clear. But, unfortunately for the defender, the ball only went as far as Hibbitt who this time made no mistake.

Kindon tested McFaul with a first-time shot after a run and cross from Sunderland, but with 15 minutes remaining, Tudor netted his, and his team's, second of the afternoon when he took a pass from Burns and found himself in the clear before placing the ball well wide of the isolated Parkes. And, just two minutes later, Terry Hibbitt's centre struck the top of the bar before bouncing to safety.

Newcastle were enjoying their best spell of the game and Macdonald should have equalised when he ran onto a through pass. Parkes ran way out of his area and although Macdonald ran past him he had been forced wide and his shot from an acute angle to the left of goal was wide of the target. It was left to the gold-and-black clad member of the Hibbitt clan to wind up proceedings three minutes from time when he cracked home a tremendous 20-yard shot that flashed past McFaul.

Hibbitt became the first Wolves man to hit four goals since Ted Farmer had achieved the feat against Manchester City 12 years earlier.

Wolves: Parkes, Palmer, Parkin, Bailey, Munro, McAlle, K Hibbitt, Powell, Richards, Sunderland, Kindon.
Unused sub: Daley.
Newcastle: McFaul, Nattrass (Craig), Kennedy, McDermott, Keeley, Howard, Burns, Smith, Macdonald, Tudor, T Hibbitt.
Attendance: 23,526.
Referee: R Tinkler.

Wolves 7 (Richards 2, Carr, Hibbitt, Bailey, Kindon, Wagstaffe)
Chelsea 1 (Garner)
Football League First Division
Saturday 15th March 1975

FEW DEBUTANTS could have enjoyed a game more than Willie Carr did following his £100,000 move across the Midlands from Coventry to Wolves two days before Wolves faced Chelsea at Molineux. The Scot had been brought in by Bill McGarry to spice up the midfield of a team who hadn't progressed following on from the League Cup success of the previous season.

McGarry had tried to sign Carr five months earlier with the fee then set at £230,000 only for the deal to fall through when he failed a medical with a knee problem. His form for the Sky Blues since then had been outstanding negating any doubts about his fitness and when financial problems at Highfield Road prompted his sale for less than half of the original price, the offer was too good to refuse.

Wolves went into the game on the back of successive 1-0 defeats – at home to Birmingham and away to Sheffield United – and were eight places off the bottom of the division, two points better off than Chelsea. Nigel Williams, sent off at Bramall Lane, was suspended and Geoff Palmer came in at right-back while Steve Daley was the man who forfeited his place to Carr.

Carr was involved in the first move of note in the game when he took a pass from John McAlle and pumped the ball downfield to Steve Kindon whose header into the box was cleared. However, by and large, play in the opening minutes was largely confined to midfield with the opening threat to the Chelsea goal being of their own making. John Hollins obviously didn't spot John Richards lurking behind him and his back-pass only just eluded the Wolves striker.

Kenny Hibbitt fired into the side netting after he had been set up by Carr, and he went close once more after taking a return pass from Richards and hitting a powerful drive inches wide. Chelsea were a whisker away from taking the lead in the 17th minute after John Sparrow's long throw was headed on by Steve Finnieston to Ian Britton who rattled the bar with a terrific overhead kick.

It was Wolves, through Richards, who went ahead in the 23rd minute following a fine move initiated by Carr, Kindon and Hibbitt. The ball was played out to Dave Wagstaffe and his cross was met by Kindon whose bullet header was brilliantly turned against the post by John Phillips. However, unfortunately for the Chelsea keeper, the loose ball rebounded to Richards and he made no mistake, blasting it home from close in.

Just two minutes later the score was doubled as Carr marked the occasion with a superb goal. Richards shielded the ball from John Dempsey deep in the Chelsea area before pushing it back to Kindon who, in turn, spotted Carr in open space. The Scot ran in and curled the ball beyond Phillips's dive from 20 yards out to

Wolves' Greatest Games

the delight of the crowd and his team-mates who immediately mobbed their new colleague.

There was a slight blot on Carr's copybook, however, as he conceded the foul on Gary Locke that led to Chelsea pulling one back in the 36th minute. Charlie Cooke's free kick into the box was headed in by Bill Garner who looked to push Frank Munro as he went for the ball. The goal stood but it just seemed to inspire Wolves to bigger and better things. It took them just four more minutes to regain their two-goal advantage.

The move was started and finished by Hibbitt who set Kindon off on a run down the right wing. His centre went behind Carr but Wagstaffe took possession and he held the ball up for a few seconds before slipping it to Hibbitt who beat Phillips from ten yards out. After the break, Finnieston missed a good chance of bringing his team back into contention when he rode two tackles before shooting over the bar.

It wasn't long though, before the home side resumed their assault on Phillips's goal. The keeper made another magnificent save, again to keep out a Kindon header that was arrowing towards the corner of the net, after a trademark cross from Wagstaffe. A fourth goal had to come and when it arrived, in the 58th minute, it proved well worth the wait as Richards's cross was met on the volley by Mike Bailey with the ball a blur as it flashed past Phillips. It was the skipper's first league goal in three-and-a-half years.

Richards had the chance of a fifth but his shot lacked the power to beat Phillips while Chelsea's chances were restricted to long-range efforts from Hollins and Ray Wilkins. The visiting defence were struggling every time that Wolves went on the attack and when Derek Parkin ventured upfield to support his forwards, he sent a cross-shot dipping narrowly over.

Two goals in a three-minute spell rammed home the superiority that Wolves were enjoying. The first saw Kindon finally breaking through with an unstoppable shot after one of his swashbuckling runs. Then the burly striker set up Richards who had little difficulty in converting his second of the match. It was left to Wagstaffe to wind up the scoring seven minutes from the end when he made a perfect connection to beat Phillips with a fierce drive. It was Wolves' biggest win since they beat Cardiff by the same score in 1966.

Wolves: Pierce, Palmer, Parkin, Bailey, Munro, McAlle, Hibbitt, Carr, Richards, Kindon, Wagstaffe.
Unused sub: Withe.
Chelsea: Phillips, Locke, Sparrow, Hollins, Dempsey (Kember), Harris, Britton, Wilkins, Finnieston, Garner, Cooke.
Attendance: 21,649.
Referee: G Kew.

68
Burnley 1 (Hankin)
Wolves 5 (Richards 2, Daley, Hibbitt 2)
Football League First Division
Saturday 15th November 1975

WOLVES MADE a drastic start to the season in 1975, winning just two of the opening 15 fixtures up to the start of November. A last-minute goal from Steve Daley against Ipswich Town at Molineux heralded a third triumph but Wanderers remained in the bottom three as they journeyed to Turf Moor to take on a Burnley side who were also struggling albeit just above the drop zone.

The midweek trip to Mansfield for a League Cup fourth round tie had seen Wolves at their worst and the struggling Third Division side progressed to the quarter-finals of the competition after a 1-0 win. Bill McGarry dropped Willie Carr and Alan Sunderland after the Field Mill debacle and brought in former Claret Steve Kindon and winger John Farley, naming Carr as a substitute.

On a dour, rain-swept Lancashire afternoon, it took Wolves just 15 seconds, a record fastest goal for the club, to open their account. Kindon slipped a pass to Farley on the left and he beat Michael Docherty before hitting a low, hard cross into the box. Burnley keeper Alan Stevenson could only push the ball out and John Richards, from the edge of the six-yard box, had the easiest of tasks in finding the net.

On the saturated surface, Kenny Hibbitt tried his luck with a skidding shot but this time Stevenson managed to keep hold of the ball. But the keeper was left helpless in the 12th minute as Daley made it two with a tremendous effort. He took possession from Farley's throw-in and brushed off Brian Flynn's challenge before launching a spectacular drive from 20 yards that flew into the net.

The humour of the home supporters was tested in the 19th minute after a Frank Munro challenge on Burnley's Welsh international winger Leighton James. The referee, who was not up with the play, pointed to the spot but, after protests from the visiting players, he was persuaded to consult his linesman who had taken up position for a corner. And, after a brief exchange between the pair, a corner was the decision.

Burnley finally threatened through Willie Morgan, whose centre was headed goalwards by Ray Hankin, forcing Gary Pierce to make a diving save. At the other end, Daley went close with a header after a cross from Mike Bailey as Wolves stepped it up again. After 24 minutes Hibbitt thought he had added a third goal after he had taken a pass from Richards just inside the Burnley half.

He ran to a point just outside the home area, with the Burnley defence in hot pursuit, before shooting past Stevenson. But no-one had heard the referee's whistle as Hibbitt was ruled to be just offside when he took Richards's pass.

Hankin was close with a header after a Doug Collins free kick and, as Wolves immediately hit back, Colin Waldron almost turned the ball into his own net as

Wolves' Greatest Games

he tried to clear for a corner. Wanderers had a second goal wiped out when Farley strayed marginally offside as he ran on to a Kindon pass before netting, but in the 43rd minute Richards screened the ball before laying it into the path of Hibbitt who cracked a left-footed drive past Stevenson – and this time it did count.

Three minutes into the second half, Burnley gave their fans a little hope by pulling a goal back. Pierce made a brilliant save as he turned Hankin's header over the bar. From James's corner Kindon headed out but only as far as Waldron and as he attempted to put the ball back into the middle, Kindon handled and the referee had no hesitation in pointing to the spot. Morgan took the penalty and struck the post but Hankin beat Pierce to the rebound and forced the ball home.

Just a minute later Hankin almost added to his tally but his shot flew a foot wide. Hibbitt, who had taken a knock in the first half, was replaced by Carr as the rain continued to fall. But Wolves didn't let the conditions hamper some play that belied their lowly league position and they went 4-1 up in the 59th minute as Daley scored his second of the afternoon. Richards began the move when he found Kindon unmarked on the left. He advanced before hitting a low cross that was side-footed home by Daley.

But Wolves weren't finished just yet and Richards notched a fifth in the 70th minute after a move instigated by Carr and Bailey, who passed for the centre-forward to drive a low shot home. Two minutes later Kindon's fierce shot beat Stevenson but a team-mate had strayed offside and for the third time in the afternoon, a Wolves score didn't count. The visitors were then forced to play the final three minutes with ten men after Munro hurt himself stretching in stopping Morgan from breaking through. Later that night, Molineux fans were able to watch highlights of the game on *Match of the Day*.

The win was one of four high-scoring victories that Wolves enjoyed that season having beaten Sheffield United 5-1 and 4-1, at home and away respectively, and Newcastle 5-0 at Molineux shortly before the season's end. But the wins weren't enough to stave off relegation with the team finishing three points short of the safety mark. It was enough to cost manager Bill McGarry his job after almost eight years in charge.

Burnley: Stevenson, Docherty (Casper), Newton, Flynn, Waldron, Thomson, Morgan, Summerbee, Hankin, Collins, James.
Wolves: Pierce, Palmer, Parkin, Bailey, Munro, McAlle, Hibbitt (Carr), Daley, Richards, Kindon, Farley.
Attendance: 14,559.
Referee: M Sinclair.

Wolves 3 (Richards 3)
Charlton Athletic 0
FA Cup fifth round
Saturday 14th February 1976

WOLVES' LEAGUE form in the 1975/76 season had been, to say the least, a mixture of disappointing and erratic. The first 15 games of the campaign had seen nine defeats and only two wins and, ultimately, the team didn't recover from such a poor start and come the following May it was to cost the club their place in the top flight and manager Bill McGarry, after almost eight seasons at Molineux, his job.

The main source of enjoyment for supporters was a healthy run in the FA Cup which began with a comfortable third round home victory over Arsenal who conceded three without reply. Then came a goalless draw against Ipswich at Portman Road with Bobby Gould grabbing the only goal of the game in the replay. The fifth round draw saw Wanderers at home once more, this time paired with Charlton Athletic.

Despite the poor league form that saw McGarry's side locked in the relegation zone along with Burnley and Sheffield United, Wolves were favourites to progress to the last eight against a Charlton team who were in the lower reaches of the Second Division. To reach the fifth round the Addicks had disposed of Sheffield Wednesday at The Valley and, after a replay at Fratton Park, Portsmouth.

McGarry made just one change to his starting line-up following a 4-2 reversal against Queens Park Rangers with Dave Wagstaffe making a return after five months out of the side, and John Richards being relegated to the substitute's bench. Richards had gone ten games without finding the back of the net but he was to have the perfect response for his manager.

Virtually straight from the start of the game Norman Bell got a shot away when he ran on to Willie Carr's centre but the striker's volley went high over the bar. Graham Tutt had to have his senses about him when Wagstaffe touched a free kick into the path of Frank Munro who, from 35 yards out, hit a drive that drew a fine save from the Charlton keeper.

From the corner conceded, taken by Wagstaffe, Munro was there again, this time chesting the ball down before hitting a shot that was cleared off the line by Peter Hunt. Then Jimmy Giles had to head over his own crossbar to clear the danger when Gerry O'Hara's deep centre dropped into the six-yard box. O'Hara, a bright young midfielder, was making only his fourth senior appearance and he almost set up an opening goal when he cleverly controlled a Munro clearance before setting up Carr whose shot was blocked.

Mark Penfold struck his own player, George Hope, with a dangerous-looking shot before returning to his defensive position where he was beaten by Wagstaffe whose cross was just out of reach for the incoming Kenny Hibbitt. The winger injured himself in crossing the ball and with the half midway through, he limped off to be replaced by Richards.

There was another potential headache for McGarry when Munro went down with a knee injury but he was able to carry on after treatment albeit, at first, with a limp. A long ball from Hibbitt led to Wolves going ahead in the 28th minute. Phil Warman's attempted clearance was charged down by Richards who suddenly found himself with just Tutt to beat and he made no mistake in slotting the ball home.

Vociferous Charlton appeals for a penalty when Derek Hales went down under a challenge from John McAlle were ignored by the referee and Tutt pulled off a great save from Hibbitt who had enjoyed a spell of inter-passing with Richards that had carved open the visiting defence seven minutes before the interval.

Two Carr corners came to nothing although from the second, had McAlle been two or three inches taller, he would surely have profited at the far post. Giles was penalised for pulling Bell back by his shirt but Hibbitt's free kick came to nothing before a breakaway almost saw the Addicks drawing level as Hope's header from Colin Powell's cross landed on top of the bar. On the stroke of half-time, Tutt had to dive full length to gather a misdirected back-pass from Warman.

Shortly after the restart, Phil Parkes had to fist clear a long throw from Penman. The ball landed at the feet of Hunt who hit a first time shot two yards wide. O'Hara was causing untold trouble for the Charlton defence and after making space for himself he tried a shot that was deflected for a corner. Carr took the kick but Richards's header was too high.

Tutt saved at O'Hara's feet after the Wolves man had shrugged off the attentions of Bobby Curtis in chasing Hibbitt's through ball, before Richards notched his second goal in the 56th minute with a sweetly struck shot from the edge of the box that veered away from Tutt's outstretched hand. And just two minutes later, he had the chance of completing his treble when Gould's centre found him just eight yards out but he snatched at the shot and lifted the ball over the bar.

Charlton attacks at this stage were sporadic although Parkes was forced into a full length save from Powell. However, Wolves looked to have the game sewn up before Richards eventually became the only Wolves substitute to complete a hat-trick when he took a pass from Carr and fired across Tutt into the far corner of the net from the 18-yard line.

Wolves: Parkes, Sunderland, Parkin, O'Hara, Munro, McAlle, Hibbitt, Carr, Bell, Gould, Wagstaffe (Richards).
Charlton: Tutt, Penfold, Warman, Hunt, Giles, Curtis, Powell, Hales, Hope, Peacock (Young), Flanagan.
Attendance: 32,301.
Referee: R Matthewson.

Hereford United 1 (McNeil penalty)
Wolves 6 (Sunderland, Kindon, Gould 2, Carr, Daley)

Football League Second Division
Saturday 2nd October 1976

FOLLOWING THE relegation of 1976, Wolves had made a solid start to their Second Division campaign as they looked for an instant return to the top flight. The first six games had yielded three wins and three draws with just three goals conceded. Then came a shock reminder that it wasn't going to be a cakewalk to promotion as Luton came to Molineux and took advantage of an unconvincing Wolves performance by winning 2-1.

Manager Sammy Chung did not panic and he kept faith with the players that had fallen to the Hatters by naming an unchanged side for the trip to Hereford – the first ever senior meeting between the clubs. Veteran winger Terry Paine, a member of England's World Cup squad in 1966 and with over 700 appearances for Southampton under his belt, was in the Hereford line-up.

The Edgar Street ground was packed for the game with a sizeable contingent having made their way from the West Midlands for the fixture. In the opening seconds Derek Parkin's under-hit back-pass was intercepted by Peter Spiring but John McAlle had spotted the danger and he was in position to clear the short cross that followed. Then Paine almost gave the Bulls a second-minute lead when he volleyed Roy Carter's pass inches wide of the post.

After a Paine free kick had been cleared, Steve Daley raced towards the home goal and his shot drew a fine save from former Wolves junior keeper Kevin Charlton. After weathering the early storm, Wanderers moved into a sixth-minute lead. Willie Carr looked to be yards offside as Daley pushed the ball forwards to him. However, mid-pass, the ball struck a Hereford defender, playing Carr onside. He drew Charlton from his line and slipped past the keeper before squaring the ball to Alan Sunderland who side-footed it into the vacant net.

Good work by Gary Pierce prevented Dixie McNeil from levelling matters. The striker ran through on goal but he was forced wide by the keeper and although he managed to force the ball towards goal, Geoff Palmer was there to clear from in front of the line. With the game passing the 20 minutes mark, there was a loudspeaker announcement urging supporters to move forward as there were still people outside queuing to get in. Midway through the half, a deflected shot from Paine bounced off the bar and dropped down for Pierce to punch clear. Les Briley was yellow-carded for body-checking Bobby Gould before Wolves moved into a two-goal lead through Steve Kindon who won possession back off Briley before sending a vicious cross-shot past Charlton and into the far corner of the net.

There was a chance for Spiring when he beat Mike Bailey and ran into the Wolves box. However, Pierce had run from his line to narrow the angle and Spiring's shot

Wolves' Greatest Games

bounced wide. Perhaps a little unfortunate not to have got a goal themselves, Hereford found themselves three down in the 38th minute. Kenny Hibbitt crossed from the right and Gould's back-header beat Charlton who appeared to get a touch but couldn't keep the ball out.

The happy mood of the travelling fans was muted at the interval when one of their number ran on to the field waving his scarf. His treatment by the stewards, believed to be members of the SAS and stationed in the town, bordered on brutal and there were some ugly scenes as the Wolves supporters threatened a mass invasion to exact their revenge. There were several arrests but thankfully, by the time the players took to the field again, peace had been restored.

Gould had a chance of grabbing a fourth for Wolves after he had run onto Daley's through pass but, from the right of goal, he fired into the side netting. A further goal wasn't far away although when it arrived, in the 53rd minute, it went the way of Hereford. The referee had no hesitation in pointing to the spot after Spiring had gone down under a challenge from Carr and McNeil sent Pierce the wrong way with the penalty.

Kindon left Dudley Tyler in his wake as he sprinted down the left flank before delivering a low cross that Gould somehow missed from just a yard out. However, Wolves restored their three-goal advantage in the 62nd minute after Bailey's free kick beat Hereford's offside trap. The defence moved forwards but Carr ran from an onside position to take possession and blast the ball past Charlton.

Five minutes later Gould atoned for his earlier miss by scoring his side's fifth goal when he touched in a cross from the lively Kindon whose power and pace had been tormenting the home rearguard throughout the game. With Gould's strike, you sensed that the spirit shown by Hereford was finally slipping away.

Eight minutes from the end came goal number six with Gould and Kindon combining to present a chance for Daley. The midfielder, positioned near to the penalty spot and with his back to goal, quickly swivelled and squeezed the ball between the outstretched fingers of Charlton and the post. Amazingly, after scoring six goals away from Molineux, three days later Wolves entertained Southampton and the Saints left town having scored six themselves with Chung's men hitting two in reply.

Hereford: Charlton, Briley, Burrows, Tucker, Galley, Lindsay, Paine, Spiring, McNeil, Tyler, Carter.
Unused sub: Walker.
Wolves: Pierce, Palmer, Parkin, Daley, Bailey, McAlle, Hibbitt, Carr, Gould, Kindon, Sunderland.
Unused sub: Bell.
Attendance: 13,891.
Referee: K Ridden.

Bolton Wanderers 0
Wolves 1 (Hibbitt)
Football League Second Division
Saturday 14th May 1977

IN THE three years that followed Nottingham Forest's promotion to the First Division in 1977, the Trentside club won the Football League championship, two European Cup finals and two League Cup finals. And yet it was only thanks to a backs-to-the-wall performance by Wolves at Bolton on the final Saturday of the season that Forest achieved top flight status that year.

Seven days earlier Wolves had drawn with Chelsea at Molineux, assuring Sammy Chung's men of the Second Division title and the Londoners of promotion. The remaining place in the top flight was to go to Bolton or Forest, who had finished their campaign early. They weren't involved on the day and Brian Clough had taken his squad for a break in Majorca in the knowledge that Bolton needed three points from their games against Wolves and at Bristol Rovers on the following Tuesday to take third spot and promotion.

Backed by around 8,000 supporters at Burnden Park, Wolves began strongly and could have been ahead in the first minute after Gary Jones tackled John Richards from behind as the Molineux striker took Steve Daley's pass in his stride and advanced into the area. But referee Pat Partridge waved away the appeals that followed.

In the next attack from the visitors, Ken Hibbitt sent Alan Sunderland on a run down the left wing and his cross was headed narrowly wide by Richards. Colin Brazier had to look sharp to prevent Peter Reid from reaching a misplaced pass from Daley. The young defender won the race and shepherded the ball back to his keeper, Gary Pierce.

In the 12th minute Gary Jones drove a shot narrowly over the bar from just inside the area, and for Wolves Martin Patching made good contact as he ran onto a square pass from Sunderland but his shot bounced clear off a defender. The champions threatened again when Patching returned the favour for Sunderland with a centre that the striker headed no more than a foot wide of the post.

Wolves took a deserved lead in the 20th minute after Richards had been fouled by Gary Jones outside the home area. Hibbitt touched the free kick to Willie Carr who charged in as if to have an attempt at goal. But, as he reached the ball, he checked and chipped it over the defensive wall for Hibbitt to hit a shot that Jim McDonagh managed to get a hand to. But such was the power of Hibbitt's effort, the keeper was unable to stop the ball from going into the net.

Five minutes later Neil Whatmore had a chance of equalising but he headed over after he had run in to connect with Peter Nicholson's cross. Hibbitt's goal seemed to spark some urgency into the home players and Sam Allardyce, with a firm header from Willie Morgan's corner, was literally inches away from scoring.

Wolves' Greatest Games

Whatmore did beat Pierce in the 34th minute but as he put the ball into the net the offside flag was raised against Gary Jones. Then an incident between Hibbitt and Allardyce led to both players being shown the yellow card by the referee with the Wolves man pointing out to the official a mark on his knee. Allardyce was getting forward in support of his strikers and two minutes before the interval he headed wide after meeting a lofted free kick from Morgan.

The Wolves goal had come under heavy pressure as the half had drawn to a close and, if anything, the threat grew even more on the restart with a prolonged assault that was only relieved when Pierce saved from Gary Jones. The popular keeper then had to scramble across his line after Allardyce got a firm head to Roy Greaves's corner but once again the burly defender was just off target.

Frank Munro picked up a knock in a game that was growing ever more physical and, after treatment, he tried to continue but on the hour mark he limped off to be replaced by Bobby Gould. Derek Parkin moved into the middle of the defence to cover with Hibbitt filling in at left-back. Then Pierce was hurt as he collided with Geoff Palmer as they cleared a Greaves header.

Whatmore fired wide as the home players and spectators grew more and more anxious for the goal that could keep their promotion hopes alive. Wolves looked happy to sit back and soak up the pressure although Gould broke from defence and set Sunderland off on a run and his pass inside gave Carr a chance but he drilled the ball wide.

Pierce had been outstanding for Wolves but he was limping heavily and clearly suffering and after further treatment he tried to continue but was carried off with three minutes and a lengthy spell of injury time remaining. Gould went in goal but the ten men held firm and the final whistle was the signal for an ugly pitch invasion with celebrating Wolves fans and despondent Bolton supporters clashing. Police with batons and others on horseback broke up the numerous scuffles that took place.

Bolton boss Ian Greaves, later to have a short tenure at Molineux, couldn't hide his disappointment. He said: "It's a cruel game. I sold Gary Pierce from Huddersfield to Wolves for £40,000 and I have never known a goalkeeper have so much go for him as he did today. Also, if Wolves' goal was not offside then I'm a Japanese coalminer."

The defeat meant Bolton had to win 21-0 at Bristol to better Forest's goal average. They drew 2-2.

Bolton: McDonagh, Ritson, Nicholson, Greaves, P Jones, Allardyce, Morgan, Whatmore, G Jones, Reid, Train.
Unused sub: Taylor.
Wolves: Pierce, Palmer, Parkin, Daley, Munro (Gould), Brazier, Hibbitt, Richards, Sunderland, Patching, Carr.
Attendance: 35,603.
Referee: P Partridge.

Everton 2 (Kidd, Ross penalty)
Wolves 3 (Gray, Daniel penalty, Richards)
Football League First Division
Saturday 15th September 1979

THEY WERE heady days at Molineux in the summer of 1979. A brand new stand, the signing of the charismatic Liverpool and England skipper Emlyn Hughes, Crazy Horse himself, and then, shortly after the season's start, the British transfer fee record was broken as Andy Gray joined Wolves from neighbours Aston Villa. It all seemed a little unreal.

September was a week old when Gray was introduced to the crowd at Molineux, who looked on as he completed his move by signing on the pitch near the players' tunnel prior to the game with Crystal Palace. Gray then took a seat in the stand and watched his new team struggling to take a point with a Wayne Clarke goal cancelling Dave Swindlehurst's opener for the Londoners.

The Scot's debut was to be the following week at Everton and in the Wolverhampton area an air of enthusiasm and optimism was growing with regards to the team and especially the new striking partnership of Gray and John Richards, who at the time of the trip to Goodison Park, hadn't kicked a ball in anger as he had been recovering from close-season knee surgery. They were both destined to make their mark on Merseyside on that sunny September afternoon.

Hughes received a predictably hostile reception from the Evertonians as he led the team out. John Barnwell had made three changes to the team who had drawn against Palace with Clarke and Billy Rafferty making way for Richards and Gray. On the left of midfield, Mel Eves came in for Martin Patching.

Paul Bradshaw made an early save as he bravely dived at the feet of former Wolf Peter Eastoe who had run on to an Andy King flick. It took a while but gradually the visiting midfield began to get the upper hand and consequently the attack started to look far more threatening after a somewhat tepid start and although Gray and Richards were both winning aerial challenges, neither of them was getting much of a clear sight at goal.

Just as they were beginning to assume command, Wanderers fell behind to a 19th-minute goal from former Manchester United star Brian Kidd. There was a hint of controversy about the goal as Kidd looked at least a yard offside when he took possession just inside the Wolves half. He sprinted past Hughes to a position to the left of the Wolves area before hitting a terrific cross-shot beyond Bradshaw and into the roof of the net.

Everton keeper George Wood made two unorthodox saves after Geoff Palmer launched a long through ball into the path of Kenny Hibbitt. Wood had spotted the danger and ran from his area to head clear. The ball came back again and although still out of his area, Wood managed to hack it into the stand.

Wolves' Greatest Games

Wolves continued their search for an equaliser and twice Willie Carr got in shots that were off target. As the game headed towards half-time, it was the Everton midfield who began to look steadier and the more productive. However, the break arrived with Kidd's strike the difference between the teams and little of note to report on the Richards/Gray threat.

From the start of the new half there was much more urgency about Wolves' play and following a corner the ball was half cleared to Hibbitt who, from 20 yards, unleashed a volley that flashed just past the post with Wood beaten. Then, in the 49th minute, came the moment that the sizeable travelling support had been waiting for as Gray opened his account for the club.

It all followed a neat build-up that was started by George Berry and Palmer and carried on by Eves and Derek Parkin, who played the ball to Peter Daniel. He spotted Gray and passed the ball through the home defence to Gray who ran in and side-footed past Wood into the bottom corner.

Their tails up, it took Wolves just another ten minutes to go ahead after Mike Lyons, under pressure from Richards, blatantly handled in the area. The offence was pretty clear but the referee looked as if he was going to play on until he spotted that the linesman had signalled and then put the flag across his chest. Daniel stepped up to take the spot-kick and he beat Wood with relative ease.

Wolves' joy proved to be short-lived as it took just four minutes for Everton to pull level when they too were awarded a penalty after Berry was adjudged to have fouled Kidd just inside the box. Trevor Ross took the kick and, like Daniel moments before, he had little trouble in converting.

After a mundane first half, the game had turned into a toe-to-toe battle and Wolves were back in front on 67 minutes. Both Richards and Gray went up for a long through ball and when Wood failed to collect properly Richards stabbed the ball into the net. With nine minutes remaining, the tiring Wolves striker was replaced by Colin Brazier who helped bolster the defence for the frenetic climax of the contest.

Tempers had become frayed during the course of the second half and two minutes from time Hughes fouled Andy King who took exception and retaliated. He was immediately sent off and the crowd's hostility towards the former Liverpool defender grew ever more so and he left the field at the end of the game to a chorus of boos and a hail of missiles.

Everton: Wood, Wright, Bailey, Lyons, Higgins, Ross, Hartford, Stanley, King, Kidd, Eastoe (Barton).
Wolves: Bradshaw, Palmer, Parkin, Daniel, Hughes, Berry, Hibbitt, Carr, Gray, Richards (Brazier), Eves.
Attendance: 31,807.
Referee: TL Morris.

Norwich City 0
Wolves 4 (Hibbitt 2 (two penalties), Eves, Richards)
Football League First Division
Saturday 23rd February 1980

WITH A place secured in the 1980 League Cup Final, and handily placed in the top half of the First Division, things were looking rosy for Wolves and a place in the last eight of the FA Cup beckoned after being given a home fifth round tie against Second Division side Watford. However, 'one of those afternoons' saw the Hornets cruise to a 3-0 victory in a game that saw stalwart defender John McAlle wave goodbye to a second Wembley appearance as he was carried off on a stretcher with a broken leg after coming on as a substitute.

So, in the face of adversity, how would John Barnwell's team react the following week when they ventured to East Anglia to take on a Norwich side who were on the same points total as Wolves but had a slightly better goal difference? In short, Wanderers silenced the critics and the sceptics with a performance that left the Carrow Road supporters targeting Paul Bradshaw as the man to vent their anger and frustration on with objects thrown at the keeper by a section of disgruntled supporters.

Barnwell made just the one change to the team who had failed against Watford with Bradshaw fit again, after injury had forced him to miss the cup tie, coming back in place of Mick Kearns. Included in the Canaries' line-up was World Cup winner Martin Peters.

The game was held up after just 25 seconds when Emlyn Hughes went down holding his knee after a tackle from Peter Mendham. It took several minutes of treatment before the skipper could return to the fray and when he did so one of his first acts was to foul Justin Fashanu who was on a run to goal. Then George Berry won possession but lost it when he tried to dribble past Kevin Reeves and Bradshaw had to run from his area to boot the ball clear.

In the tenth minute Derek Parkin's well-placed pass put John Richards through on goal but the striker hesitated and Roger Brown got back to win the ball. From the second of consecutive corners from Steve Goble, Peters headed narrowly wide before Wolves moved into a 15th-minute lead after Brown had felled Richards in the area. Kenny Hibbitt nonchalantly despatched the spot-kick.

Bradshaw, again, had to leave his area, this time to clear from Goble who had been put through by Fashanu before the Wolves keeper pulled off a superb save as he smothered a shot from Jones who had been set up by Mendham. Willie Carr had to turn the ball behind after Goble had got past Hughes, and it then took a combination of Hibbitt and Parkin to halt the lively midfielder who was charging through the middle.

From a Hibbitt corner the ball was played out to Parkin who struck a fierce drive that was destined for the net until Kevin Bond stuck out a foot and deflected it for a corner. Parkin figured again moments later when Andy Gray pushed a Geoff Palmer centre into his path. Again the full-back struck the ball well and City keeper Roger Hansbury could only parry the ball. Gray rifled the rebound back towards goal but Hansbury regained his feet and managed to block.

Bradshaw was at full stretch as he saved a Brown header and, for Wolves, Mel Eves drew a fine save from Hansbury. Bradshaw saved from Reeves just before Wanderers went two up in the 40th minute. Peter Daniel, Palmer, Hibbitt and Carr were all involved in the build-up before Parkin crossed to Richards who set up Daniel. His shot struck Jones and rebounded to Eves who scored with a low right-foot shot.

There should have been a third goal before the break. Hansbury somehow turned Gray's drive round the post and from the corner, taken by Hibbitt, Berry had a great chance but he put the ball over the bar from just a few yards out. However, from the restart after the interval, Wolves did go three up. Carr released Gray who passed to Hibbitt and he found Richards who tapped home.

Three minutes later and the game was up for the Canaries as a combination of Jones and Greg Downs sandwiched Daniel as he ran into the box and Hibbitt was left to successfully convert his second penalty of the game. Wolves were, by now, in a rampant mood and only a timely intervention by Jones thwarted Daniel who would otherwise have been clean through as he ran onto Gray's pass. Then Graham Paddon had to get back and break up a Hibbitt-inspired attack after the Molineux veteran intercepted a Peters pass.

A Peters free kick was cleared with little difficulty and Paddon was wide with a wild shot as City looked to gain a consolation goal. Downs almost capitalised on a moment's hesitation in the visitors' defence, with Parkin running across to clear the danger. Then Bradshaw had to punch away a Brown header that was arrowing towards the top corner of the net. The keeper then caught a full-blooded drive from Jones under the bar.

Just before the end, a scramble in the Wolves goalmouth saw Daniel and Hughes both flat out on the ground as the ball bounced around them. The danger was eventually cleared and Wolves made the trip back along the A14 with the three points secured helping to move them up to eighth place in the table.

City: Hansbury, Bond, Downs, Mendham, Brown, Jones, Goble, Reeves, Fashanu, Paddon, Peters.
Unused sub: Nightingale.
Wolves: Bradshaw, Palmer, Parkin, Daniel, Hughes, Berry, Hibbitt, Carr, Gray, Richards, Eves.
Unused sub: Humphrey.
Attendance: 17,063.
Referee: P Reeves.

Nottingham Forest 0
Wolves 1 (Gray)
Football League Cup Final
Wembley
Saturday 15th March 1980

THE ROUTE to Wembley and League Cup glory involved ten games against teams from three of the Football League's four divisions. The final hurdle was provided by a Brian Clough and Peter Taylor-inspired Nottingham Forest side who had not only won the trophy on each of the previous two seasons, but were also the reigning European Cup holders. So, while Wolves were enjoying their best league season in the top flight for six years, it was easy to see why the bookmakers had Clough's men as out-and-out favourites to make it a hat-trick of triumphs.

Andy Gray, enjoying his first season at Wolves following his record-breaking transfer from Aston Villa, was the man destined to seal the cup's destiny and yet he almost missed the match through suspension. Wolves were due to meet Aston Villa in a league game on the Monday before the final and Gray could have served his suspension in that. The problem was that if Villa's FA Cup tie at West Ham ended in a draw, then the replay would have meant the Wolves game would be off and Gray would miss Wembley. It couldn't have been closer with a last-minute Ray Stewart penalty giving West Ham the win and Gray the chance of Wembley history.

Paired with Second Division Burnley in their opening round, Wolves had fallen behind to a Martin Dobson header but equalised in the 65th minute as Geoff Palmer collected Kenny Hibbitt's through ball and fired past Alan Stevenson. Palmer was on target again in the return leg, netting a 63rd-minute penalty after Hibbitt had given Wolves the lead with a free kick. The 3-1 aggregate win was rewarded with a third round tie at Crystal Palace who were ahead though Mark Flanagan after just two minutes. However, goals from Hibbitt and Mel Eves in the last 14 minutes saw Wolves through.

Another trip to London followed and only a last-minute goal from Hibbitt kept Wolves alive after Clive Allen had scored for Queens Park Rangers. The replay was decided by a Willie Carr header to set up a quarter-final against Third Division promotion chasers Grimsby Town. On a bitterly cold night at Blundell Park the game finished without a goal and, in the replay, after Gray had given Wolves the lead, Gary Lovell's deflected shot gave the Mariners another crack with the second replay, at Derby's Baseball Ground, where Hibbitt and John Richards fired Wolves into the last four and a meeting with Swindon Town.

At the County Ground, Andy Rowland's header was cancelled out by one from Peter Daniel before Alan Mayes sent the home crowd wild with a winner three minutes from time. In the second leg, goals after the break from Richards and Eves put Wolves in front before Ray McHale converted a penalty for Town. However, in the 73rd minute, Richards struck again to send his team to Wembley.

Wolves' Greatest Games

Leaden skies looked down on the twin towers as Clough, unpredictable as ever, allowed trainer Jimmy Gordon to lead out the teams. Clough had done so himself before the 1978 final against Liverpool and his assistant Taylor had the honour a year later when Southampton were in opposition. But with Gordon due to retire at the season's end, the Forest boss decided to pay tribute to his long-time aide.

Emlyn Hughes won the toss and set Wolves to defend the south end of the stadium which was a sea of gold and black. Forest had the first attack led by Trevor Francis and when Carr intervened, his ball back to Bradshaw only reached the keeper a fraction ahead of Garry Birtles who threatened again moments later before Hughes cleared the ball to Parkin. Richards then dropped back into defence for a Kenny Burns free kick and he needed attention after being fouled by Dave Needham as he attempted to run clear after taking possession.

Needham conceded another free kick, this time on Gray who won the first corner of the game after Hibbitt had lofted the ball into the area. Hibbitt's flag-kick was played short to Derek Parkin but his cross drifted behind. A strong Forest attack featured a spell of inter-passing between John Robertson and Frank Gray and although Hughes stepped in, his back-pass eluded Bradshaw and went out for a corner that came to nothing.

Peter Shilton dropped the ball when challenged by Gray for Parkin's deep cross, but luckily for the keeper no Wolves played had followed up. The contest had something of a chess game feel about it with both sides making cautious probes although play was constantly broken up as Wolves and Forest players continued to concede free kicks.

Daniel went on a 40-yard run, eluding tackles as he did so, before hitting a left-foot drive fractionally wide of the post. Another move involving Frank Gray and Robertson saw the ball transferred to Martin O'Neill whose cross was intercepted by Paul Bradshaw before Birtles had the chance to prosper. Then Forest broke from defence with Gray holding off the close attentions of George Berry and Palmer before attempting a lob that went wide as Bradshaw left his line.

The Forest defence had started to look decidedly edgy when Wolves went forward and after Carr had fired wide following Gray's flick on, Richards was fouled by Needham just two yards outside the box. Carr and Hibbitt played a short free kick routine before teeing the ball up for Richards whose effort was blocked by Burns. When the ball ran to Daniel he fed Carr whose lob into the area was ushered back to Shilton by Robertson, who had dropped back.

Then it was Forest's turn to win a free kick in a dangerous position after Hughes had felled Francis outside the Wolves box. O'Neill took the kick and his low right-footed effort was covered all the way by Bradshaw who got his body behind the ball. Like Shilton, Bradshaw had enjoyed a fairly comfortable opening half with little by way of direct saves for them to deal with. However, the second period was to prove an entirely different matter.

Almost straight from the restart Wolves won a free kick after Burns had fouled Gray. Palmer's kick was headed across goal by Berry and Richards got in a shot that

v Nottingham Forest, 1980

didn't have the power to beat Shilton, who had little trouble in saving. Another Needham foul, his time on Gray, led to Carr lifting the ball into the Forest box but there were no gold shirts there to take advantage.

A mix-up in the Wolves defence gave Birtles a chance but before he could react Palmer got in a telling tackle to avert the danger. Hibbitt struck a low shot across the face of goal and then John McGovern had to concede a corner after Daniel's cross caused problems as Wolves upped the ante. Hughes was hurt after breaking up a Forest counter-attack and although he was able to continue after treatment, he was limping as he did so.

It looked as if the stalemate had been broken as Richards and Shilton went up for a Daniel cross and the ball dropped into the net with Carr making sure. But celebrations from Wolves players and supporters alike were quickly stifled when the referee blew for an infringement. The ball was back in the Forest net in the 66th minute, and this time it did count as Gray scored probably the easiest, and yet most important goal of his career.

Daniel, deep inside his own half and on the right, lifted a long though ball towards the Forest area. Needham was there and Shilton raced from his line but the two got into an awful tangle as communications broke down and the ball bypassed them both as they collided, leaving Gray with the simplest of tasks in prodding the ball over the line as it rolled towards the net.

The goal sparked a siege on Bradshaw's goal and it began with a cross-shot from Francis that flew wide. In the next attack Francis found O'Neill whose shot bounced off Berry's back and hit Hughes before rolling to Birtles who saw his low effort smothered by Bradshaw. After Eves had conceded a corner, virtually every man on the field was packed into the Wolves area for Robertson's kick. However, when the ball fell at Birtles' feet, he shot straight at Bradshaw.

In a brief respite Wolves broke to force a corner and they almost hit Forest with a sucker punch as Berry headed Hibbitt's kick against a post. It was back to absorbing more waves of Forest attacks with Bradshaw trapping a McGovern shot between his legs as he lay on the floor before throwing himself in the way of goal attempts from McGovern, again, and Birtles.

It looked for all the world, in those seemingly endless final minutes, that an equaliser must come. However, Barnwell's defence were magnificent with the 'they shall not pass' attitude of Hughes spreading throughout the team and they were rewarded when the referee blew the final whistle. The beaming Hughes led his men up the Wembley steps to collect the only trophy that had eluded him in his illustrious career.

In the post-match inquests, Shilton shouldered the blame for the confusion that led to the game's only goal, saying: "Yes, it was all my fault. I thought I could help David out and shouted at him to leave the ball but, because of the noise, he didn't hear me. We nudged each other and left the way open for Andy."

Gray added: "I knew there was something when I saw Peter coming so far out. I was left with the simplest of chances and even I don't miss those!"

Wolves' Greatest Games

Delighted skipper Hughes said: "I never, ever thought I would complete my set of medals after leaving Liverpool. But once we got to Wembley, we had to have a chance. The odds on Forest were ridiculous for a two-horse race. It felt like going home when I went up the steps to collect the cup. It was a great moment. In football, the prize you've just won is always the greatest.

"The young lads in the side, the ones people had reservations about, came through magnificently. George Berry was my man of the match. He never put a foot wrong and Daniel and Bradshaw were not far behind."

As for the respective managers, John Barnwell said: "Andy Gray does not miss many chances like that. I do not normally single out individuals for praise but George Berry deserves some today. I though he was superb."

Clough lamented: "We have taken defeat very badly. Needham was blameless for the goal. I do not think you can call at Wembley. Nobody can hear anything. At the moment I could not even lift a glass of champagne."

The Forest boss did have the best of consolations though, as his team retained the European Cup while Wolves finished a creditable sixth in the First Division.

Forest: Shilton, Anderson, F Gray, McGovern, Needham, Burns, O'Neill, Bowyer, Birtles, Francis, Robertson.
Unused sub: O'Hare.
Wolves: Bradshaw, Palmer, Parkin, Daniel, Hughes, Berry, Hibbitt, Carr, Gray, Richards, Eves.
Unused sub: Brazier.
Attendance: 96,527.
Referee: D Richardson.

West Bromwich Albion 1 (Thompson)
Wolves 3 (Crainie 2, Clarke)
Football League First Division
Saturday 26th November 1983

THE OPENING game of the 1983/84 season gave little notice of the horrific campaign that lay in wait for Wolves and their supporters. Fresh back from a year in the Second Division, a Geoff Palmer penalty gave Wanderers a point when they met reigning league champions Liverpool at Molineux. However, with Allied Properties at the helm, what followed, not only in that campaign but the two after it, was unpalatable to say the least.

In the 13 games that came after the visit of the Merseysiders, there were ten defeats and three draws and going into the local derby against West Bromwich at The Hawthorns at the end of November, Wolves were stuck at the bottom of the table with just four points to their name. Added to the misery were home and away defeats to Third Division side Preston North End in the League Cup.

A goalless draw with Coventry at Molineux seven days earlier did nothing to raise the spirits of anyone concerned with Wolves but it did prompt manager Graham Hawkins to name an unchanged side. Albion, who were hovering in mid-table, had lost 1-0 at Southampton and 2-0 at Norwich leading into the game.

On a dismal Black Country afternoon Wolves began with more purpose than their hosts and there was an early chance when Ken McNaught headed out Ian Cartwright's long throw. The ball went as far as Danny Crainie who was on loan to Wolves from Celtic. Crainie slipped inside to find a shooting position but Clive Whitehead managed to block the Scot's 15-yard drive.

Aston Villa's Andy Blair, another loanee at Molineux, fed a low through pass to Steve Mardenborough who outpaced Ally Robertson but then had the ball taken from his feet by Baggies keeper Paul Barron who had advanced from his line. In Albion's first major attack they almost took the lead. Barry Cowdrill found Noel Luke who skipped past Dale Rudge and hit a low shot that Paul Bradshaw blocked.

The keeper couldn't hold on to the ball, which bounced to Garry Thompson who had a clear shot at goal but failed to get any power behind the ball allowing Bradshaw the opportunity of recovering to save. Then, after Alan Dodd's poor challenge on Mick Perry, Gary Owen's free kick fell to Whitehead who succeeded only in running the ball out of play.

A Robertson challenge on Mardenborough drew an angry response from the Wolves striker. Ken Hibbitt took the free kick, finding Wayne Clarke, but he had run into an offside position. After a spell of Albion pressure Wolves broke away and Robertson had to head a Blair cross behind for a corner that was taken short by Crainie. He played the ball to Blair, whose cross was headed wide by Dodd.

Wolves' Greatest Games

Midway through the half Blair set up Cartwright who ran through and hit a low shot that drew a tremendous save from Barron. Play quickly switched to the opposite end and Bradshaw's quick throw out to Hibbitt set up a lightning Wolves raid. Hibbitt passed to Blair and his cross was hammered clear by Whitehead before Cartwright hit a cross-shot that flew wide as the visitors continued to have the better of things. When Albion did go forward, the Wolves defence looked well capable of absorbing any threat.

The second half opened with a move involving Hibbitt and Mardenborough who crossed for Clarke whose header bounced clear off McNaught. The former Villa defender was soon in the thick of things again with a free kick that caused a scramble in Bradshaw's area before Dodd booted the ball to safety. Then there was a chance for Mardenborough who was put through by Blair but the youngster hesitated, allowing Barry Cowdrill to get back and clear.

It had been almost nine hours since Wolves had last scored a goal but, in the 51st minute, Crainie broke the spell as he put his side ahead. Whitehead's attempted clearance of Hibbitt's cross dropped nicely for Crainie who rifled a left-footed shot into the top corner of the net before Barron could move.

Just three minutes later he did it again after receiving a pass from Blair and taking a few paces as the Albion defence retreated before lashing a 25-yard shot, again from his left foot, past the bemused Albion keeper. In the 59th minute Albion looked to have won a penalty when Thompson went down under a challenge from John Pender but, much to the annoyance of the home supporters, the referee waved play on.

Albion sent on Derek Monaghan in place of Perry and within minutes of his introduction he picked out Luke who was unmarked and just 12 yards out. Any hopes of pulling a goal back, however, evaporated when the ball struck Thompson and ran to Pender who gratefully cleared upfield. To make matters worse for the Albion fans, Clarke put Wolves three up in the 71st minute.

He ran onto Mardenborough's excellent crossfield pass and drew Barron from his line before stroking the ball into the net. Albion did grab an 88th-minute consolation from Thompson who headed in a cross from Martin Jol, but by then Wolves had the game well and truly in their pockets. It was one of few bright spots in an awful season at the end of which the team plummeted back into the Second Division after finishing bottom of the table a full 20 points short of the safety mark.

Albion: Barron, Whitehead, Cowdrill, Zondervan, McNaught, Robertson, Jol, Thompson, Perry (Monaghan), Owen, Luke.
Wolves: Bradshaw, Humphrey, Rudge, Blair, Pender, Dodd, Hibbitt, Clarke, Cartwright, Mardenborough (Palmer), Crainie.
Attendance: 17,947.
Referee: K Hackett.

76
Liverpool 0
Wolves 1 (Mardenborough)
Football League First Division
Saturday 14th January 1984

THE MID-1980s years under the ownership of Allied Properties have to rank as the worst in the history of Wolverhampton Wanderers. After an unimpressive promotion from the Second Division in 1983, three seasons of misery followed with each ending in relegation in a trip from the top tier to the bottom one.

The top flight campaign got off to a satisfactory opening with a home draw against the reigning league champions, Liverpool. But it proved to be a false dawn as, by the time Wanderers travelled up to Merseyside for the return the following January, Graham Hawkins's men were rooted at the bottom of the table having won just three games while Liverpool were top, having lost only three.

Wolves had had to wait until the end of November to register their first success which came against arch rivals West Bromwich Albion at The Hawthorns. Home wins over Norwich and Everton over the Christmas holiday had given fresh hope, but a narrow defeat at Queens Park Rangers preceding the trip to Anfield had ended hopes of moving off the bottom rung at the start of the New Year.

Liverpool, on the other hand, were looking a sure-fire bet to retain their championship. Their side were laced with household names and seven of the line-up that faced Wolves had played in every game for them at that stage of the season with an eighth, Ian Rush, having been absent just the once and that was for a League Cup tie. If there was any comfort that could have been gleaned by the faithful few that followed their team up to the north-west, it was that the legendary Kenny Dalglish was still ruled out by injury.

Wolves made just one change from the side that had drawn with Coventry in an FA Cup third round tie with Steve Mardenborough a late replacement for Mel Eves who had suffered an injury in training. Mardenborough, who had been released by Coventry City, had written to Wolves asking for a trial and he was taken on at the start of the season.

He was to write himself into the history books with his only goal for the club as David slew Goliath in his own backyard. No-one, even the most patriotic of supporters, could have given Wanderers a prayer that afternoon but football isn't perhaps as predictable as it may seem. Defending the Kop end, Wolves' two opening attacks came to an end when Mardenborough strayed into offside positions.

It turned out to be third time lucky for the Birmingham-born youngster as he stunned Anfield into silence by giving the visitors the lead in the ninth minute. Alan Hansen headed clear Wayne Clarke's centre but only as far as Danny Crainie who returned the ball into the middle for Mardenborough to send a looping effort past

Wolves' Greatest Games

Bruce Grobbelaar. He had attempted a header but the ball appeared to go in off his shoulder.

Needless to say, the goal only served to stir up the hornets' nest and then began the task of protecting it with a massed defence facing 80 minutes of almost constant pressure with just the odd breakaway relieving the tension. Geoff Palmer had to make an acrobatic clearance to prevent Rush from reaching Graeme Souness's deep pass, and then Steve Nicol fired wide. John Humphrey twice cleared the lines as the onslaught continued. First he headed out a dangerous Sammy Lee cross and then he blocked after Craig Johnston and Phil Neal had set up a shooting chance for Alan Kennedy.

Keeper John Burridge punched clear as Michael Robinson challenged for Souness's centre, and Alan Dodd got in the way of a Johnston shot as the snow began to fall. The Liverpool pressure was constant and there was another chance for them when Robinson headed on a Kennedy centre to Johnston. But he failed to make a proper connection and Palmer was able to clear.

In a rare break from defence, Sammy Troughton cleared to Mardenborough and his shot was scrambled away by Grobbelaar before another series of home attacks were soaked up by the Molineux defence. Another break saw Mardenborough sending Crainie away on the left and his cross just eluded Clarke with Nicol having to head over his own bar to ease the situation. In the dying seconds of the half, Souness was just wide with a left-foot drive and Burridge saved well from Robinson.

After the break the pattern continued although the valiant Wolves defence this time also had to combat the strong wind that was blowing into their faces. Nicol wasn't far away with a low shot after he had intercepted a Humphrey clearance, and after Burridge had punched away a Lee corner, he then caught a speculative lob from Hansen.

Clarke almost gifted Liverpool an equaliser when his attempted back-pass to Burridge was short of the mark. He hadn't noticed Robinson who would have had a free shot at goal had Burridge not spotted the danger to race from his line and claim the ball in the nick of time. But the keeper earned the plaudits of the home crowd with a fantastic save to thwart Nicol.

The Scottish international met Lawrenson's cross on the volley and with The Kop preparing to celebrate Burridge made a tremendous one handed save and then quickly scrambled across his line to claim the loose ball. Just before the end, a header from substitute Ronnie Whelan hit the post but Wanderers held on for the unlikeliest of victories.

Liverpool: Grobbelaar, Neal, Kennedy, Lawrenson, Nicol (Whelan), Hansen, Robinson, Lee, Rush, Johnston, Souness.
Wolves: Burridge, Humphrey, Palmer, Daniel, Pender, Dodd, Towner, Clarke, Troughton, Mardenborough, Crainie.
Unused sub: Cartwright.
Attendance: 23,235.
Referee: A Saunders.

Wolves 3 (Thompson, Holmes, Bull)
Stockport County 1 (Moss)
Football League Fourth Division
Saturday 7th February 1987

IT SAID much of the perilous state of the club that a crowd of just 3,238 was scattered around the two sides of Molineux that were open to the public when Stockport County came visiting in the winter of 1987. Saved from the clutches of the receiver the previous summer, Wolves sat below the halfway mark of the old Fourth Division table after a first half of the campaign that at best was inauspicious and, with the inclusion of the Chorley debacle, woeful at its worst.

The arrival of Stephen George Bull from West Bromwich Albion did raise spirits a little as he began a career at Molineux that was to earn him cult status. His first 14 league and cup games leading up to the visit of County had yielded seven goals and yet everything was still unpredictable leaning towards cloudy, rather than bright, prospects.

Results from the month of January proved the point with just one win, two goalless draws and two defeats. The losses both came at Molineux where the hardy few loyal supporters had been starved of success, having not seen their team win on home soil in six attempts. When County took the lead shortly after half-time, it looked odds-on that the winless spell at Molineux was destined to continue.

Yet a late revival that afternoon was to see the start of the club's comeback from the depths and although they were to be thwarted come the end of the campaign, the dark skies were beginning to clear. The County game would be looked back upon as the beginning of happier days and the end of the darkest of times for Wolverhampton Wanderers.

There was a chance for Wolves after just five minutes when Bull broke away but, although he got plenty of power behind his shot, he completely mishit it and the ball screwed well wide of the target. County, who were even lower in the league than Wolves were, struggled to cope with the Bull and Andy Mutch spearhead and keeper Andy Gorton had to dive to keep out a glancing header from Mutch after Neil Edwards had lifted a free kick into the visitors' area.

Mutch threatened again when he cut inside but his tame finish dribbled wide. Stockport finally gave Mark Kendall something to think about when Ernie Moss ran through and fired at goal but the Welsh keeper pushed the ball behind for a corner that was cleared with little fuss. A mistake by Ally Robertson then let in Vernon Allatt but he hesitated, allowing Kendall to close him down and scramble the ball away.

After Mutch had shot high over the bar when connecting with Bull's cross, there was a moment of light relief for the home fans when Allatt beat Chris Brindley but then completely missed the ball as he tried to shoot past Kendall. But the laughter

Wolves' Greatest Games

turned to groans of despair just two minutes after the interval as Stockport moved into the lead.

The goal came seconds after Gorton had prevented Mutch's shot on the turn going into the net with an outstretched leg after Nicky Clarke's cross had fallen nicely for the striker. Edwards followed up to take possession but he was denied by a goal-saving tackle from Ian McKenzie. From the clearance, County moved ahead as Moss sent a superb header past Kendall after a cross from Clive Evans.

At the time, a goal in the debit column was very much par for the course for the long suffering few and they looked on as Brindley's smart piece of defensive work averted what could have been a second County goal. Wolves started to regain the initiative though and but for a bad miss from the usually reliable Bull, they would have been level. Mutch's clever flick opened up the County defence and Bull tore in but, with the goal at his mercy, he shot straight at Gorton.

Relief, in the shape of a spot-kick, arrived in the 78th minute. The referee didn't hesitate in the award after Evans felled Purdie in the area and Andy Thompson sent the keeper the wrong way to even things up. Three minutes from time, Bull headed a deep Purdie cross back into the goalmouth where Micky Holmes was waiting to nod over the line.

Virtually from the restart, the shell-shocked County defence were undone again as Bull raced clear onto Mutch's pass and, as Gorton left his line, the striker lobbed the ball over him into the vacant net to complete the late comeback.

The effect that the win had was a remarkable one. There were 18 league games remaining in the season and incredibly Wolves were to win 14 of them and lose out in just two. Unfortunately, the second of those setbacks came at promotion-chasing Southend – a single-goal defeat at Roots Hall.

The result, two weeks before the campaign's climax, was a significant one as the Shrimpers finished in third place, a single point above Wolves who were condemned to the newly-introduced play-offs. Had it been the season before, they would have gone up automatically in fourth spot. After beating Colchester to get through to the final, Wolves lost out to an Aldershot team against whom they had done the double and finished nine points above.

However, better days lay in wait and that Stockport victory is looked upon as the game that saw the birth of the revival.

Wolves: Kendall, Stoutt, Clarke, Thompson, Brindley, Robertson, Purdie, N Edwards, Bull, Mutch, Holmes.
Unused sub: Forman.
County: Gorton, Evans, McKenzie, L Edwards, Matthewson, Williams, Hodkinson, Moss, Allatt, Robinson, Brown.
Unused sub: Entwhistle.
Attendance: 3,238.
Referee: P Don.

Burnley 0
Wolves 2 (Mutch, Dennison)
Sherpa Van Trophy Final
Wembley
Sunday 29th May 1988

WOLVES AND Burnley were two of the founder members of the Football League and yet, 100 years later, they both found themselves wallowing in the Fourth Division after what can only be described as hard times. The renaissance began for both clubs in 1988 as they reached a Wembley final with Wolves already having captured the bottom tier's title.

A measure of the tradition of Wolves and Burnley was shown in the 80,000 gate that descended on Wembley for the Sherpa Van Trophy – a sponsored competition that involved clubs from the Third and Fourth Divisions. Whereas Wembley was four-fifths full for the game, the opening round of the competition for Wolves was played out in front of a much smaller audience.

Just 2,886 were at the Vetch Field for the preliminary round tie with Swansea City. After a dour opening half, Swansea took a 53rd-minute lead through Joe Allon who shook off challenges of Andy Thompson and Floyd Streete before shooting past Mark Kendall. The equaliser came seven minutes from the end when Steve Bull beat two men before, from a tight angle, hitting a fierce right-foot shot that flew between home keeper Mike Hughes and his near post.

The second preliminary game took place at Molineux with Bristol City providing the opposition. Bull shook off the effects of a calf injury to take part and he played a major role in steering Wolves through to the last 16 of the competition. However, it was Nigel Vaughan that opened the scoring when he tapped the ball home after City keeper Mark Prudhoe had failed to hold on to a rasping drive from Andy Mutch.

Prudhoe was beaten again five minutes before the break as Bull connected with Robbie Dennison's cross from the right to send a low, angled shot into the net. The game was wrapped up 14 minutes from the end when Bull converted from close range after Mutch, as he had done and was to do so many times, created the opening for his strike partner.

After Swansea and Bristol City had suffered at the hands of Bull, next up came the turn of Brentford with the tie once again taking place at Molineux. It took Bull just nine minutes to open Wolves' account and his goal was the deciding factor at half-time. However, 45 seconds after the restart he hammered a drive against the post and Dennison tucked away the rebound to ease any fears of a Brentford comeback.

Bull struck again in the 77th minute with a close-range finish after Bees keeper Gary Phillips had pushed out his initial header following a Dennison centre, and five minutes from time he completed his hat-trick with a stunning strike from 20 yards. There was still time for Streete and Mutch to have efforts cleared off the line as Wolves finished the game with a flourish.

Wolves' Greatest Games

Just three days after a shock 4-1 home reversal against Cardiff had brought about a temporary hiccup in the charge towards promotion, Peterborough visited Molineux on a bitterly cold February evening for the Southern Area quarter-final of the competition. Anxious to put the Welsh nightmare behind them Wolves were soon in front with Bull, inevitably, the scorer.

Just four minutes had gone when he converted after the Peterborough defence had failed to clear Vaughan's corner. Seven minutes after the break Mutch set up the chance for Bull to smash a second from ten yards and moments later Dennison's free kick made it three. Mutch rounded things off in the 70th minute, heading into an empty net after keeper Kevin Shoemake could only parry Vaughan's shot.

The draw gave Wolves a home tie once again, for the area semi-final against Torquay, and although they bossed most of the game, just one goal separated Graham Turner's men from the South Coast team at the end. It came in the 18th minute after an exquisite build-up involving Mutch, Phil Robinson, Micky Holmes and Dennison who crossed for Bull to glance a header beyond Kenny Allen in United's goal.

The win left only Notts County, in the two-legged area final, standing between Wolves and Wembley. Watched by a crowd of 10,000 at Meadow Lane, of which 4,000 had made the trip from Wolverhampton, it was an hour before the stalemate was broken as Bull took advantage of a sliced clearance from Paul Smalley by hitting a fearsome half-volley past County keeper Mick Leonard. Six minutes from the end Ian McParland gave the home fans something to cheer about when he squeezed the ball past Mark Kendall after Gary Mills had intercepted Thompson's back-pass and centred.

Two goals from Bull in the opening 26 minutes of the second leg allayed any fears that may have been harboured by the home supporters. His first, eight minutes in, was a low finish into the bottom corner aafter he had run on to Holmes's through ball. Then he took possession after Mutch had flicked on Streete's deep pass and held off the dual challenge of Paul Hart and Chris Withe before blasting the ball past Leonard.

It was left to County old boy Keith Downing to wind things up after 63 minutes when he volleyed home from ten yards after Dennison's corner was only half-cleared. So Wolves were Wembley bound having beaten a team who were scrapping for promotion a division higher, 4-1 on aggregate.

Burnley fans were outnumbered by their Molineux counterparts on the big day but there was something of a carnival atmosphere as the teams strode out into the sunshine. Gary Bellamy had recovered from an eye injury allowing Turner the luxury of fielding his strongest side.

With just two minutes gone Andy Farrell rose to meet Ray Deakin's cross but his header was well wide of Kendall's goal. Then Steve Davis headed straight at the Welsh keeper after he had met Ian Britton's centre as Burnley made the more positive start to the game. Having weathered the early pressure Wolves almost moved ahead after 12 minutes when Bellamy's free kick almost caught the Burnley

v Burnley, 1988

defence napping and keeper Chris Pearce was forced to turn the ball onto the top of the bar before his defenders scrambled it clear.

When Mutch nodded down Streete's long through ball into the path of Bull, the striker wasn't far from giving Wolves the lead with a right-footed drive that flashed a few inches wide. After their shaky start Wolves had, by now, begun to take a grip on the game and they moved ahead in the 22nd minute through Mutch. Dennison's right-wing corner was headed on by Streete and the ball eluded a posse of defenders before going to Bull who flicked it back across the face of goal, as he fell, to Mutch, who steered a header between Pearce and full-back Deakin into the net.

Holmes had to leave the field for treatment to an ankle injury as Bull and Mutch began to assert their authority on proceedings with the Clarets defence at full stretch in trying to contain them and as frustrations began to seep through, Davis went into the book for a blatant foul on Bull. Holmes returned to the battle but almost immediately there was another hold-up after a heavy challenge from Farrell left Ally Robertson in need of treatment from the physio.

Just before the interval a downcast Holmes limped off to be replaced by Vaughan and worse was to follow for Wolves as they lost the services of skipper Robertson less than a minute after the start of the second half. The veteran defender fell to the ground clutching his knee with Jackie Gallagher, Wolves' second and final substitute, taking his place. Turner quickly reorganised his defence with Bellamy moving into the middle, Thompson switching to right-back and Downing dropping from midfield to the left-back spot.

However, the changes didn't ease the grip that Wolves had on the game and they went two up in the 50th minute after Steve Gardner had fouled Vaughan just outside the Burnley box. In front of the end of the ground that was a sea of gold and black, Dennison flighted a copybook free kick into the Burnley net – the accuracy and pace of his effort leaving Pearce with no chance.

With a virtual last throw of the dice, Burnley threw on veteran winger Leighton James. However, the Wanderers defence were in no mood to let things slip and there could have been a third goal after Bull and Dennison combined to open up a chance for Robinson who drilled his shot no more than a foot wide. And, in the final minute, Mutch saw his close-range angled effort come back off the outside of the post. Minutes later, a jubilant Robertson limped up the steps to the Royal Box to receive the trophy.

Bull had scored in each of the rounds leading up to the final with a tally of 12 goals. Although he had to be satisfied with an assist on the big day, he was nevertheless delighted with the outcome of the game.

He said: "If someone had told me last August that by the end of May Wolves would have won the Fourth Division title and the Sherpa Van Trophy, and I would score 52 goals, I would have laughed at them and told them they were mad. But it's happened and it's a dream come true. I only hope I shall still be with Wolves next season as we try to win the Third Division. I love the club and want to stay. If I have my way I shall be going nowhere.

Wolves' Greatest Games

"Naturally, I was a little disappointed I didn't get among the goals. I had a couple of half chances but the main thing is we won. To walk out for the start of the match in front of 80,000 supporters was another quite unbelievable and unforgettable experience."

On his free kick, Dennison revealed that his manager hadn't wanted him to take it. The winger explained: "I had been missing the target all week with free kicks in training and was not a popular choice to take any more. But the goals are a bit bigger at Wembley and this one went in. It looked a bit dodgy when we lost Ally Robertson straight after half-time, but the goal took a bit of pressure off."

When asked if he felt that Wolves were always in control, boss Turner responded: "No, not until the final whistle. Burnley had a spell in the second half where they caused us problems and we certainly knew that we had been in a game. Going to Wembley has provided us with a lot of new finance. Maybe now I can think about buying a centre-forward who scores goals!"

Burnley: Pearce, Daniel, Deakin, Britton, Davis, Gardner, Farrell, Oghani, Taylor, Comstive, McGrory (James).
Unused sub: Hoskin.
Wolves: Kendall, Bellamy, Thompson, Streete, Robertson (Gallagher), Robinson, Dennison, Downing, Bull, Mutch, Holmes (Vaughan).
Attendance: 80,841.
Referee: R Milford.

Wolves 6 (Bull 3, Mutch, Gooding, Thompson)
Mansfield Town 2 (Coleman, Leishman)
Football League Third Division
Saturday 17th December 1988

WOLVES WERE in a fantastic vein of form and were perched at the top of the Third Division when they suffered a shock reversal against Northampton Town at the County Ground. The defeat ended a run of eight consecutive league victories including a 6-0 demolition of Preston North End in the game before the trip to face the Cobblers.

Smarting from the defeat, Graham Turner's men had to wait a fortnight for their chance to make amends against Mansfield Town. They had a blank weekend before Town's visit as it was second round FA Cup day and a 1-0 defeat at Grimsby had brought a surprise and early exit from the competition. One thing was for sure though, when the Stags arrived at Molineux Wolves were in a hungry mood. Turner made just one change, bringing in Mick Gooding for Keith Downing who was named as a substitute.

When Andy Mutch was fouled by Mark Kearney it gave Wolves a first sight of goal. Andy Thompson chipped the free kick into the area where Ally Robertson and Floyd Streete made strong challenges before the ball ran to Steve Bull who uncharacteristically sliced it high and wide of the target. Then came Mansfield's first threat as Craig McKernon sprinted past Robbie Dennison and delivered a cross that Streete and Mark Kendall had difficulty in dealing with as Keith Cassells closed in.

To relieve the danger the ball was turned behind but from the corner Mansfield stunned the home crowd by taking a seventh-minute lead. Dave Hodges took the flag-kick and Kendall was beaten by a Simon Coleman header that flew high into the net. Wolves quickly won a corner at the other end when George Foster ended Thompson's raid down the right wing. From the kick Mutch got in a header which Brian Cox, in the Town goal, dived to save.

Mark Venus was fouled by Hodges as he cut in from the left and when Dennison tapped the free kick into the path of the full-back, he fired wide of the far post. The pressure was building up on the Town defence and Wolves got the equaliser they deserved in the 26th minute with Bull sending a low header past the outstretched fingers of Cox. The striker immediately acknowledged the contribution of Gooding whose superb cross had forged the goal.

Gooding had a shot at goal himself shortly afterwards after Dennison's persistence had created the opportunity. He got plenty of power behind his effort but the ball struck Stephen Charles's back and bounced to safety. Cox just beat Gooding to Gary Bellamy's through ball and then the keeper managed to get enough on Phil Robinson's left-foot drive to deflect the ball onto the post, allowing a defender to run in and hack clear.

Wolves' Greatest Games

It was just a matter of time before the Town defence capitulated and they did so in the 37th minute. Bellamy crossed from the right and Bull nodded the ball on to strike partner Mutch who headed past Cox from the edge of the six-yard box. A third goal arrived just three minutes later with Bellamy once again providing the ammunition in the shape of a cross to Gooding who scored with a great header from near the penalty spot.

The Town players were desperate for the interval but they were made to suffer once again before they could find the sanctuary of the dressing room as Bull made it 4-1 in the 43rd minute. Streete's deep through ball into the box was chested down by the number nine who lashed a rising drive into the top right corner of the net. It was a quite superb finish – Bull at his best.

After the break, Cassells had the chance to cut the deficit but he fired straight at Kendall after connecting with a Hodges free kick. Another Bull hat-trick seemed inevitable and it duly arrived in the 58th minute with Bellamy completing a treble of assists. Mutch headed on the defender's through ball and Bull, in full flight, ran on for a few yards before despatching a low shot just inside the far post.

With 62 minutes gone Thompson got a sixth when he took Cox by surprise as he let fly from 30 yards although, in fairness to the keeper, the ball did take an unkind bounce just before it flew past him. The goal was the signal for Wolves to ease off the throttle and Town substitute Graham Leishman pulled one back when he shot past Kendall after a free kick from McKernon.

By completing his hat-trick, Bull became the first Wolves player to score three in three successive home games. It also took him to within one of a century as, in league, cup and play-offs, he had scored three for West Bromwich and 96 for Wolves. His quest to join the '100 club' had taken just 127 games spread over less than a three-year period. He didn't have to wait too long for the 100th, which arrived in the 2-2 draw with Brentford at Griffin Park on New Year's Eve.

Bull also dispelled worries from his adoring fans that he could be tempted away from Molineux. He said: "I've got this year and two more left on my contract, but if someone offered me another five years at Wolves, I'd sign tomorrow. I've just had nearly 13,000 people chanting 'Bully for England' so why should I want to leave?"

Wolves: Kendall, Bellamy, Venus, Streete, Robertson (Downing), Robinson, Thompson, Gooding, Bull, Mutch, Dennison (Vaughan).
Mansfield: Cox, McKernon, Kenworthy, Lowery, Foster, Coleman, Hodges (Leishman), Charles, Ryan (Garner), Cassells, Kearney.
Attendance: 12,134.
Referee: P Wright.

West Bromwich Albion 1 (Talbot)
Wolves 2 (Dennison, Bull)
Football League Second Division
Sunday 15th October 1989

AFTER A four-season absence, Wolves returned to The Hawthorns to renew acquaintances with one of their oldest and fiercest rivals, West Bromwich Albion. Since the last meeting between the clubs, in the First Division, Wolves had endured the indignity of three successive relegations. Now, however, fortunes had improved and under the guidance of Graham Turner, the team had climbed back up two rungs of the ladder.

The trip to Albion meant that for many there was going to be a late Sunday lunch as, to lessen the risk of crowd trouble, the kick-off was scheduled to take place at noon. Getting anything of a positive result from the game looked to be a tall order for Wolves as the Baggies went into the game on the back of three consecutive away victories – 3-2 at West Ham, 5-3 at Bradford in the League Cup, and 2-0 at Watford.

However, their home form wasn't quite so impressive with one win, two draws and two defeats from the five games played. For Wolves, the return to the second tier of English football had been far from easy in the first instance with the opening five games yielding just two points. Then came a four-game run of three wins and a draw before, eight days prior to the trip down the A41, Turner's men succumbed to Sheffield United at Molineux.

The atmosphere was heightened as Albion and Wolves took to the field as included in the visiting line-up were three former Hawthorns players – Steve Bull, Robbie Dennison and Andy Thompson. Albion player-manager Brian Talbot made just one change to the side that had won at Vicarage Road with Don Goodman replacing Kevin Bartlett. Wolves, too, made one change after the poor showing against the Blades with Thompson coming in for Phil Chard.

The first half belonged very much to the Baggies although, with local pride at stake, neither side settled particularly well in the opening stages. When the breakthrough did arrive though, given the pressure that had been building up, it didn't come as a shock that it was the home supporters who were celebrating.

Shane Westley fouled John Thomas and Stacey North pushed a low free kick through to Thomas who had advanced to the edge of the Wanderers box. He took the ball to the byline and, despite an attempt to block by Gary Bellamy, crossed for Goodman to back head into the path of Talbot who volleyed into the net from 12 yards.

The pressure intensified and after Goodman had taken a return pass from Thomas, he fired inches over the bar from the edge of the area. Then Mark Barham missed an absolute sitter as he met Goodman's cross from the left and sliced the ball horribly wide.

Wolves' Greatest Games

After absorbing the pressure, Wolves pulled level in the final minute of the half in controversial circumstances. North turned an Andy Mutch centre behind for a corner that was taken by Dennison. Albion keeper Stuart Naylor easily claimed the ball but then dallied in releasing it. After 12 seconds referee Kelvin Morton blew and awarded Wolves a free kick for the keeper's time-wasting.

The Albion players protested as the crowd in the Birmingham Road end behind the goal made their feelings known. Their mood didn't improve as Thompson tapped the ball into the path of Dennison and he drilled it home from two yards inside the Baggies box.

Shortly after the interval Floyd Streete had to head behind a Barham cross. Tony Ford's corner was half-cleared to Bernard McNally who hit a 20-yard shot that was deflected narrowly wide. That effort was struck with McNally's right foot and, after Ford's next corner was again scrambled clear to him, this time McNally hit a left-footed volley that clipped the top of the angle.

Dennison's angled through ball gave Mutch the chance to hit a low cross that Chris Whyte cut out for a corner. Had he failed to do so, Bull was positioned just behind him and a goal would have been a certainty. Then the introduction of substitute Keith Downing seemed to enhance Wolves' attacking play. The midfielder almost marked his introduction with a goal with a header that had Naylor back-pedalling to tip the ball over the bar, after Dennison's cross had been half cleared.

Bellamy's long pass gave Mutch the chance to advance into the home area and hit a low shot that was just wide of the far post. Mr Morton then angered the Albion players once again after he refused them a penalty after Westley had appeared to handle. Then there was another chance for Mutch who was played in by Thompson's long through ball. He looked a certain scorer but Naylor pulled off a terrific save with North completing the clearance.

Mutch did find the net only to have his celebrations cut short by the offside flag before Albion were awarded a penalty when Ford went down under the softest of challenges from Thompson. McNally took the spot kick but Mark Kendall guessed correctly, making a wonderful save as he dived to his left.

In the dying seconds, Downing won the ball from Ford and passed to Mick Gooding. He found Mutch who crossed for Bull to chest the ball down and smash it past Naylor in front of a Smethwick end that held a sea of delirious supporters celebrating the sweetest of returns for their idol.

Albion: Naylor, Bradley (Robson), Burgess, Talbot, North, Whyte, Barham, Thomas, Goodman, McNally, Ford.
Unused sub: Bartlett.
Wolves: Kendall, Bellamy, Venus, Streete, Westley, Vaughan (Downing), Thompson, Gooding, Bull, Mutch, Dennison.
Unused sub: Paskin.
Attendance: 21,316.
Referee: K Morton.

81

Newcastle United 1 (Brock)
Wolves 4 (Bull 4)

Football League Second Division
Monday 1st January 1990

HUNDREDS OF Wolves fans were well and truly on cloud nine, quite literally, as they made their way back from Newcastle on New Year's Day 1990. Masterminded by the Wolves Supporters' Club, seven planes were chartered to ferry the fans up to Tyneside for a game that Wolves weren't expected to win. The flight cost £73 a head for the 45 minutes each way trip but it was to be money well spent.

Although the team had enjoyed a 3-1 home win over Bournemouth two days earlier, it preceded away draws at Brighton and Oxford and then a poor display against Hull City at Molineux on Boxing Day with Steve Bull's first goal in over seven weeks not enough to prevent a 2-1 reversal. Bull had missed home games against Blackburn and Middlesbrough, and one at Watford, through suspension leading into December by which time he had netted 11 league and cup goals.

The air travellers met those who had travelled to St James' Park by more conventional methods to form a large, noisy and festive delegation. The start of the game was none too convincing from the visitors' point of view and only a seventh-minute penalty save from Mark Kendall prevented an early setback.

Wayne Fereday nodded the ball inside to Micky Quinn who lobbed it forward into the path of Mark McGhee. The man destined to become manager at Molineux went down under Floyd Streete's challenge and the referee pointed to the spot. Quinn hit the penalty too close to Kendall who beat the ball away and then easily caught Fereday's half-hearted follow-up.

Kevin Brock's cross from the left almost led to an opening goal for the Geordies as Liam O'Brien steamed in to deliver a rocket header that was brilliantly turned over by Kendall. The action was taking place in front of the massed Wolves support behind the goal and while the opening 45 minutes had given them little to shout about, they were to have an excellent view of far more encouraging aspects of play after the break.

The opening goal arrived in the 50th minute after an awful blunder by Bjorn Kristensen. The Dane took a terrible touch as he attempted to clear Robbie Dennison's cross and Paul Cook quickly took advantage to fire in a short, low cross that Bull, running in, lashed into the net from little more than three yards out. South African striker John Paskin was inches away from a second after Cook had laid a free kick, from near the right-hand corner flag, into the path of Andy Thompson.

His low shot struck a defender and ballooned in the air. As it dropped Paskin swivelled and struck a shot that clipped the bar and went over. A second goal wasn't far away though and, in the 55th minute, Bull struck again, this time after he collected

Wolves' Greatest Games

Keith Downing's measured through ball as he just beat the offside trap before skilfully taking the ball around Newcastle keeper John Burridge and rolling it into the empty net.

The striker then completed a nine-minute hat-trick with a far post header after Dennison's corner came off the head of a defender who had impeded Burridge's path to the ball. The way that Bull had despatched his goals must have brought back memories for the older home fans of the late, great Tyneside legend, Jackie Milburn. And Bull wasn't finished yet!

Before completing a quartet of goals Bull did have to restart the game after Kevin Brock's 74th-minute free kick from the edge of the area swerved around the wall and beat Kendall. However, there was no stopping Wolves and Dennison, who was enjoying a fine game on the left, almost hit a fourth when he turned inside the box and lashed a shot from a tight angle against the bar.

The rampant Bull completed the scoring in the 76th minute with a goal that was almost a replica of his first although it was Dennison this time who provided the through pass. Bull held off the attention of three defenders as he again took the ball past Burridge before slipping it into the net. While the home crowd were making it known in no uncertain terms what they thought of their own team's performance, they sportingly gave a huge ovation to Bull as he wheeled away after scoring his fourth.

It was the third time that he had scored four in a game for Wolves and his first hat-trick for nine months. The three points lifted Graham Turner's team up to eighth in the First Division just a place below Newcastle and it reignited hopes of a place in the end-of-season play-offs.

Turner said of his centre forward: "When he's at his best he will score goals even against the best defenders. But he had not been playing well and hadn't looked particularly sharp. In this game though, his finishing was terrific. He was a different man in the second half and looked red-hot again.

"His second and fourth goals were first class. He could have done the same at Brighton a few weeks ago, but the ball wouldn't run for him. To score four and win at Newcastle, though, is not a bad start to the year."

Nine hundred fans, a few thousand feet up as they made their way back to Birmingham Airport, would have heartily agreed with Turner's sentiments.

Newcastle: Burridge, Anderson, Stimson, Bradshaw (Gallacher), Scott, Kristensen, Fereday, Brock, Quinn, McGhee, O'Brien.
Unused sub: Sweeney.
Wolves: Kendall, Bennett, Venus, Bellamy, Downing (Jones), Streete, Paskin, Cook, Bull, Mutch, Dennison (McLoughlin).
Attendance: 22,054.
Referee: K Lupton.

82
Derby County 1 (Kitson)
Wolves 2 (Birch penalty, Bull)
Football League Second Division
Saturday 21st March 1992

THE 1991/92 season was one of mid-table mediocrity for the Wolves team as were the two other campaigns since their elevation from the Third Division at the end of the 1980s. But the scoring feats of Stephen George Bull continued unabated albeit if not in quite such a prolific manner as had been the case in the promotions from the fourth and third tiers of the Football League.

In his first two seasons in the Second Division, Bull had scored 27 and 26 goals respectively and it was clear that it would be just a matter of time before he became the club's all-time top scorer. The record was held by John Richards who found the net 194 times in his lengthy Molineux career. He headed a list of some of the game's great goalscorers including the likes of Billy Hartill, Jimmy Murray, Derek Dougan, Tom Phillipson and Roy Swinbourne.

Bull equalled Richards's record with a goal in the draw against Bristol Rovers in March 1992, but he failed to hit the target in the two matches that followed – a home victory over Plymouth and an away defeat at Bristol City. Then came another away game with a short journey up the A38 to take on Derby County at the Baseball Ground. Derek Mountfield was missing through injury and Andy Thompson was ill so manager Graham Turner drafted Mark Burke and Andy Mutch into the team.

The visitors found themselves under intense pressure from the start with skipper Mark Venus stopping the progress of Tommy Johnson and Kevin Ashley doing likewise when Michael Forsyth went through. Mutch carried Wolves' first major threat with a run from inside the centre circle but his long-range shot cannoned off the legs of Derby defender Simon Coleman.

Paul Kitson headed narrowly wide following a Geraint Williams cross and after two Paul Birch corners had been cleared at the opposite end, Venus had to head behind a dangerous looking cross from Paul Simpson. After the nervy start, the Wolves team began to settle down and cause some moments of concern for the home rearguard with Mutch hitting a left-footed drive that struck Bull who had no time to get out of the way, and then Bull himself volleying over from Birch's centre.

Wolves won three corners in quick succession and, from the last of them, home keeper Martin Taylor plucked the ball off the head of Mutch. Ashley's foul on Paul Williams led to a free kick to the side of Mike Stowell's area. Simpson lifted the ball across and Tom Bennett did well in deflecting Marco Gabbiadini's header over the bar.

After 35 minutes Stowell came to the rescue when he blocked Gabbiadini's shot with his body after the Derby man had broken clean through having taken a return pass from Kitson. A foul by Andy Comyn on Bull gave Birch the chance with the free

Wolves' Greatest Games

kick from 20 yards but he was well off the mark and when Geraint Williams felled Bull outside the box, Paul Cook's kick hit the defensive wall and was cleared.

Gabbiadini's defence-splitting pass put Kitson in the clear but a poor first touch allowed Stowell to collect. The keeper was beaten, though, as Derby took the lead in the 44th minute. Johnson hit a shot that swerved at the last minute and Stowell could only palm the ball away and Kitson reacted quickly to hit a first-time effort past the grounded keeper.

The second half opened with Burke clearing a Simpson corner and, two minutes later, Stowell had to dive and cut out a low cross from the winger. Bull, fully aware that the travelling fans were awaiting the history-making moment, squandered a chance when he blasted the ball high and wide after chesting down a pass from Birch.

It took a remarkable goal-line clearance from Bennett to stop County from doubling their advantage. Gabbiadini found Kitson who ghosted past Lawrie Madden before hitting a low drive that Stowell, at full stretch, managed to get a hand to. But the momentum of the ball was carrying it towards the line and as the Derby supporters began to celebrate, Bennett appeared from nowhere to hook clear.

After Cook had shot wildly over the bar, Wolves suddenly turned the game on its head with two goals in little over a minute. The equaliser came in the 72nd minute when a long-range shot from Cook was blocked by Forsyth. But the referee deemed that the full-back had used his hands in doing so and pointed to the spot. Birch took the spot-kick responsibility and he duly lifted the ball past Taylor and high into the net.

Straight from the restart Mutch, as he had done innumerable times during his partnership with Bull, laid an inch-perfect pass into his team-mate's path and as Taylor advanced the number nine slipped the ball past him from ten yards before sinking to his knees, arms raised, in front of the Wolves supporters amassed behind the goal. Derby lost their spark after the double setback with the only real moment of danger coming when Simpson fired just wide.

Bull went on to add a further three goals to his tally in what remained of the season at the end of which Wolves finished in 11th spot having won 18 and lost 18 of their 46 games. Bull continued with his goalscoring heroics, eventually finishing with a grand total of 306 when injury forced his retirement in 1999.

Derby: Taylor, Kavanagh, Forsyth, G Williams, Coleman, Comyn, Johnson, Kitson, Gabbiadini, P Williams, Simpson.
Unused subs: McMinn, Micklewhite.
Wolves: Stowell, Ashley, Venus, Bennett, Rankine, Madden, Birch, Cook, Bull, Mutch, Burke.
Unused subs: Simkin, Downing.
Attendance: 21,024.
Referee: M James.

Wolves 6 (Mutch 3, Bennett, Cook, Bull)
Newcastle United 2 (Quinn, Peacock)
Football League Second Division
Tuesday 31st March 1992

ANDY MUTCH was the perfect foil for Steve Bull and the two formed a partnership feared by opposition defences. Mutch had joined Wolves in February 1986, some nine months before the arrival of Bull. A Merseysider, he had served as an apprentice at both Liverpool and Everton before joining non-league side Southport. He joined a sinking Wolves side from the Sandpipers for a relatively low fee and in the 15 games he played that season, he scored seven goals. However, they weren't enough to prevent Wolves from slipping into the bottom tier of English soccer. His contribution to the club's climb to better times, though, was a valuable one and he made over 300 appearances with a strike rate of almost one every three games.

His efforts earned him international rewards at both England B and Under-21 levels and he won Third and Fourth Division championship honours as well as a Sherpa Van Trophy winner's medal after he had opened the scoring against Burnley at Wembley.

While his strike partner regularly celebrated hat-tricks, Mutch only managed one treble and that came against a Newcastle United team managed by former England and Liverpool idol Kevin Keegan. Neither team were having a particularly impressive campaign and hopes of promotion had long since disappeared when they met at Molineux with Wolves looking for revenge after going down 2-1 at St James' Park on Boxing Day.

The first goal arrived in the sixth minute when Mutch passed to midfielder Paul Cook. He took the ball to the edge of the box before laying a short low cross into the path of Mutch, who had continued his run. Keith Scott dived in with a last-ditch tackle and the ball appeared to hit Mutch, who was in the process of shooting, and fly past Geordie keeper Tommy Wright.

Mutch was soon involved again when he laid the ball into the path of Mark Venus whose mishit cross still fell for Cook to turn and hit a shot that Wright kept out with his leg. The pressure on Wright's goal in front of the partly constructed Stan Cullis Stand continued and Paul Birch's left-wing corner in the 11th minute led to a second goal from Mutch as he headed in at the far post after Lawrie Madden had helped on the flag kick.

However, with Newcastle's first goal attempt of the game, just two minutes later, Micky Quinn reduced the arrears when the striker took a lofted pass from the halfway line and, as he spotted Mike Stowell off his line, he executed a perfect lob over the stranded keeper. Stowell soon made amends with a smart save off his former Everton team-mate Kevin Sheedy before Tom Bennett restored the two-goal cushion in the 26th minute.

Wolves' Greatest Games

The goal came from yet another corner, this time taken by Cook. Derek Mountfield headed the ball down to Bull who hooked it over his shoulder into the heart of the six-yard box for Bennett to run in and convert from close in.

The brisk action continued and after Kevin Brock had shot against the post, the rebound fell to Scott and his first time effort drew a fine save from Stowell. Then it was the turn of Bull to chance his luck as Cook's pass from the centre circle was knocked on by Mutch to the centre-forward and, like his counterpart at the other end of the field, Wright had to be at his best to turn away the fierce shot that followed.

The Molineux supporters had seen just three goals from their team in the five home games leading up to Newcastle's visit. However, that total was beaten in the 49th minute as Cook made it 4-1. An attack from the visitors was broken up and Bennett took a return pass from Bull as he sprinted into the opposition half. He laid the ball off for Birch to cross and when Mutch went up to challenge Wright, the keeper could only half clear to Cook who volleyed into the opposite corner of the net.

There was still a threat from United when they went forward and in the 73rd minute they once again pulled a goal back. Liam O'Brien went on a fine run through the middle of the home defence and Gavin Peacock escaped the close attention of Keith Downing to rifle the ball home. However, Wolves, and in particular Mutch, weren't quite finished.

Just five minutes remained when he completed his treble. Wolves were awarded a free kick 25 yards out and in a central position. Downing and Birch stood either side of the ball and they touched it to each other, allowing Cook to run and fire over the defensive wall for Mutch to deflect it past Wright.

Two minutes later Bull wound up the scoring for the evening when Venus's deep cross bounced down in front of him before he hit a shot on the run that just beat Wright and squeezed inside the far post. The game had long gone for Newcastle and yet Keegan remonstrated with the referee that Bull was offside when he took possession.

The inconsistency in Wolves' play returned in the following two games – away defeats at Oxford and Ipswich. The season finished with the team just inside the top half of the table having won 18 and lost 18 of their fixtures while Newcastle were down in 20th just four points above the drop zone.

Wolves: Stowell, Ashley (Kelly), Venus, Bennett, Madden, Mountfield, Birch, Cook, Bull, Mutch, Downing.
Unused sub: Steele.
Newcastle: Wright, Watson, Stimson, O'Brien, Kilcline (McDonough), Scott, Quinn, Peacock, Kelly, Sheedy, Brock.
Unused sub: Clark.
Attendance: 14,480.
Referee: R Gifford.

Wolves 3 (Burke, Bradbury 2)
Millwall 1 (Allen)
Football League First Division
Saturday 1st May 1993

THERE DIDN'T appear to be much significance to Wolves' final home game of the 1992/93 season. The opposition was provided by Millwall who had an outside chance of scraping into the end-of-season play-offs, while that opportunity for Graham Turner's team had disappeared with a mid-table finish guaranteed.

The game, however, was destined to go down in the history books not so much for what occurred on the pitch, more than the event that took place off it. There was an air of sadness in the South Bank because the fixture marked the end of watching games at Molineux from the terraces. The vast spaces of the hotel end were to make way for a smaller, all-seated commodity.

Following the Bradford fire tragedy in 1985, half of Molineux was closed by the local authorities as a fire risk. The Waterloo Road Stand and the enclosure in front of it were shut down, as was the much-loved North Bank. Supporters who followed the club on their travels in the Third and Fourth Divisions asked, with some justification, why the Cow Shed was out of bounds when many of the grounds they visited while following Wolves looked to provide far more hazardous accommodation.

The result was that the only seating at Molineux was in the relatively new John Ireland Stand while the South Bank, with a vast swathe down the middle cordoned off for segregation purposes, provided the only standing view of games. The once proud Molineux looked, and was, a mess and with work to convert the stadium into a modern, all-seat facility, it was time to say goodbye to a traditional method of watching the game in Wolverhampton.

Of the 12,000 supporters who turned up to watch the game, many were packed in to the home section of the South Bank and it came as something of a surprise to them when it was announced that Shaun Bradbury would be playing up front. Birmingham-born, the 19-year-old had played just once before at senior level in a League Cup tie against Shrewsbury Town in October 1991.

He was one of three changes made by Turner as he tried to halt a run of three consecutive defeats with five goals conceded and none scored. Paul Jones replaced injured keeper Mike Stowell, while Lawrie Madden and Derek Mountfield were omitted with Bradbury and Paul Blades coming into the team.

Wolves attacked the South Bank end and there was almost a memorable start for Bradbury in the opening seconds. Robbie Dennison sent Paul Edwards away on the left and his excellent cross looked destined for the head of the young striker until Ian Dawes intervened to head behind. Then a Paul Cook corner eluded Lions keeper Kasey Keller and Mark Burke before going behind just beyond the far post.

Wolves' Greatest Games

Two Millwall corners, both conceded by Blades, were cleared by the home defence and Jones was called upon for the first time when he held a low drive from Andy Roberts before Cook, Edwards and Burke combined to set up Andy Mutch whose far-post header was wide of the mark. Cook was then high and wide with a first time shot after a pass from Dennison, but the offside flag had been raised anyway.

With 20 minutes gone, Bradbury opened the scoring after he had taken a short pass from Burke midway inside the Millwall half. There seemed little danger to the visitors but Bradbury took a few paces before letting fly from 22 yards with a shot that whistled past three defenders on its way into the top corner of the net.

Millwall weren't posing much of a threat and they could have gone further behind when Mutch's centre presented Burke with a free header that he guided wide of the near post. Wolves kept up the pressure and Bradbury struck again in the 28th minute. He took a Mutch pass in his stride and, with his confidence high, blasted a right-footed drive across Keller and into the far corner of the net.

A penetrating pass from Burke opened up the Millwall defence. Mutch, to the left of the area, rolled the ball into the path of Dennison who got plenty behind his shot which went straight into the arms of Keller. Considering that the play-off door hadn't closed on the Londoners, they were showing little in terms of determination or as an attacking force and they fell three behind a minute before the break. Darren Simpkin won a tackle with Colin Cooper and crossed for Burke to lash the ball into the roof of the net from close in.

After the restart, Bradbury spurned the chance of a hat-trick when he miskicked with an attempted volley from Cook's cross. The loose ball ran to Dennison but he shot over from a good position. Following their first-half domination, and attacking the vacant North Bank end, Wolves seemed to lose some of their spark and there was a chance for Millwall when Kenny Cunningham's cross ran through to Dawes who snatched at his shot and was off target.

Bradbury, who had taken a knock, was replaced before Malcolm Allen pulled one back in the 67th minute when he volleyed home Phil Barber's cross to conclude the scoring for the afternoon. Bradbury played in the following week's defeat at Derby, but that was to be his final appearance for the senior squad before he moved to Hereford a year later.

Wolves: Jones, Simkin, Edwards, Burke, Blades, Venus, Bradbury (Roberts), Cook, Thompson, Mutch, Dennison.
Unused sub: Steele.
Millwall: Keller, Cunningham, Dawes, Roberts, Cooper, Maguire, Rae, Moralee, Allen, Goodman, Barber.
Unused subs: Dalby, May.
Attendance: 12,054.
Referee: K Cooper.

85

Wolves 1 (Kelly)
Sheffield Wednesday 1 (Bright)

Wolves win 4-3 on penalties. FA Cup fourth round replay, Wednesday 8th February 1995

TWO GOALS down at the break against Third Division side Mansfield Town, it looked as if Wolves' 1995 FA Cup interest was going to come to a sudden and ignominious end at Field Mill. However, a 'few words' from manager Graham Taylor during the interval obviously hit home as his talk sparked a revival that saw Wolves emerge as 3-2 victors.

While that comeback emerged over a 45-minute period, it wasn't as dramatic as the one that lay in wait when Wolves were paired with Premiership opposition in the shape of Sheffield Wednesday in the fourth round of the competition with the draw giving the Owls home advantage. Yorkshire-born Lee Mills had the chance to give Wolves the lead inside three minutes. He ran on to Robbie Dennison's through ball but with only Kevin Pressman to beat, his tame shot was easily gathered by the keeper.

Twice more in the next few minutes Mills had attempts at goal and both were a lot closer than his initial effort as Wolves looked anything but fazed playing on an away ground against top flight opposition. Guy Whittingham did head narrowly over the bar for Wednesday and from another of his efforts, Gordon Cowans cleared off the line. However, generally speaking Wolves looked comfortable and Neil Emblen almost broke through with a fierce shot that forced a fine save from Pressman as he clawed the ball away.

Wolves fully deserved a second bite of the cherry but they were almost denied a replay by a controversial refereeing decision three minutes from time. Chris Bart-Williams had dribbled the ball to the byline when he was challenged by Emblen. With the Wednesday players getting in position for a corner, they suddenly realised that the official had pointed to the spot. Emblen was entirely blameless and like the rest of the Wolves team, he was incensed. Bart-Williams took the kick aiming for the top corner but Paul Jones pulled off a fantastic save to ensure that justice was done.

The first goal of the tie came after 12 minutes of the replay at Molineux. Pressman completely missed Dennison's corner from the left and David Kelly nodded the ball over the line from point-blank range. Don Goodman almost made it two when he clipped the outside of a post, and Pressman denied the striker with a terrific save from a well struck half-volley after 36 minutes.

After being on the back foot for much of the opening half, Wednesday began to push Wolves back following the break and they equalised in the 56th minute. Cowans did well to block Graham Hyde's shot on the line but he could do nothing as Mark Bright ran in to force the ball into the net from a yard out. Ten minutes later,

Wolves' Greatest Games

Pressman was at his best again as he somehow got a hand to Kelly's close-range shot and turned the ball on to the post.

Neither side could find a winner in the 90 minutes so the game went into extra time during which Wednesday had three good chances to settle matters. Bright headed over from Chris Waddle's centre, Jones only just got a hand to Andy Sinton's low drive, and in the 119th minute Bright missed an absolute sitter as he shot over the bar after being set up by Whittingham. It was to prove a costly miss as the game moved to a penalty shoot-out – only the second at Molineux after a Birmingham Senior Cup tie against VS Rugby in 1989.

The South Bank was the end of the ground designated for the kicks to take place and Wednesday took the first through Bright who sent the keeper the wrong way to give the visitors a confident start. For Wolves, regular penalty taker Andy Thompson looked to level things up but he was left holding his head in anguish as his shot rebounded off the crossbar.

Whittingham made it 2-0 with a kick that was almost identical to Bright's, slotting the ball to the keeper's left as he dived the other way. When Dennison's effort was beaten down by Pressman, things began to look bleak for the home side and even more so after the Wednesday keeper took the next kick himself, launching a rocket of a left-footed shot into the top corner leaving Jones without a prayer.

At 3-0 down it looked like it was game over for Wanderers as the Owls just needed to net one of their remaining kicks, or for Wolves to miss one of theirs. There was a glimmer of hope when Cowans beat Pressman and when Pearce's kick hit the top of the bar and went over, the confidence seemed to drain out of the Wednesday players.

Kelly pulled it back to 3-2 when he hammered the ball into the roof of the net but it just needed Bart-Williams to convert to leave the visiting supporters celebrating. However, his kick was too close to Jones who fell to his left to save. When John de Wolf took his turn his shot into the corner was out of Pressman's reach even though the keeper guessed correctly.

With the scores even it was now down to sudden death and Waddle's body language as he stepped up to the plate spoke volumes. His kick lacked power and was virtually straight at Jones who moments later was joining his team-mates as they engulfed Goodman who had sealed matters with a penalty over Pressman's head and into the top of the net.

Wolves: Jones, Blades (Mills), Thompson, Emblen, de Wolf, Law, Rankine (Bennett), Kelly, Goodman, Cowans, Dennison.
Unused sub: de Bont.
Wednesday: Pressman, Atherton, Nolan, Hyde (Whittingham), Pearce, Walker, Waddle, Bart-Williams, Ingesson (Sheridan), Bright, Sinton.
Unused sub: Woods.
Attendance: 28,136.
Referee: A Wilkie.

Port Vale 2 (Naylor, Kent)
Wolves 4 (de Wolf 3 (one penalty), Bull)
Football League First Division
Saturday 25th February 1995

IN DECEMBER 1994, manager Graham Taylor made a double signing when he bought Don Goodman from Sunderland and added a surprise choice to bolster his defence, Dutchman John de Wolf from Feyenoord. While Goodman was a familiar figure in the West Midlands, de Wolf was less so although a check through the record books revealed that he had played eight times for Holland prior to Taylor laying out £620,000 for him.

Easily recognisable with his beard and flowing locks, he quickly became a firm favourite of the female supporters at Molineux and there was little doubt that he could be a commanding figure in defence. However, injuries were to mar his stay with the club and he returned to his homeland after just 18 months.

His 15th game in Wolves colours saw him creating a little bit of history when he became the first post-war defender to score a hat-trick for the club – the last man to have achieved the feat being Ted Pheasant back in 1902 in a home game against Newcastle. De Wolf's venue for his treble was the wide open spaces of Vale Park in north Staffordshire.

While Wolves' FA Cup form was up to speed, their league performances had been indifferent in the games leading up to the visit to the Potteries with a 5-1 humbling against Bolton at Burnden Park and a 2-0 home reversal against Middlesbrough, sandwiching a Molineux win against Bristol City. After the Boro setback, Taylor made changes with Geoff Thomas, Brian Law and Mark Venus being replaced by Steve Bull, Peter Shirtliff and Paul Blades. Bull's return came after a two-month absence following heel surgery.

The afternoon didn't get off to the greatest of starts for de Wolf with Shirtliff taking over the captaincy from him. However, after just 85 seconds he had a broad grin on his face after giving Wolves the lead. Kevin Kent conceded a corner and from Robbie Dennison's inswinging kick, David Kelly headed towards goal only for Steve Guppy to clear off the line. But Vale couldn't get the ball away and de Wolf smashed it into the roof of net from the heart of a crowded box.

Ray Walker sliced a shot wide and Paul Jones collected a low centre from Guppy as Vale tried to hit back before a lineman's flag denied Wolves a second goal. Andy Thompson's shot struck a defender but when the ball rebounded back to the utility man he drilled it past Paul Musselwhite in the home goal unaware that a team-mate had strayed offside.

Vale too had a goal rubbed out but it wasn't a difficult decision for the referee to make as Martin Foyle clearly handled as he knocked the ball out of Jones's hands after the keeper had collected a cross from Kent. Jones then needed two attempts to collect the ball after Foyle had headed Guppy's deep corner back into the goalmouth. But he was beaten in the 18th minute after he failed to hold on to Walker's 25-yard drive and Tony Naylor ran in to force home the rebound.

Goodman struck a low drive wide of the near post, and Jones punched clear a Guppy free kick and then saved after Kent had swooped on the loose ball. He then had to save at the feet of Foyle after his poor clearance had gone straight to the Vale striker. Only the woodwork denied Wolves a second goal with Kelly's header from Dennison's corner coming back off the crossbar.

Jones saved acrobatically as he palmed away a deep swerving cross from Guppy, before a mistake by his counterpart in the Vale goal led to Wolves' second two minutes before the break. Musselwhite left his line to try to gather another Dennison corner but was left stranded as de Wolf headed home with the ball having just crossed the line before Guppy hooked it clear. In stoppage time Bull added a third as he ran on to Goodman's nod on from de Wolf's through pass and chipped the ball over Musselwhite.

Wanderers started the second half strongly and Thompson and Bull set up Kelly for a low drive that was only taken with a degree of difficulty by Musselwhite. Then Bull, with a typical piece of bustling play, created an opening for himself but his drive was inches wide of the near post. After absorbing heavy pressure, Vale pulled a goal back in the 56th minute.

Foyle had seen his shot blocked in front of the line by Shirtliff, and with his next attempt the striker miscued his shot. However, the ball fell invitingly for Kent to score from close range. Kent then turned creator with a neat pass to Naylor who was thwarted by Jones. As Wolves attacked, Shirtliff headed against the post after getting on the end of Mark Rankine's high ball into the box.

De Wolf completed his hat-trick in the 68th minute after Kevin Scott handled just inside the area as he tried to fend off Bull's challenge. De Wolf assumed spot-kick duties ahead of Thompson and he expertly sent Musselwhite the wrong way as he completed his treble.

Just two games later, playing against Sunderland, de Wolf landed awkwardly from an aerial challenge, and he didn't play again for the remainder of the campaign. After making sporadic appearances the following season, he returned to Holland having failed to get on with Taylor's replacement Mark McGhee.

Vale: Musselwhite, Sandeman, Tankard, Walker (Glover), Aspin, Scott, Guppy, Van Der Laan, Foyle (Allon), Naylor, Kent.
Unused sub: Van Heusden.
Wolves: Jones, Blades, Thompson, Rankine, de Wolf, Shirtliff, Goodman, Kelly, Bull (Venus), Cowans, Dennison.
Unused subs: Stowell, Smith.
Attendance: 13,676.
Referee: J Lloyd.

Wolves 3 (Goodman, Thompson penalty, Bull)
Birmingham City 2 (Devlin 2, one penalty)
Football League First Division
Saturday 5th March 1996

JUST 18 days before Birmingham City's visit to Molineux, Wolves had lost 2-0 to them at St Andrew's. And in the return fixture it looked odds on that Blues were going to do the double over their near neighbours until Wolves got their revenge in one of the most dramatic endings to a game ever seen between the teams.

There were two changes to the Wolves team who had lost to City with Darren Ferguson and Brian Law making way for Steve Froggatt and Jamie Smith. In that season's FA Cup Wolves and Blues were paired together in the third round and, after a 1-1 draw in Birmingham, Wolves edged the replay 2-1 before going out to Tottenham Hotspur in the next round. In the league things were pretty bleak with no hope of even reaching the play-offs as the season entered the home straight.

Before the game, charismatic City boss Barry Fry was advising people to put £50 on Steve Bull scoring the first goal. He was to find out, to his team's cost, that it should have been the last goal and not the first!

With a little over a minute gone, Birmingham skipper Gary Breen was lucky to escape with just a yellow card after he lost the ball to Froggatt and then halted the winger's clear run at goal by pulling him back. Simon Osborn's free kick was half-cleared to Neil Emblen whose close-range shot was gathered by keeper Bart Griemink. Play was somewhat feisty in the opening minutes of which just seven had gone when the visitors moved ahead.

Jonathan Hunt took a pass from Vinny Samways and crossed to lanky striker Kevin Francis who helped the ball on into the path of Paul Devlin and he drove the ball past Mike Stowell from ten yards out. Steve Corica earned Wolves a free kick shortly after the restart with a run that took him past three defenders before he was finally hauled down but Don Goodman's kick was way too high.

Luck was against Wolves in the 16th minute when Goodman nodded Stowell's clearance on to Bull who sped past Michael Johnson before hitting a shot from 20 yards that struck the inside of the post and rolled along the line to the relieved Griemink. Devlin was then well wide with a close-range header following a cross from Steven Barnes.

Wolves were far from being at their best but chances were coming their way and after Froggatt fired wildly over the angle, Dean Richards headed narrowly wide after a free kick from Osborn. Richards figured again with a low left-footed shot that Griemink saved at his near post. Stowell dived to save a long-range shot from Hunt before Wolves drew level five minutes before the break.

Smith pushed the ball forward to Corica and the Australian found Goodman who took a touch before drilling home an angled shot that went in off the foot of the far post. It was the striker's 20th goal of the season. Blues almost regained the lead moments later when Steve Castle met Andy Legg's cross with a header that forced an acrobatic save from Stowell.

Goodman's penalty appeal after he had been pulled down by Richard Forsyth was ignored by the referee and then Stowell cut out a dangerous cross from Samways at his near post. Breen headed behind a Smith centre at the other end as Goodman threatened and, from the corner conceded, Osborn played a short ball to Corica whose cross was just too high for the incoming Richards.

City should have been back in front after 61 minutes when Francis, just eight yards out and unmarked, blasted the ball over the bar. Wolves went close when Smith met Bull's centre and miscued his shot. Legg made a hash of his clearance, giving the ball back to Smith who volleyed against the outside of the near post.

With six minutes remaining Blues were awarded a penalty in farcical circumstances. Francis was just six yards out when he took an air-kick at Legg's cross. He completely missed the ball but the referee thought that he had been fouled by Thompson and to the amazement of everyone, he pointed to the spot. Amid all the protests, Devlin kept his nerve to beat Stowell with the penalty.

Two minutes later, Breen was adjudged to have handled Richards's overhead kick in the box. Again it seemed to be a harsh decision but Andy Thompson netted the kick to tie things up again although there were a few flutters as Griemink touched the ball with his arm but was unable to prevent it from going in.

Still the drama wasn't over. Osborn played the ball over the Blues' defence and Bull, in full flight, left Johnson in his wake as he careered towards Griemink's goal. The Dutch keeper stood little chance as the Molineux ace arrowed an angled shot just inside the post to trigger a cacophony of noise from the elated home supporters.

After the final whistle, manager Mark McGhee conceded: "I think we are not much better than Birmingham City but both teams are in their rightful position in the middle of the table. We both still have a lot to do but I have to commend Barry Fry for his attitude. To be able to smile as he did at the final whistle, in the wake of such a disappointment, says a lot for the man."

Wolves: Stowell, Smith, Thompson, Young (Atkins), Emblen, Richards, Corica, Goodman, Bull, Froggatt, Osborn.
Unused subs: Williams, Pearce.
Blues: Griemink, Forsyth, Legg, Samways, Breen, Johnson, Hunt, Devlin, Francis, Barnes, Castle.
Unused subs: Donowa, Bowen, Edwards.
Attendance: 26,256.
Referee: J Kirkby.

West Bromwich Albion 2 (Hamilton, Taylor)
Wolves 4 (Roberts 3, Bull)

Football League First Division
Sunday 15th September 1996

WOLVES HAD made a fairly convincing start to the 1996/97 campaign, losing just one of their opening six league games when an Ian Crook penalty at Carrow Road was enough to give Norwich the three points. Then, five days before the derby at West Bromwich, Iwan Roberts had scored the equalising goal at Oxford's Manor Ground, his first for the club since he signed from Leicester City in the summer of 1996. However, the Welshman's contribution at The Hawthorns was to earn him a mention in the history books.

Like Wolves, Albion had lost just one game although they had played one fewer than their arch rivals. It all looked like the crowd were in for a typical closely-fought derby game but with Roberts and Steve Bull leading the charge, the visitors swept into a three-goal lead with less than 30 minutes gone.

A slip by Roberts set Paul Peschisolido on a run at goal but Dean Richards got back and won possession from the Canadian. Roberts quickly atoned for his error by giving Wolves a fourth-minute lead. Steve Froggatt launched an inswinging corner from the right and Roberts ran in unmarked to head home from close range.

Albion tried to hit back through Richard Sneekes who had been set up by Peschisolido but Mark Venus tackled the Dutchman on the edge of the area and denied him the opportunity of getting a shot in. Shane Nicholson made a desperate clearance as Bull homed in on the Albion area and the frenetic start to the game continued as Daryl Burgess headed Ian Hamilton's corner down to Sneekes who fired high over the bar into the massed ranks of Wolves supporters in the Smethwick End.

On 15 minutes Bull got a second goal for the visitors when, from six yards out, he turned and hit a left-footed shot past Albion keeper Paul Crichton following Froggatt's long throw. Andy Hunt's low drive from the 18-yard line didn't give Mike Stowell any reason for concern but as Albion tried desperately to get back into the game, Bull had to fall back and clear a dangerous centre from Paul Holmes after another Hamilton corner had been played back to him.

The home defence were struggling to contain the dual threat of Bull and Roberts and they capitulated once more in the 28th minute as Roberts grabbed a third with a virtual replica of the first goal – a close-range header after a Froggatt corner. Within a minute it took a smart save from Crichton to thwart Bull who had taken a pass from Steve Corica.

Stowell made light work of taking a cross from Holmes and when Peschisolido broke through and fired at goal the whistle blew as he had handled the ball. Paul Groves headed narrowly over the bar after a cross from Holmes and then Hunt set up David Smith on the 18-yard line but his shot was deflected away from goal by Venus.

Wolves' Greatest Games

Roberts was just beaten to Simon Osborn's free kick by Crichton before Albion pulled a goal back three minutes before the interval with the unmarked Hamilton heading in Smith's centre from the left. Buoyed by the goal, the Baggies started the second period on the front foot and the visiting defence had to clear Nicholson's through ball as Hunt ran in on it. Then Richards had to head away a dangerous cross from Nicholson.

Twice in the matter of a minute, long throws from Froggatt had the Albion backline in panic mode and when they broke from defence, Groves released Holmes on the right and his cross was cut out by Andy Thompson. In the 53rd minute Roberts completed his hat-trick and in doing so became the first Wolves player to hit a treble at The Hawthorns. Froggatt delivered a cross that was missed by Bull but not Roberts who side-footed home from the edge of the six-yard box.

Three minutes later another Froggatt cross was met by Bull who deftly laid the ball off for Corica to crack a shot that wasn't too far away. Bob Taylor, an interval substitute for Peschisolido, headed narrowly wide after a centre from Hunt. Osborn had a shot blocked on the edge of the box by Groves, before Albion reduced the deficit in the 66th minute when Taylor's angled shot went in off the far post.

Albion poured forward and Sneekes had a shot charged down by Richards, Hunt headed just over the bar from a Nicholson cross and Taylor was narrowly wide with a shot on the turn. Froggatt hit a searing drive narrowly over although his effort would not have counted as the referee had blown for an infringement, and at the other end Stowell made a fine save to turn away a drive from Sneekes.

Seven minutes from the end Taylor thought he had netted Albion's third but he was flagged offside as he put the ball past Stowell who then had to be at his best as he pushed Hamilton's shot behind for a corner. The terrific pace continued right up until the final whistle with Groves hooking a shot just off target and, in the final minute, Stowell saving Taylor's flick. However, there was no denying Wolves and, in particular, Iwan Roberts.

Albion: Crichton, Holmes, Nicholson, Sneekes, Mardon (Donovan), Burgess, Hamilton, D Smith (Gilbert), Peschisolido (Taylor), Hunt, Groves.
Wolves: Stowell, J Smith, Froggatt, Atkins, Venus, Richards, Thompson, Corica, Bull, Roberts, Osborn.
Unused subs: Ferguson, Segers, Wright.
Attendance: 20,711.
Referee: M Pierce.

Norwich City 0
Wolves 2 (Keane 2)
Football League First Division
Saturday 9th August 1997

AS PART of the pre-season warm-up in 1997, Wolves went on a brief two-match tour of Scotland. Included in the travelling party was a Dublin-born youth apprentice by the name of Robbie Keane. Boss Mark McGhee had obviously seen enough of him in training to warrant taking him north of the border and his decision turned out to be fully justified.

Keane started in both friendlies and he was at the heart of some promising moves in the 1-0 victory over Dundee United. In the second game, at Stirling Albion, he gave an even stronger performance and he showed a coolness that belied his tender years when he took a pass from Darren Ferguson and lobbed the ball over advancing Stirling keeper Mark McGeown for Wolves' first equaliser. He then supplied the cross for Glen Crowe to level again with 2-2 the final score.

Keane's man of the match performance at the tiny Forthbank Stadium left the group of Wolves supporters who had made the trip to Scotland in no doubt that he had to be in with a shout of at least being on the bench for the season's opening league game at Norwich. McGhee obviously felt that the youngster could handle the pressure and, just a month after his 17 birthday, Keane was given a full debut. He made a start that, in all probability, surpassed his wildest dreams as he trotted out into the Norfolk sunshine at Carrow Road.

Also making their debuts for the club that afternoon were summer signings Steve Sedgley and Dariusz Kubicki, the Polish defender. Sedgley, because of his playing days at Ipswich, was a target for the home fans to voice their disapproval while Iwan Roberts, after his season at Molineux, took plenty of stick from the Wolves contingent in the crowd.

There was an early chance for Steve Bull but his header from Steve Froggatt's centre went straight to Andy Marshall. Then Roberts, a month after his move from the Midlands to East Anglia, saw his deflected shot on the turn well held by Mike Stowell. Then it was Bull again, with a volley that flew across the face of goal after he connected with Ferguson's quickly-taken free kick.

Wolves were looking much the better side and Bull was giving the home defence plenty to think about. He was inches away from the opening goal after he had chested down Jamie Smith's centre. However, it was the youngest player on the pitch who made the breakthrough in the 34th minute. Don Goodman headed down Keith Curle's deep free kick and from 20 yards Keane hit the back of the net with a dipping left-footed shot.

Some neat interplay between Mark Atkins and Smith opened up a chance for Bull to grab a second goal but, surrounded by defenders, he could only stab the ball wide.

Wolves' Greatest Games

Then, after being fouled some 25 yards out from goal, Keane tapped the ball into the path of Goodman but the home defensive wall did its job.

Shortly after the interval, Keane was again in the thick of things, this time inside his own area where he was on hand to clear a free kick from Neil Adams. He then showed that despite his age he wasn't to be taken lightly when he became involved in a heated exchange with Craig Fleming.

There was a chance for the Canaries after Curle's aerial challenge on Rob Newman was penalised. Adams took the free kick quickly and his low shot from 22 yards was only just wide of the far post. Norwich should have been level after a move instigated by Keith O'Neill. He found Victor Segura with a long, accurate pass and the Spaniard's centre was headed a yard wide by Darren Eadie who couldn't have been better positioned.

City had started to gain the upper hand and after Goodman had pulled a shot wide after being set up by Keane, there was another moment of danger in Stowell's goalmouth as Roberts headed down Eadie's cross and the ball just eluded Newman as he ran in at the far post. After enjoying their best attacking spell of the game, Norwich went two behind in the 65th minute.

Again it was Keane who did the damage as he took an intelligent pass from Atkins and breezed past Segura into the City area where a cluster of defenders lay in wait. Undeterred, Keane toe-poked the ball past Marshall for a finish that any seasoned striker would have been proud of.

Goodman, his way to goal blocked, almost fashioned a third when he spotted Bull to the right of the box but his angled drive flew wide of the far post. O'Neill went close to putting Norwich back into the game with a dipping effort that just cleared Stowell's bar, and then Adams dragged a shot wide when well placed.

Wolves held on to their advantage quite comfortably with Stowell only having the one real save to make in a solid team performance. However, there was only going to be one man, or teenager, who was going to grab all the headlines at the start of a career that was to see him become the first man to score over 50 goals for the Republic of Ireland in over 120 games for them. Wolves had indeed given birth to a prodigious talent in Robbie Keane.

Norwich: Marshall, Newman, Fleming (Bellamy), Sutch, Segura, Polston, Adams, Mills, Roberts (Fleck), Eadie, O'Neill.
Unused sub: Scott.
Wolves: Stowell, Smith, Kubicki, Atkins, Sedgley, Curle, Ferguson, Keane, Bull, Goodman, Froggatt.
Unused subs: Robinson, Crowe, Westwood.
Attendance: 17,230.
Referee: M Bailey.

Leeds United 0
Wolves 1 (Goodman)
FA Cup quarter-final
Saturday 7th March 1998

FEW GAVE Wolves a chance when they were given an away tie at Premiership side Leeds United in the quarter-final of the FA Cup. Given that the Molineux team had been booed from the field by their own supporters after conceding a last-minute goal to struggling Stoke City three days earlier, as Leeds were beating Tottenham Hotspur 1-0 at Elland Road, the omens weren't looking good.

The path to the last eight had seen Wolves beat Darlington, Charlton Athletic and Wimbledon – the latter two after Molineux replays, while Leeds had overcome Oxford United, Grimsby Town and Birmingham City. The draw with Wolves meant that all four of the ties they played were at home and against non-Premiership opposition.

Wolves began encouragingly with Lee Naylor starting a move down the left, feeding Dougie Freedman who beat Robert Molenaar before sending in a cross that just evaded Steve Bull in the six-yard box. Jimmy Floyd Hasselbaink got in Leeds' first effort with a tame header that was easily gathered by Hans Segers after a throw from Martin Hiden. There was a much greater threat when Rod Wallace raced past Dean Richards and drilled a shot not far wide of the far post.

Don Goodman started a flowing move which involved Bull slipping the ball to Freedman who fired over from a good position. As Wolves performed with a confident air against their higher ranked opponents, Bull almost got on the end of Simon Osborn's through pass. The home crowd were strangely subdued as Keith Curle marshalled his defence superbly, absorbing any pressure with little difficulty.

Leeds were struggling to make the final pass count and when an opportunity did come their way Hasselbaink fired high over Segers's bar. However, in their next attack, the Yorkshire side almost broke through as Harry Kewell shrugged off the challenge of Adrian Williams and hit a low shot that Segers did well to turn away. When Williams ventured upfield his goal attempt hit Molenaar but rather than deflecting the ball past Nigel Martyn, it simply took the sting out of the shot allowing the England keeper an easy claim.

Kewell was close with a curling effort that skimmed the top of Segers's crossbar, and the Wolves keeper made an instinctive save as he collected a deflected shot from Gunnar Halle. At the other end Goodman won possession from Molenaar and fed Freedman who drove well wide. However, Leeds were beginning to turn the screw and two corners and a free kick had to be cleared by the Wolves defence before Kewell sent a volley into the crowd behind Segers's goal.

It had been all Leeds in the period leading up to the break but, in the final minute of the half, Osborn's free kick gave Freedman a half chance but he couldn't get his shot away. Then Kevin Muscat didn't get enough power behind his drive, affording Martyn a relatively easy save. The resumption saw Segers racing from his line to cut out Hasselbaink's through ball as Wallace homed in, before a slip by Lucas Radebe almost gifted Wolves the lead.

The South African failed to deal with Muscat's cross, allowing the ball to run through to Goodman who drove fractionally over. Then Martyn had to concede a corner after a dangerous cross from Naylor. When Leeds attacked Wallace had a half-chance but he scooped the ball over the bar and after a Goodman pass had been intercepted, Molenaar raced upfield and hit a volley that went straight to Segers.

Alf-Inge Haaland tried a long-range drive that was well off target before Kewell and Radebe also had goal attempts that Segers was able to watch pass harmlessly past the post. However, the Dutch keeper was forced to clutch a curling shot from Hasselbaink right on the line. Then on 82 minutes, Goodman, who was born just a few miles from Elland Road, wrote the Sunday newspaper headlines as he put Wolves ahead.

Carl Robinson played a superbly weighted ball into the Leeds box, leaving the home defence flat-footed and allowing Goodman to run in and lift the ball over Martyn to send the 5,000 travelling supporters into raptures. However, with two minutes remaining they looked on in horror as the referee pointed to the spot after Robbie Keane, on as a substitute for Bull, had been adjudged to have tripped Hasselbaink in the area.

It was a debateable decision but after Hasselbaink had picked himself up to take the spot-kick, he was denied by Segers who threw himself to his left to save and put Wolves into the semi-final and a meeting with Arsenal at Villa Park.

Speaking after the game, Goodman, who as a youth had acted as a ball boy at Elland Road for the team he had supported, said: "I was rejected by Leeds on account of my size at 15 or 16, and once or twice when I was at West Bromwich and Sunderland, I heard they were watching me or making bids. There was a time that I would have walked here to play for them but that time has passed me by."

His goal had put Wolves one step from Wembley with the chance of their first final in the competition in 48 years. But a Christopher Wreh goal, the only one of the game, saw McGhee's men fall at the final hurdle.

Leeds: Martyn, Hiden, Molenaar, Radebe, Harte, Halle, Haaland, Ribeiro (Kelly), Kewell, Wallace, Hasselbaink.
Unused subs: Wetherall, Bowyer, Hopkin, Beeney.
Wolves: Segers, Muscat, Naylor, Williams, Richards, Curle, Goodman, Robinson, Bull (Keane), Freedman, Osborn.
Unused subs: Stowell, Simpson, Atkins, Roberts.
Attendance: 39,902.
Referee: P Durkin.

Bristol City 1 (Hutchings)
Wolves 6 (Whittingham, Connolly 4, Robinson)

Football League First Division
Saturday 7th November 1998

WOLVES BEGAN the 1998/99 season in top form, winning their opening four league games without conceding a goal. However, their time at the top of the division proved to be brief as the next 12 fixtures yielded just two wins and ten points from a possible 36.

The defeat at Ipswich at the beginning of November proved to be the last straw for the club's board and manager Mark McGhee was fired after just two complete seasons at Molineux. He did lead the club to third place in the first of them only to lose out in the play-offs to Crystal Palace, and to the FA Cup semi-final in 1998. But after such a bright start to the campaign, the plummet down the First Division table had inevitable consequences for the Scot.

Colin Lee had been McGhee's assistant at both Reading and Leicester and had followed him to Molineux. After the dismissal, Lee was asked to take over team affairs on a temporary basis. He made such a successful start in the manager's chair that he was soon offered the job on a full-time basis.

Lee's first game at the helm was against Bristol City at Ashton Gate where he spent his early days as a player serving his apprenticeship. And the day before the game was his 23rd wedding anniversary with the reception having been held in one of the function rooms at the ground. In his wildest dreams he couldn't have envisaged the start he was going to enjoy on his first game in charge.

He made just two changes from the team who had lost at Portman Road – one of them enforced. Lee Naylor came in for the injured Michael Gilkes while Fernando Gomez returned from a one-game injury break to take the place of Carl Robinson who was named as a substitute.

City were lucky to be left with a full complement of players in the opening minute after Mark Shail caught David Connolly with an awful late challenge. The defender seemed fortunate to just be shown the yellow card but Connolly was to gain his revenge as the game progressed. The Irish striker had moved to Wolves on loan from Feyenoord and in seven starts and half a dozen substitute appearances prior to the Bristol game, he was still to find the net. But all of that was about to change.

The early stages of the game belonged to the home side and they took the lead after 12 minutes. Michael Bell crossed from the left and Carl Hutchings was afforded too much time and space as he took aim and buried a low, right-footed shot past Mike Stowell in the Wolves goal. It took just six minutes for the visitors to pull level with Guy Whittingham, two games into his second loan spell at Molineux, the man on target. Steve Corica pushed the ball to Simon Osborn on the right side and his cross was side-footed into the roof of the net from an acute angle by the former soldier.

Wolves' Greatest Games

Three minutes later and Wanderers were in front. Kevin Muscat's through ball was snapped up by Connolly who cut inside before despatching a low, left-footed drive out of the reach of City's keeper, Keith Welch. Full-backs Muscat and Naylor looked bright when they pushed forward although when City attacked the Wolves defence had something of a nervous look about them. However, there were no further additions to the score come the interval.

With 57 minutes gone Wolves, and Connolly, took control of proceedings. Corica, having his best game for the club since signing from Leicester three years earlier, laid a perfect through ball into the path of the predatory Connolly who beat the advancing Welch with a right-foot finish. With Osborn and Corica commanding figures in midfield, it wasn't long before Wolves went even further in front.

This time, with the half at its midway point, it was Naylor who provided the telling cross that enabled Connolly to complete his hat-trick as he hooked the ball home from close quarters. With the City defence in tatters, Connolly added a fourth to his personal account and the fifth for Wolves, in the 76th minute, when he finished clinically after running on to Whittingham's short ball into the area.

With 12 minutes remaining, Robinson, on as a replacement for Gomez, wound up the scoring with Wolves' sixth. In front of watching Welsh manager Bobby Gould, Robinson did his international prospects a power of good as he fired home after a build-up involving Connolly and Corica. Australian Corica deserved a goal himself and it looked like he was about to get one until Welch pulled off an excellent save to deny him with just a few minutes left.

After the final whistle, Lee remarked: "I think the result here would have been the same regardless of what had happened in the week. For myself, I'm delighted and could never have imagined that it would go so well. I wondered if it was going to be my day, but, as the goals went in, the confidence came and their confidence suffered.

"David Connolly has never given up. He is probably the one guy that works more than any other at the club after training, practising his finishing. His confidence could have drained away but he has never let his lack of goals affect him."

City: Welch, Murray, Bell (Hill), Hutchings, Shail, Carey, Goodridge, Thorpe (Cramb), Akinbiyi, Andersen (Torpey), Tinnion.
Wolves: Stowell, Muscat (Robinson), Naylor, Emblen, Sedgley, Curle, Corica, Fernando (Ferguson), Connolly (Jones), Whittingham, Osborn.
Attendance: 15,432.
Referee: P Taylor.

Wolves 3 (Ince, Kennedy, Ndah)
Newcastle United 2 (Jenas, Shearer penalty)
FA Cup third round
Sunday January 5th 2003

DESPITE BEING cast very much in the role of underdogs, in a game of high drama at Molineux Wolves progressed to the fourth round of the FA Cup after a terrific display against Premiership giants Newcastle United. A measure of the gulf between the clubs at the time was that the Geordies were fourth in the Premiership on the back of a home victory over Liverpool, while Dave Jones's men were tenth in the Championship, four points adrift of a play-off place.

Jones opted to keep the same 11 who had drawn with Derby County at Molineux four days earlier. The game was broadcast on live television with a teatime kick-off and it began against the background of a deafening noise. The volume increased dramatically as Wanderers moved into a sixth-minute lead after Mark Kennedy had played a short corner to Colin Cameron. The ball was laid back to Kennedy whose cross was headed back by Paul Butler into the path of Paul Ince who beat Shay Given with a low 12-yard drive.

United, attacking the North Bank end, almost pulled level following Ince's foul on Laurent Robert. The Frenchman took the free kick himself and lofted the ball into the area where Alan Shearer got in a diving header that went wide of the far post. Kenny Miller took a knock after a collision with Given as he chased Shaun Newton's through pass although the striker had strayed into an offside position anyway.

George Ndah then pressurised Aaron Hughes into conceding a corner and, from Kennedy's kick, Butler hit a shot with the outside of his right foot that went wide. Virtually all the attacking play was coming from Wolves and after good work on the right from Newton, Cameron tried to loop a header over Given but the keeper saved at full stretch. Ince powered a tremendous shot from fully 30 yards only just over but, in the 28th minute, Wolves deservedly moved into a two-goal lead. Newton ran down the right before feeding Cameron who lashed over a low centre. The ball went behind Miller but not Kennedy who ran in to fire an angled shot into the far corner of the net.

In their next attack Wanderers almost made it three when Newton centred to Kennedy whose header went into the side netting. But two goals in two minutes saw the Magpies back on level terms. Just five minutes of the half remained when Craig Bellamy crossed from the right. Shearer's shot bounced off Butler but the ball landed invitingly for Jermaine Jenas who headed into the empty net from eight yards out.

Worse was to follow with Joleon Lescott appearing to tug Bellamy's arm just to the side of the home box. The Welshman went down and the referee immediately pointed to the spot – Shearer giving Matt Murray no chance with a rasping shot into the top corner. The excitement of a classic cup tie continued after the break and,

Wolves' Greatest Games

within five minutes of the new half, Wolves were back in front. But before Molineux erupted again it was the visitors who almost took the lead after Lescott had been penalised 25 yards out for a tackle on Robert.

When Shearer fired the free kick through the wall his shot was kicked off the line by Lescott and when Clarence Acuna tried to convert the loose ball it was Lescott who cleared off the line again. Moments later Kennedy tore down the left flank and hoisted a perfect cross to Newton who nodded down for Ndah to convert from close range. Mark Clyde replaced Butler before the game could restart, the club captain having pulled a muscle in his side.

A Kennedy corner was deflected towards goal after the ball had landed amongst a throng of players. It was unclear who the ball had come off but Nolberto Solano managed to hack it off the line. Another Kennedy corner, in the 55th minute, was headed out to Cameron whose first time volley curved just the wrong side of the far post.

From yet another Kennedy corner, Ince powered in a flying header. Given looked to gather the ball safely but he appeared to let it slip from his grasp and there was a tremendous scramble before it was cleared. Wolves continued to create the better openings and Lee Naylor fired a rocket of a shot narrowly over from 30 yards, before, in the 73rd minute, Given made a first class save to deny Newton whose thunderous shot looked destined for the back of the net after Kennedy had picked him out with a pinpoint pass.

But Wanderers were almost caught out as United broke through Bellamy who ran clear only for Murray to heroically block his close-range shot. Lomana LuaLua must have thought that he had scored with his first touch after he had replaced Solano in the 75th minute. Bellamy squared the ball to the man who had scored two against Wanderers in a pre-season friendly. He tried to turn the ball in at the back post but Naylor brilliantly blocked on the line.

Miller did beat Given ten minutes from the end, but he was penalised for pushing, before Kevin Cooper came on as a late replacement for Newton. Newcastle won a succession of corners in the closing minutes as they tried desperately to force a replay, but it was Wolves who almost went further ahead, only Given's alertness denying Cooper deep into injury time.

Wolves: Murray, Irwin, Naylor, Cameron, Lescott, Butler (Clyde), Newton (Cooper), Miller, Ndah, Ince, Kennedy.
Unused subs: Oakes, Rae, Andrews.
Newcastle United: Given, Griffin, Bernard, O'Brien (Dabizas), Hughes, Solano (Lu Lua), Jenas, Acuna (Ameobi), Shearer, Bellamy, Robert.
Unused subs: Harper, Kerr.
Attendance: 27,316.
Referee: R Styles.

Sheffield United 0
Wolves 3 (Kennedy 6, Blake 22, Miller 45)
First Division play-off final
The Millennium Stadium
Monday 26th May 2003

WOLVES FINALLY made it back into football's top flight after a 19-year absence thanks to a devastating opening 45 minutes at the Millennium Stadium that left Sheffield United dead and buried in the First Division play-off final. Mark Kennedy, Nathan Blake and Kenny Miller were all on target as the travelling Molineux supporters danced and sang with delight as the Premiership dream was finally realised.

After finishing fifth in the First Division, Wolves had to overcome a tough hurdle if they were to make it through to Cardiff. In the play-off semi-final they met Reading who had finished one place higher and, in the league encounters between the sides, each had enjoyed a single-goal away victory. So it was fair to say that things were pretty evenly matched.

And that's how it turned out with it taking two goals in the last 15 minutes at Molineux to give Wolves a slight, but crucial, advantage to take into the second leg. During a somewhat flat first half, Wanderers had fallen behind in the 25th minute when Nicky Shorey's low cross was deflected by Matt Murray's legs to Nicky Forster at the far post and he had time to control the ball before rifling it into the roof of the net.

The equaliser arrived in the 75th minute after Paul Ince went down under a challenge from Steve Brown in the Reading box. With cries for a penalty ringing in the air, Shaun Newton kept his mind on the game and drove an angled shot into the net via Graeme Murty who deflected the ball over the line. Nine minutes later, Steve Brown upended Ince right on the edge of the Reading area. Lee Naylor, with a low free kick that flew through the wall and nestled into the far corner of the net, gave Wolves the advantage.

Everything was set for a tense second half of the contest at the Madejski Stadium four days later. Just 15 minutes of the game remained when substitute Alex Rae was sent on for Miller in what proved to be a masterstroke by Wolves boss Dave Jones. The popular Scottish midfielder sent the travelling fans into ecstasy in only his sixth minute on the pitch when he took a Colin Cameron pass and jinked past a defender before firing low past Marcus Hahnemann into the corner of the net

The streets of Cardiff were awash with supporters from both camps as the atmosphere built up over the course of the morning. The roof of the Millennium Stadium was open on a fine afternoon in South Wales as the teams took to the field to the background of a sea of colour and an incredible noise from the full house. Dave Jones sent out the team who had overcome Reading in the semi-final with George Ndah, who had been suffering from a knee injury, not having recovered sufficiently to even take a place on the bench.

Wolves' Greatest Games

Wolves kicked off defending the end that was packed with their supporters who had to wait for just 40 seconds before they saw the first goal attempt from their side – Miller's chip being easily gathered by Paddy Kenny. Play then went straight to the other end and a heavy United attack ended with Steve Kabba shooting well wide.

Michael Brown fired high over the bar from 30 yards before Blake was a whisker away from giving Wolves a fifth-minute lead. Denis Irwin's long through ball picked out Miller and his square pass found Blake whose low shot from the edge of the box couldn't have been more than a foot wide. Paul Butler had to put a Kabba cross out for a corner that was easily cleared and then, to a deafening roar, Wolves took the lead with just six minutes gone. Miller pushed a sideways pass to Kennedy who came steaming in to drill the ball past Kenny from 18 yards.

Only a fine piece of defensive work from Phil Jagielka prevented a second after Kenny misjudged a long ball out of the Wolves defence as he ran out of his area in attempting to clear. Blake tried to capitalise on the error but he was thwarted by Jagielka who cleared for a throw-in. After Blake had received lengthy treatment following a mid-air challenge, Peter Ndlovu hit an angled shot wide. But the action soon switched to the opposite end and a Kennedy corner led to Wanderers going two clear in the 22nd minute.

Cameron ran from the halfway line and unleashed a shot that Kenny did well to push around the post. There was no reprieve for United as Ince nodded on Kennedy's flag-kick and Blake completed the job by heading in from six yards. United went in search of a goal but they were finding it difficult to break down a resolute Wolves defence although there was a scare on 37 minutes when John Curtis's centre took Ndlovu by surprise at the far post – the ball bouncing off the winger's foot and running away for a grateful Murray to gather up.

Murray was soon in action again, this time with a fine save from one of his own men. Kabba's cross hit the head of Ince and was destined for the net until the Wolves keeper used every inch of his 6ft 4in frame to paw the ball away. Irwin was yellow-carded for a late challenge on Ndlovu who needed treatment before he could continue. The veteran defender was soon joining in the celebrations as Wolves went three goals up just as the first half entered stoppage time. Blake did well in helping the ball on to Newton who drilled in a low cross that Miller slotted high into the net from point-blank range.

As play resumed after the break, it emerged that United boss Neil Warnock had been banished to the stand during the interval for something he said to the referee as the teams had left the field. Stuart McCall came on for former Wolf Mark Rankine for the start of the new half, which was just three minutes old when United were awarded a penalty after Butler was deemed to have handled although he looked to be trying to move his hands out of the ball's path. However, Murray came to the rescue with a great save – the popular keeper beating down Brown's spot-kick before Kabba blazed the loose ball over. As in the first period Wolves seemed happy enough to absorb United pressure and, the penalty apart, Murray's main task was in fielding crosses.

v Sheffield United, 2003

Paul Peschisolido replaced Ndlovu as the half neared its midway point and then Curtis did well to cut out a Kennedy cross as Miller closed in for the kill. Wanderers were sharply reminded that the game wasn't over as the Blades went as close as they possibly could have to pulling one back in a frenetic two-minute spell. From Michael Tonge's corner, Peschisolido got in a firm header that Murray got down to but he couldn't prevent the loose ball from running to Jagielka. He lashed in a shot that Kennedy scrambled off the line but still the danger wasn't cleared.

United were awarded a free kick some 30 yards out and Brown's shot curled around the wall and looked destined for the net until Murray dived to tip it onto the bottom of the post. The rebound fell to Robert Page who looked a certain scorer but he ballooned the ball over the bar. That was to prove to be the last real danger from United as Wanderers regained their grip on the game for the final 20 minutes.

Kenny collected a Miller header following a deep cross from Newton, and then both sides made substitutions – Wayne Allison coming on for Carl Asaba for the Blades, and Dean Sturridge going on up front in place of Miller. Two Naylor free kicks came to nothing and Tonge was booked for flooring Kennedy.

Murray 'lost' a Tonge corner but Naylor was on hand to clear before Irwin tried his luck with a free kick which took a deflection and passed just wide of Kenny's right-hand post. Then the United keeper had to race from his area to clear from Sturridge. From a Kennedy corner Blake headed over and shortly afterwards the Welsh international was replaced by Adam Proudlock for the final moments.

Sturridge, with some fine ball control, looked like he was going to finish the afternoon off in style as he jinked his way past three challenges. But just as he was about to shoot Rob Kozluk managed to prod the ball behind. Seconds later referee Steve Bennett signalled the end of Wolves' exile from football's top flight, and the party began. The two Pauls – Butler and Ince – were jointly presented with the play-off trophy before the players and backroom staff performed a dance of joy in front of their celebrating supporters.

After the final whistle an emotional Dave Jones said: "When I came to Wolves it wasn't just a case of rebuilding a club it was a case of rebuilding my life." The Liverpudlian had suffered an awful experience when he was falsely accused of child abuse – a total fabrication that was thrown out by the high court. He continued: "I'm pleased for my family and friends, for those who know me, that this moment has arrived – and I include my players in that.

"The last thing I said to them before they went out was that I wished them everything that they wished for themselves. And the reward is a big, big prize for this football club. There has been a lot of talk about pressure but the players have shown their true selves by handling it."

Sir Jack Hayward joined the celebrations on the pitch before talking to reporters. He said: "It's wonderful, it's a dream come true, it really is fantastic – I didn't think it would end like this. But if we were going to go up, this was the way to go up. I would have liked to have relaxed over the last month but it was exciting. There were times when the ball was in our half a lot but our defence has been tremendous this season.

Wolves' Greatest Games

The penalty save was absolutely vital because if they had scored they could have come back quickly for another one – Matt Murray was definitely man of the match."

Two days later an estimated 45,000 people crammed the streets of Wolverhampton to welcome the team home. Two open-topped buses ferried players and backroom staff through the city centre and then back to Molineux where every seat in the stadium was taken up as the players did a lap of honour. The return to the top flight proved to be short lived, but they were a magical few days at the end of May.

United: Kenny, Kozluk, Curtis, Page, Jagielka, Tonge, Brown, Ndlovu, Kabba (Peschisolido), Asaba (Allison), Rankine (McCall).
Unused subs: Kelly, Montgomery.
Wolves: Murray, Irwin, Naylor, Cameron, Lescott, Butler, Newton, Ince, Blake (Proudlock), Miller (Sturridge), Kennedy.
Unused subs: Oakes, Rae, Edworthy.
Attendance: 69,473.
Referee: S Bennett.

Wolves 4 (Cameron 2 (one penalty), Rae, Camara)
Leicester City 3 (Ferdinand 2, Scimeca)
Premiership
Saturday 25th October 2003

SEEMINGLY DEAD and buried at the interval after conceding three goals to bottom-placed Leicester, Wolves staged a miraculous second-half comeback that culminated in Henri Camara's winner five minutes from time.

With Paul Ince ruled out because of a chest infection following the one-match suspension that saw him missing the defeat at Fulham, Dave Jones named an unchanged side for the visit of the Foxes. The first real chance fell to Jamie Scowcroft who hooked a shot goalwards from just inside the box with Denis Irwin managing to block from close range.

Worse almost followed when Muzzy Izzet ran past Jody Craddock and thumped a shot against the post from six yards out. Then, in the space of just a few seconds, Wolves had the chance to go ahead before falling behind. Eleven minutes had gone when Camara left Matt Elliott for dead as he chased a through ball from Lee Naylor but Ian Walker smothered the striker's low angled shot.

City went straight to the other end and won a corner which was taken by Izzet whose flag-kick was powerfully headed home by Les Ferdinand. Just four minutes later an identical situation saw the Foxes double their advantage. This time Izzet's corner was from the left but again Ferdinand rose to head in.

Joey Gudjonsson tested Walker with a low shot as Wanderers tried to find a response but the Icelandic midfielder was replaced as the half reached its midway point by Shaun Newton. Naylor and Colin Cameron combined before finding Camara who squared the ball to Alex Rae. However, Walker was equal to the Scot's low shot.

City were looking dangerous every time they went forward and Irwin had to head a cross from Keith Gillespie over his own bar for the first of two consecutive Leicester corners. Ten minutes before the interval a bad situation for Wolves got even worse when the home defence failed to clear their lines and Ferdinand's lay-off gave Ricky Scimeca the chance to drill the ball past Michael Oakes from 20 yards.

Nathan Blake just failed to reach a Naylor centre and although Gerry Taggart put the ball behind, Rae's corner came to nothing as a shell-shocked Wanderers team fought to get back into the game. Three minutes before the break Ferdinand had the chance of completing his hat-trick when he ran on to a pass from Gillespie but, with just Oakes to beat, he shot straight at the keeper. In stoppage time of a bitterly disappointing first half for Wolves, Paul Butler did well to block a Paul Dickov shot. Hassan Kachloul was an interval replacement for Kenny Miller and two crosses from the Moroccan in his first two minutes on the field had the City defence struggling to clear their lines, with Blake testing Walker with an angled shot following the second.

Wolves' Greatest Games

Seven minutes into the half the home fans were given hope as Cameron pulled a goal back when he tucked away a low cross from Blake who had run in from the left. It was all Wolves now and after Izzet was penalised for hands, Rae saw his free kick blocked. However, in the 59th minute Molineux erupted as Cameron again hit the back of Walker's net – this time with a well taken penalty after Gillespie had clearly handled Newton's cross.

Newton then had Walker stretching with another teasing centre that landed on the roof of the net and Camara drove wide as Wolves continued to pour forward. After 64 minutes Leicester boss Micky Adams made wholesale changes, replacing Ferdinand, Dickov and Gillespie with Marcus Bent, Craig Hignett and Lilian Nalis respectively.

Just three minutes after their introduction the roof almost came off the stadium as Rae directed a superb header past Walker after a probing cross from Irwin. City were, by now, like a punch-drunk boxer on the ropes and after Taggart had headed behind a cross from the tricky Camara, Craddock headed over from the resulting corner which was taken by Kachloul. The visitors had spent almost all of the second period on the back foot but Irwin had to be at his best to head away a dangerous cross from Bent.

Then Bent outpaced Butler and lashed in a shot from the finest of angles that Oakes parried, allowing Butler to nod the ball back to the keeper. Irwin was soon in action at the other end with a cross that Kachloul nodded narrowly wide and then Camara ended a short sprint through the visiting defence with a drive that flew past the far post.

The pressure had to tell and it did with just five minutes left when Elliott only half-cleared a Newton free kick into the path of Irwin. The full-back, with a brilliant piece of work, nodded the ball down as he ran round a defender before crossing low into the six-yard box. Kachloul allowed the ball to go through his legs and Camara, who was right behind him, lashed it into the roof of the net to spark joyous scenes.

From the restart an Izzet free kick caused a few moments of concern in the Wolves box but when the ball was played upfield, Camara had a shot on the turn well saved by Walker. Scowcroft was uncomfortably close with a header from an Izzet corner and then, in stoppage time, Camara wasn't far away after his original shot had bounced back into his path off a defender.

Wolves: Oakes, Irwin, Naylor, Cameron, Craddock, Butler, Rae, Blake, Miller (Kachloul), Gudjonsson (Newton), Camara.
Unused subs: Murray, Iversen, Luzhny.
City: Walker, Elliott, Taggart, Izzet, Gillespie (Nalis), Ferdinand (Bent), Scowcroft, Rogers, Scimeca, Dickov (Hignett), Curtis.
Unused subs: Coyne, Stewart.
Attendance: 28,578.
Referee: P Walton.

Wolves 1 (Miller)
Manchester United 0
Premiership
Saturday 17th January 2004

WOLVES DEFIED the odds in their bottom versus top clash with Manchester United by taking all three points thanks to a Kenny Miller goal midway through the second half.

Just six of the team that began the midweek FA Cup tie against Kidderminster Harriers were in the starting line-up against the reigning Premiership champions and current leaders. Back into the side came Lee Naylor, Alex Rae and Steffen Iversen along with the former United duo Denis Irwin and Paul Ince.

United kicked off attacking the North Bank end and after just 14 seconds Rae went down after challenging Phil Neville. It looked serious at first but the midfielder slowly got to his feet, rubbing his hip as he did so, before play resumed. After a Ronaldo centre had drifted wide, it was Rae who got in the first shot of the game but his 22-yard drive was well off target.

Ince blasted a long-range shot over the bar and then Rio Ferdinand hurt himself after a tackle on Miller. The England defender had to receive treatment both on and off the field before he was able to continue. Roy Keane had to boot a Naylor cross out of the six-yard box for a throw after a neat Mark Kennedy flick had released the Wolves full-back. But United were soon back on the attack and after a Darren Fletcher shot had been deflected behind for a corner, Rae was on hand to head clear Ronaldo's kick.

Fletcher was figuring heavily in the visitors' attacks and from one of his centres Ruud Van Nistelrooy tried an overhead kick that just cleared the bar. Paul Scholes headed well wide from another Fletcher cross and, in the 28th minute, Rae got in the game's first on-target shot – a 20-yard drive that Tim Howard gathered easily. There was a scramble in the Wolves box when Kennedy skied an attempted clearance but the danger was eventually cleared. Kennedy was soon in action at the other end with a low cross that John O'Shea put behind for the first home corner of the contest.

Kennedy's flag-kick was cleared but Iversen soon pressured Mikael Silvestre into conceding another and this time Shaun Newton's kick was headed out to Rae who handled as he controlled the ball before getting his shot in. Five minutes before the break Naylor was penalised for hands to the side of the home area but Ronaldo's free kick went straight to Michael Oakes.

A minute later Ronaldo saw his low shot deflected just wide following a cross from O'Shea. From the corner conceded, which was taken by Ronaldo, Keane helped the ball on to Van Nistelrooy who, from point-blank range, headed over the bar. After Miller had a shot charged down by Keane, Naylor picked up the loose ball and returned it into the box. It was headed out to Kennedy whose shot flew through a sea of legs into the arms of Howard.

The game had been played at a breakneck pace and it continued to do so after the break. Oakes dealt comfortably with a 20-yard drive from Fletcher then, after Kennedy had obstructed O'Shea, the Wolves keeper pushed away Ronaldo's free kick as Van Nistelrooy came in at the back post.

A mix-up between Irwin and Oakes almost let in Van Nistelrooy, but the keeper recovered to snatch the ball away from the prolific striker's feet. Then, four minutes into the half, Ince had the home supporters, in a record crowd for the rebuilt Molineux, on their toes when he hit a terrific shot from 25 yards that smacked against the post with Howard beaten. Ferdinand finally limped off to be replaced by Wes Brown before first Ronaldo and then Scholes fired in shots that were well off target.

Oakes came to the rescue in the 57th minute with a brilliant save. Van Nistelrooy laid a Fletcher cross into the path of Scholes whose shot had 'goal' written all over it until Oakes pushed the ball away.

In the 67th minute Molineux erupted as Wolves took the lead. Paul Butler headed the ball forward to Miller and the Scot took full advantage of Brown's slip to run on and side-foot past the advancing Howard. After Scholes had miskicked after taking a pass from David Bellion, there was the chance for Irwin to make his mark against his old club after Bellion had fouled Ince outside the United area. The veteran defender curled his shot over the wall and Howard had to turn the ball over the bar.

From the corner conceded, taken by Kennedy, Jody Craddock ran in at the near post and prodded the ball wide. Oakes made another fine save, this time from Bellion, before Kennedy shot narrowly wide of the near post at the other end. Oakes was called into action again, as United poured forward – this time he got down low to keep out a shot from substitute Diego Forlan. Then, six minutes from the end, Dave Jones sent on Vio Ganea in place of Iversen.

In a frenetic finish, Kennedy went on a probing run that ended just outside the United box, Oakes turned aside a powerful shot on the turn from Van Nistelrooy, and Rae blocked a Ronaldo free kick after Ince had fouled the United winger 30 yards out. The final whistle sparked joyous scenes as the home fans celebrated one of the shocks of the season.

Wolves: Oakes, Irwin, Naylor, Rae, Craddock, Butler, Newton, Ince, Miller, Iversen (Ganea), Kennedy.
Unused subs: Cameron, Clyde, Kachloul, Ikeme.
United: Howard, P Neville (Forlan), Ferdinand (Brown), Ronaldo, Van Nistelrooy, Keane, Scholes, O'Shea, Fletcher (Bellion), Fortune, Silvestre.
Unused subs: Butt, Carroll.
Attendance: 29,396.
Referee: A D'Urso.

Charlton Athletic 2 (Halford, Lita)
Wolves 3 (Ebanks-Blake 2, Henry)
Championship
Saturday 29th March 2008

AS THEY travelled to The Valley to take on Charlton Athletic, Wolves still held out hopes of claiming an end-of-season play-off place. An away win at Burnley had been followed by home games against Scunthorpe and Queens Park Rangers that yielded four more points with the Loftus Road team thwarting a hat-trick of wins as Wolves shared six goals with them at Molineux.

There was to be an incredible finish to the game against Charlton with Karl Henry snatching the winning goal for Wolves almost four minutes into stoppage time after Charlton's Leroy Lita looked to have earned his side a point just seconds earlier. Twice Sylvan Ebanks-Blake had fired Mick McCarthy's men into the lead with superb individual efforts, and twice the Londoners hit back before Henry's goal gave Wanderers the points that took them back into a play-off position.

Jody Craddock kept his place after coming on as a substitute for the injured Rob Edwards in the Queens Park Rangers game in an otherwise unchanged Wolves line-up. Charlton kicked off attacking the Jimmy Seed Stand end of The Valley that housed around 1,200 visiting supporters. An early Michael Gray corner was headed wide by Seyi Olofinjana while Neill Collins did well to clear from Lita who would otherwise have been clean through.

Home appeals for a penalty when Collins ran into Lita were waved aside by the referee, and Darren Ambrose hooked a low shot well wide of the target in Charlton's next attack. Wolves moved into a 15th-minute lead thanks to a brilliantly executed goal from Ebanks-Blake. The striker controlled Andy Keogh's low cross and turned as he did so, leaving Greg Halford for dead before slamming a left-footed shot past Nicky Weaver from the edge of the box.

A slip by Ambrose gifted possession to George Elokobi who found Matt Jarvis on the left. Gray ran in to meet the winger's centre on the volley but his effort was too high. Charlton drew level in the 31st minute after a shot from Halford was deflected behind for a corner. Ambrose's flag-kick travelled to the far side of the area to Jerome Thomas who drilled in a low cross that was despatched into the corner of the net by Halford.

Gray almost restored Wanderers' lead with an angled shot that could have been no more than inches above the angle with Weaver a spectator. Two minutes before the break the home goal had an amazing escape. Jarvis pushed the ball through to Ebanks-Blake and his angled drive came back off the inside of the far post. The ball rebounded to Henry who only managed to push it wide of the open goal.

There was a chance for Wolves just 20 seconds after the resumption. Jarvis raced down the left flank before cutting into the box and pulling the ball back to Henry who shot over from 22 yards out. Then Wayne Hennessey had to be at his best to deny Halford after Craddock was harshly penalised for a challenge on Chris Iwelumo 25 yards out. Halford's free kick looked destined for the top corner until the Welsh keeper athletically tipped the ball over the bar.

Gray's long-range drive was comfortably saved by Weaver before Lita, twice in the space of two minutes, went close for the home side. First he hit a short cross straight through the six-yard box with no home player available to tap the ball home, then he broke through on goal only to be denied by Hennessey who spread himself to save with his feet.

Darron Gibson came on in place of Gray for the final 20 minutes and then Collins and Jose Semedo went into the book after a brief altercation with the Charlton man appearing to aim a headbutt at the Scot who had exchanged words with him. Home substitute Lee Cook wasn't too far off with a 25-yard drive and then he was booked for clattering into Kevin Foley just after Craddock had been shown the yellow card for persistent fouling.

Freddy Eastwood replaced Jarvis in the 80th minute seconds before Ebanks-Blake restored Wolves' advantage with a stunning goal. He took the ball to the byline, flicked it through the legs of Paddy McCarthy and ran round the defender before lashing an unstoppable shot into the roof of the net. Hennessey saved from Luke Varney but, in the second of the four added minutes, he was beaten by Lita who headed home after connecting with Sam Sodje's deep ball into the box.

Kevin Kyle, a late substitute for Ebanks-Blake, saw his header deflected onto the face of the bar following an Eastwood corner. However, the drama wasn't over and Henry won it for Wolves right in front of their delighted supporters when he raced in at the far post to turn home Kyle's low driven cross.

After the match, Mick McCarthy said: "It was a great game for the public. I thought we were excellent in the first half. You can see by the reaction of the players and the bench what it means to everyone. Maybe I'm biased but I thought we were good enough to win it without having to nick it. However, winning in the last minute can cover a multitude of sins and in spells our defending wasn't up to scratch. But at the end of the day it was a great finish and we've come away with the three points."

Charlton: Weaver, Thatcher, Sodje, McCarthy, Holland, Ambrose (Zheng), Thomas (Cook), Iwelumo, Semedo (Varney), Halford, Lita.
Unused subs: Elliot, Gray.
Wolves: Hennessey, Foley, Elokobi, Henry, Craddock, Collins, Jarvis (Eastwood), Keogh, Ebanks-Blake (Kyle), Olofinjana, Gray (Gibson).
Unused subs: Stack, D Ward.
Attendance: 23,187.
Referee: K Stroud.

Derby County 2 (Kazmierczak, Sterjovski)
Wolves 3 (Keogh 2, Jarvis)
Championship
Monday April 13th 2009

AFTER HAVING failed to qualify for the play-offs on goal difference in 2008, Wolves took a giant step towards automatic promotion following a dramatic 3-2 Easter Monday win over Derby County at Pride Park. It meant that one victory from the final three games of the campaign would guarantee the step up to the Premiership after five years in the second tier.

Wolves had held on to the number one spot in the division from the end of October despite a mid-season crisis that lasted from Boxing Day until the end of February when they managed just two wins from 11 league games. But things improved dramatically following a single-goal victory at Crystal Palace. It started a run of five wins from seven games leading up to the Derby trip.

Mick McCarthy's team were unchanged from the one who had beaten Southampton 3-0 at Molineux on Good Friday and they kicked off defending the end of the ground that housed a huge travelling support. From an early Dave Jones free kick Sam Vokes saw his header deflected behind. Then Przemyslaw Kazmierczak half-hit a 20-yard shot that dribbled wide.

Andy Keogh gave Wolves a seventh-minute lead with a tremendous goal. He held off Martin Albrechtsen's challenge and volleyed the ball home as it dropped over his shoulder after Kevin Foley had pumped a long through pass into the box.

Vokes almost made it two shortly afterwards but Matt Jarvis's left-wing centre was just too high for the Welsh striker. Derby forced three successive corners before the visiting defence eventually cleared their lines then, in the 19th minute, Kazmierczak wasn't far away with a first-time shot.

Derby were pressing hard and Rob Hulse went unwittingly close when Foley's clearance from the heart of the six-yard box struck the striker and ricocheted just wide of the post past a flat-footed Wayne Hennessey. But the pressure eventually told and Nigel Clough's team equalised in the 29th minute. Karl Henry was penalised for a challenge on Hulse 25 yards out and Kazmierczak curled the free kick round the wall and beyond Hennessey's dive.

Jody Craddock blocked a Hulse shot in the area and then the Wolves skipper booted clear a dangerous cross from Kris Commons as the home side continued to press. Hennessey parried and then claimed a rising drive from Gary Teale and, in a rare Wolves attack, Foley's cross was deflected behind for a corner that came to nothing. In stoppage time Hulse powered a header inches wide after a cross from Teale.

Three minutes after the restart Hennessey did well to clear from Hulse after Henry had blocked Commons's driven cross. Wolves were inches away from taking

Wolves' Greatest Games

a 50-minute lead after Foley had ventured upfield and played the ball wide to Jarvis. The defender continued his run into the box and when Jarvis rolled the ball back to him Foley hit an angled shot against the inside of the post.

The rebound was cleared to Hulse who raced down the left before cutting into the Wolves area where Craddock threw himself to block the Derby man's shot. Mile Sterjovski then won a challenge with Matt Hill and raced clear on goal but Hennessey was off his line like a shot to block on the edge of the area. Henry had a chance when he collected a Keogh centre at the far post but he fired over the bar from an acute angle.

On 55 minutes Derby took the lead when Commons played a corner to the unmarked Sterjovski who side-footed the ball home from just inside the area. In the minutes that followed Marlon Harewood replaced Vokes and Kyel Reid went on in place of Dave Edwards. Both players were enjoying a loan spell at Molineux – Reid from West Ham and Harewood from Aston Villa.

Keogh headed over following a Jones corner while, at the other end, Hennessey just managed to get a hand to Hulse's shot on the turn. Then a final change came when Stephen Ward went on for Hill, just before Wolves drew level in the 73rd minute. Keogh dummied Reid's low cross and the ball fell to Harewood who found his path to goal blocked. But the ball ran to Jarvis who rifled it into the net from close in, right in front of the ecstatic gold and black following behind the goal.

Three minutes from time Keogh struck again to win it for Wanderers with a close-range header after a great cross from Harewood. Despite the near hysteria from the travelling fans, McCarthy was typically restrained after the final whistle, keeping his feet firmly on the floor. He admitted: "I think we were very fortunate to win the game today. But I'm also happy, pleased, relieved, delighted – all those adjectives.

"I was disappointed with the performance but obviously happy with the result which tends to mask everything else. That's as poor as we've played for a very long time and we couldn't do any worse but do you know what? We had good front men who took their chances."

The following weekend Sylvan Ebanks-Blake scored the only goal of the game against Queens Park Rangers, his 25th of the campaign, to rubber-stamp Wolves' elevation to the top tier. And a week later came the icing on the cake as McCarthy's men were crowned champions after taking a point from Barnsley at Oakwell.

Derby: Bywater, Connolly, McEveley (Nyatanga), Kazmierczak (Eustace), Commons, Savage, Hulse, Sterjovski (Bannan), Todd, Teale, Albrechtsen.
Unused subs: Price, Villa.
Wolves: Hennessey, Foley, Hill (Ward), Jones, Craddock, Berra, Edwards (Reid), Henry, Keogh, Vokes (Harewood), Jarvis.
Unused subs: Higgs, Stearman.
Attendance: 33,079.
Referee: P Taylor.

West Ham 1 (Franco)
Wolves 3 (Doyle, Zubar, Jarvis)
Premiership
Tuesday 23rd March 2010

WOLVES LAY 16th in the Premiership when they journeyed to Upton Park to take on a West Ham side who were a point and a position worse off. And Mick McCarthy's men took a massive leap towards safety following one of their best displays of the season as they ruthlessly put the Hammers to the sword to avenge the opening day defeat at Molineux and record a first victory at Upton Park since 1978.

After six games with the same starting line-up, McCarthy made two changes with George Elokobi coming in for Stephen Ward at left-back, and on-loan Michael Mancienne in midfield for Adlene Guedioura. From the off Wolves took the game to their opponents and after James Tomkins had cleared an early cross from Matt Jarvis, Kevin Foley was inches away from opening his goal account for the season in the eighth minute as he ran onto a headed flick from Kevin Doyle. After outpacing Fabio Daprela, Foley smashed an angled volley against the bar with the ball ricocheting to safety on the far side of the area.

Home keeper Robert Green had to punch clear a Jarvis corner and Marcus Hahnemann had his first real taste of the action as he fielded a low drive from Scott Parker. Julien Faubert cut into the box after a surging run down the right wing but his final shot lacked accuracy and was well wide of the far post. Play was swinging from end to end and after another dangerous cross from Jarvis had been hooked clear, a driven centre from Faubert was deflected behind for a corner that came to nothing.

Green just beat Jarvis in a race for Doyle's through ball, but the keeper was beaten in the 28th minute as Wolves moved into a deserved lead. Tomkins's attempted back-pass to Green was intercepted by Doyle who advanced into the area and drilled a low shot that went in off the inside of the far post. West Ham looked for an immediate response and Hahnemann dived to save a Carlton Cole shot after Benni McCarthy had supplied a short pass on the edge of the box. Seconds later a low cross from Jarvis took a deflection before going behind off Matthew Upson but the corner proved to be a fruitless one.

Wolves should have been awarded a 35th-minute penalty after Radoslav Kovac had clattered into Dave Jones just inside the Hammers' box. The referee had a clear view of the incident but even the home fans looked amazed as he waved play on. A flowing Wolves move ended with a 25-yard drive from Jones that took a deflection as it flew narrowly wide. The visitors had been the dominant team in the opening half but luck was with them in the 45th minute as Parker's shot hit the inside of the far post. The ball rebounded behind Hahnemann and back to Parker who had

Wolves' Greatest Games

continued his run. He rammed a cross back into the middle and Hahnemann saved on the line with Karl Henry completing the clearance.

The Hammers made a double switch at the start of the new half with Jonathan Spector and Junior Stanislas replacing Tomkins and Kovac respectively. Valon Behrami's challenge on Jarvis resulted in a free kick to the left of West Ham's area. Jarvis took the kick himself but the ball went safely to the far side off the top of Ronald Zubar's head. McCarthy was well wide with a powerful header after Faubert had fired in a cross from the right, and Hahnemann had little difficulty in dealing with a long-range effort from Alessandro Diamanti.

Wolves went two up in the 58th minute as Zubar scored his first league goal of the campaign. He ran onto a diagonal ball from Jones and smashed a first time shot inside the far post. If the travelling supporters behind Green's goal were happy with Zubar's effort, they were positively delirious as Jarvis made it three just three minutes later. Again Jones was the architect supplying a pass that Jarvis sprinted onto, bypassing two defenders, before beating Green with a low shot from the 18-yard line.

Doyle had to receive lengthy treatment after he had been caught on the back of the calf by Diamanti. Then both sides made changes, Guillermo Franco replacing McCarthy for the home side and, for Wolves, Ward went on for Jarvis. In the 77th minute it took a superb save from Hahnemann to keep out a rising drive from Franco who had run into the area and stepped inside his marker.

Wolves made two changes in the final ten minutes with Greg Halford taking the place of Zubar and Guedioura that of Mancienne. In between the substitutions Hahnemann made another fine save – this time from Diamanti who let fly from 30 yards and in stoppage time the winger was only narrowly wide although Hahnemann had his post covered. With seconds remaining Franco grabbed a consolation goal when he beat the offside trap and lobbed the ball over Hahnemann after Behrami had threaded the ball through. The three points hoisted Wolves up a further place in the Premiership table.

The game, which was televised live, was the third in a run of ten until the end of the campaign in which Wanderers suffered just two defeats and top flight security was guaranteed with two matches still remaining.

West Ham: Green, Parker, Cole, Kovac (Stanislas), Upson, McCarthy (Franco), Faubert, Behrami, Tomkins (Spector), Diamanti, Daprela.
Unused subs: Stech, Ilan, Mido, Noble.
Wolves: Hahnemann, Zubar (Halford), Elokobi, Mancienne (Guedioura), Craddock, Berra, Foley, Henry, Doyle, Jones, Jarvis (Ward).
Unused subs: Hennessey, Ebanks-Blake, Iwelumo, Milijaš.
Attendance: 33,988.
Referee: P Dowd.

Wolves 2 (Elokobi, Doyle)
Manchester United 1 (Nani)
Premiership
Saturday 5th February 2011

AFTER THE bitter disappointment of the midweek game at Bolton when they lost to a last-minute goal, Wolves bounced back with a vengeance to inflict a first defeat in ten months on Premiership leaders Manchester United. The Molineux braves, placed 19th in the table, even came from a goal down on their way to three priceless points with headers from George Elokobi and Kevin Doyle securing a fully deserved victory.

Mick McCarthy made two changes following the Bolton defeat – both in midfield with Jamie O'Hara making his full debut and Nenad Milijaš returning in place of Dave Jones and Dave Edwards. In the opening seconds Wolves penned United back and Ronald Zubar's cross was picked up on the far side by Matt Jarvis who returned the ball into the middle.

Adam Hammill grabbed possession and he laid the ball back to Milijaš who fired high and wide from the edge of the box. But the United fans in the Steve Bull Stand were soon cheering as Nani gave their side the lead. He took the ball into the home area and cut inside Elokobi before rifling a shot home inside the near post.

Wayne Rooney almost got a second shortly afterwards after he had been set up by Dimitar Berbatov, but Wayne Hennessey plucked the striker's drive out of the air. Nani then hit a 20-yard shot that went straight to Hennessey before Wolves drew level in the tenth minute. Jarvis played a short corner to Hammill whose low cross was blocked. The ball ran back to Jarvis and this time his cross was met by Elokobi whose towering header left Edwin van der Sar clutching thin air.

Wolves were playing like men possessed and their spirit and endeavour were summed up by Jarvis who sprinted over half the length of the pitch back to the edge of his own area to win a tackle and take the ball off the threatening Patrice Evra. Doyle went to ground after trying to run between Evra and Nemanja Vidic in the United box but there were no penalty appeals. At the other end, a challenge by Richard Stearman on Rooney led to a United free kick in a dangerous position but Nani curled the ball on to the roof of the net.

When O'Hara regained possession after his corner hadn't been cleared, he drilled in a low shot from an impossible angle that van der Sar saved with his legs at the near post. Then, after Rafael had fouled Milijaš some 20 yards out, the Serb took the free kick which hit the wall and deflected a yard wide with the keeper flat-footed in the middle of his goal.

However, Molineux erupted in the 40th minute as Doyle headed Wolves in front. And it was all thanks to an enterprising run by Zubar who dispossessed Rooney just outside the Wanderers area and ran to the opposition half before slipping a pass to

Wolves' Greatest Games

Doyle. The striker returned the ball to Zubar who was bowled over by Vidic just to the side of the United box. Milijaš curled over the free kick and Doyle found the net with the ball appearing to get a touch off Elokobi on the way in.

Karl Henry became the first man to be shown the yellow card in the game after he had tripped Vidic, and then van der Sar saved a low shot from Doyle who had cut inside Jonny Evans. The opening 45 minutes ended with Nani sending a powerful header over the bar following a cross from Rafael. Paul Scholes was a replacement for Michael Carrick at the start of the new half which was three minutes old when Nani planted a shot wide of the far post.

O'Hara was harshly booked for the slightest of tugs at Darren Fletcher's shirt and then the new loan signing was denied by Fletcher who got in the way of his low drive after a move involving Doyle and Jarvis, who had pulled the ball back into the path of the midfielder. A dangerous cross from Rafael was met by Scholes who slid in but diverted the ball well wide of the target. In the minutes that followed, both sides made two changes. Kevin Foley and Stephen Ward went on for O'Hara and Hammill for Wolves, while United sent on Javier Hernandez and Chris Smalling for Evans and Berbatov.

A frustrated Rooney was shown the yellow card after barging into the back of Zubar as the home defence held firm against any United threats. Rafael was forced to try a shot from distance that was nowhere near after he failed to find a path through to goal.

Jarvis delivered a low cross that went through the United six-yard box with no-one able to get a touch, then Rooney had a shot deflected over the bar after Hennessey looked to have been impeded. Scholes was booked for trying to handle a cross into the net as United "threw the kitchen sink" at the Wolves rearguard without getting through to test Hennessey. The five minutes of stoppage time went by without Hennessey being tested other than for crosses, and the final whistle was greeted by a tremendous cheer from the home fans in the capacity crowd.

Boss McCarthy said: "My teams are built on team spirit but we've a bit more quality than just that."

Wolves: Hennessey, Zubar, Elokobi, Milijaš (Ebanks-Blake), Berra, Stearman, Hammill (Ward), Henry, Doyle, O'Hara (Foley), Jarvis.
Unused subs: Hahnemann, Edwards, Craddock, Fletcher.
United: van der Sar, Evra, Evans (Smalling), Giggs, Vidic, Carrick (Scholes), Nani, Rafael, Fletcher, Berbatov (Hernandez), Rooney.
Unused subs: Owen, Anderson, O'Shea, Kuszczak.
Attendance: 28,881.
Referee: M Oliver.

Wolves 3 (Doyle 2 (one penalty), Fletcher)
Tottenham Hotspur 3 (Defoe 2, Pavlyuchenko)

Premiership
Sunday 6th March, 2011

WOLVES ENJOYED fine home victories against some of the game's elite in 2010/11, beating the likes of Manchester United, Manchester City and Chelsea. Mick McCarthy's men only managed a point when Tottenham Hotspur visited Molineux but the sides played out a six-goal, end-to-end thriller in front of the television cameras in a game that proved to be an excellent advertisement for Premiership football.

With Ronald Zubar and David Edwards ruled out through injury, Kevin Foley and Stephen Ward came into the side while Nenad Milijaš replaced the on-loan Jamie O'Hara who was not eligible to play against his parent club.

Before the game began an emotional tribute was paid to the late Dean Richards who had given great service to both Wolves and Spurs. Always a popular figure with the fans, the defender had passed away in a Leeds hospice just eight days earlier after suffering from a long-term illness. He was just 36 years old.

When the game started, inside the first minute there was a chance for the visitors as Luka Modric laid the ball into the path of Roman Pavlyuchenko on the edge of the box. However, the Russian scuffed his shot and the ball rolled tamely wide. Wolves won a fifth-minute corner which was taken by Adam Hammill. Heurelho Gomes punched the ball clear as far as Milijaš who drilled a first-time shot over the bar from 20 yards. Gomes saved at the feet of Milijaš who then headed over the bar following a cross from Hammill. In the 20th minute Hammill threaded a ball through to Matt Jarvis whose drive was deflected into the side netting by a defender.

From Milijaš's corner the ball was headed out by Benoit Assou-Ekotto but only as far as Karl Henry. The midfielder played it wide to Milijaš and his cross was headed past Gomes by Kevin Doyle.

Steven Pienaar shot into the side netting as Spurs looked for an instant response and when another Pienaar effort was blocked by Christophe Berra, Modric hit the rebound wide. Jermaine Jenas went on a surging run from the halfway line to the edge of the home area but his final shot lacked the power to trouble Wayne Hennessey. However, the keeper was left with little chance as Jermain Defoe levelled matters on the half-hour mark. The England striker picked up a loose ball 25 yards out and hit a swerving shot into the top corner.

Five minutes later, he did it again, pouncing on a half clearance and rifling a first-time effort past Hennessey. It took just five minutes more for Wanderers to get back on even terms. Doyle's deflected cross went through to Milijaš who was clearly pulled back by Alan Hutton.

Wolves' Greatest Games

The referee pointed straight to the spot and yet only gave the defender a yellow card when Milijaš was clearly through on goal needing only to tap the ball over the line. Doyle sent Gomes the wrong way from the spot. In the final minute of the half, Milijaš was high and wide from the 18-yard line after Henry had nodded on a Hammill centre.

Just three minutes after the break, the home defence struggled to get the ball clear and Jenas played a short pass to Pavlyuchenko who smashed a shot into the roof of the net from the edge of the box. Ward glanced a header wide after a cross from Jarvis before Michael Dawson went into the book for a late challenge on Hammill.

Good work from Doyle opened up the chance for Jarvis to have an attempt at goal but, from the corner of the area, he fired high over the far angle. On the hour mark Sylvan Ebanks-Blake went on in place of Ward. Gomes rescued Spurs in the 64th minute when he touched a low shot from Milijaš onto the post and, shortly afterwards, Hennessey just managed to take the ball off Defoe's foot with Richard Stearman doing his best to intervene.

Wingers Hammill and Jarvis combined to set up a chance for Ebanks-Blake but he fired wide of the post before both teams made a change in the 74th minute with Steven Fletcher replacing Hammill and Aaron Lennon going on in place of Pavlyuchenko. At full stretch, Milijaš was wide as he connected with a Doyle cross before William Gallas became the third Spurs man to go into the book after pulling back Ebanks-Blake.

Tottenham substitute Gareth Bale shot wide of a virtually open goal after a mix-up between Henry and George Elokobi had gifted the Welsh international the opportunity. With ten minutes remaining, Stearman looked to have equalised as he headed in a Milijaš free kick only for the referee to disallow it for a foul on Gomes. Replays later showed that Stearman was more the victim than the villain.

An on-target effort from Henry bounced clear off a defender and then there was a let-off for Wolves as Defoe was inches away from completing his hat-trick as his snap-shot came back off the post. However, Wolves deserved something from the game and it arrived in the 87th minute with Fletcher looping home a precision header following a cross from Jarvis.

Wolves: Hennessey, Foley, Elokobi, Ward (Ebanks-Blake), Berra, Stearman, Hammill (Fletcher), Henry, Doyle, Milijaš, Jarvis.
Unused subs: Hahnemann, Craddock, Mouyokolo, Griffiths, Doherty.
Spurs: Gomes, Hutton, Gallas, Dawson, Assou-Ekotto, Modric (Kranjcar), Sandro, Pienaar (Bale), Jenas, Pavlyuchenko (Lennon), Defoe.
Unused subs: Palacios, Crouch, Bassong, Cudicini.
Attendance: 28,669.
Referee: M Halsey.

Also available at all good book stores

9781785314995

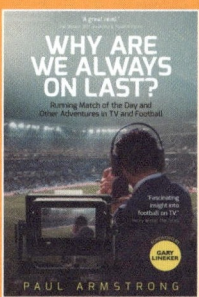
9781785314384

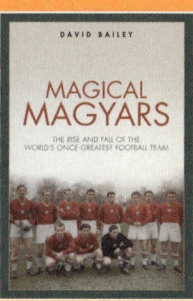
9781785315442

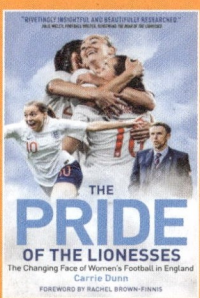
9781785315411

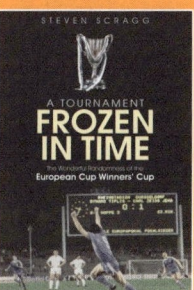
9781785315381

9781785315220

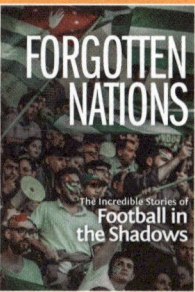
9781785314568

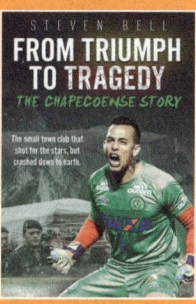
9781785315237

9781785315060

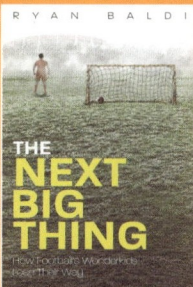
9781785315015

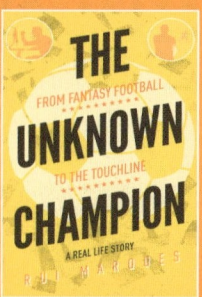
9781785315046